02/13 .

STUDIES IN POLICY-MAKING

General Editor: Anthony King, Professor of Government,
University of Essex

*Most books on British politics are concerned with political
institutions — with the cabinet, Parliament, the political parties and
so on. This new series of books approaches the same subject matter
from a different point of view. It is concerned not with institutions but
with processes — with how laws, policies and decisions are formulated
and implemented. It is hoped that the books in the series will, among
other things, make it clearer how the institutions themselves actually
function. All of the books in the series are addressed to the general
reader, to academic students of politics and also to specialists in the
fields with which the books deal — such fields as industrial relations,
the nationalised industries, health and housing.*

THE POLITICS OF INDUSTRIAL RELATIONS

The origins, life and death of the 1971 Industrial Relations Act

MICHAEL MORAN

Here one comes upon an all-important English trait: the
respect for constitutionalism and legality, the belief in
'the law' as something above the State and above the
individual, something which is cruel and stupid, of
course, but at any rate *incorruptible*.

GEORGE ORWELL
The Lion and the Unicorn

First published 1977 by
THE MACMILLAN PRESS LTD
London and Basingstoke
Associated companies in New York
Dublin Melbourne Johannesburg and Delhi

ISBN 0 333 15503 3

Printed in Great Britain by
UNWIN BROTHERS LTD
Woking and London

FOR LIAM AND JOE

Contents

Acknowledgements

A large number of very busy people were kind enough to spend time helping me in the writing of this book. I owe a particular debt to those concerned in some way with the Industrial Relations Act who were good enough to answer my questions. My thanks go to Mr Stephen Abbott, Sir Denis Barnes, Lord Boyle, Lord Carr, Mr Eric Heffer, Sir Geoffrey Howe, Mr Tom Jackson, Mr Pat Lowry, Mr John Monks, Sir Leonard Neal and Mr Harry Urwin.

I also owe particular debts to a number of other people: to Anthony King, who first encouraged me to start the project and whose comments on an early draft substantially improved the finished product; to my colleagues David Banks and Tim May, and to John Purcell of the University of Manchester Business School, for their perceptive remarks on my manuscript; and to Sandra Lowe for allowing me to consult her collection of ephemera about the Conservative Party.

A book such as this could not be written without access to good libraries. I owe a special debt to the library staff at Manchester Polytechnic, at the University of Manchester Business School and at Manchester Central Reference Library. The Board of Governors of Manchester Polytechnic were kind enough to give me a term's leave in which part of this book was written.

Since the events described in this study took place a number of the important participants have been ennobled: Robert Carr, for instance, is now Lord Carr. In order to avoid confusion I have retained the old stylings throughout.

MJM

Manchester Polytechnic
June 1976

Introduction

This is a study in the politics of public policy-making in the field of industrial relations. As a result certain matters are stressed: the links between the political ideas of the main groups involved and their proposals for the reform of industrial relations; the methods used by the relevant interest groups in arriving at and promoting their policies; and the wider constitutional questions raised by the attempted implementation of the Industrial Relations Act. Conversely, other matters are neglected. In particular, though there is some discussion of the problems involved in working the Act, there is no detailed study of its effect on industrial relations; that task has already been carried out by those better qualified to do so.

Why write a study of the 1971 Industrial Relations Act? The answer in part is that the legislation is of considerable historical interest. It came as the climax of a decade when politicians, industrialists, trade unionists and publicists became increasingly worried by the problems of industrial relations. It transformed the British workplace from one where the law played only a small part to one where legal regulation was extensive and pervasive. Many government policies arouse controversy; few could match the Act for the amount of disagreement it created. Many Acts on the statute book are not enforced; few become so irrelevant within so short a time of reaching the status of a law. Many Acts do not have the precise effect intended by their authors; few can have gone so disastrously awry.

The historical significance of the legislation is emphasised by its climactic character: it was the most serious attempt yet made to solve the problems of industrial relations by legal regulation, and its admitted failure has led to the widespread rejection of such solutions. The Labour Party, purged apparently of the forms of intervention embodied in *In Place of Strife*, committed itself to repeal even before the legislation reached the statute book, and rapidly carried out its pledge in the summer of 1974. The Conservatives, whatever their private thoughts, quickly accepted that the Act could not be revived, and indeed appear willing to let Labour's legislation remain on the statute book substantially unaltered. Prediction is a hazardous business, but it seems unlikely that any conflict between the unions and the next Conservative Government will concern the general question of a legal framework for industrial relations.

But apart from recounting events of some historical significance the present work has a second, more important, aim: to try to illuminate some general questions about British politics. In this respect the case study is a labour saving device enabling us to gain wider insights from a limited range of material. But it has its costs, the most important being that since every case is peculiar to itself any general conclusions can only be inferred with caution. It can hardly be stressed strongly enough that the Act was highly unusual, and that in examining it we are not observing a typical example of how decisions are made and responded to in British politics. The general significance of the legislation is rather the reverse. It shows the political system under stress and alerts us to likely points of breakdown in present arrangements: established methods of rule making and consultation failed, while defiance of the law was encouraged by leaders of powerful pressure groups. The willingness of the General Council of the TUC to threaten a general strike in July 1972 is but one indication that the constitution underwent its most severe crisis for a generation. The concluding chapter of this book in particular examines some of the main points of stress in our system, and attempts to indicate some of the available ways of coping with it.

One of the cliches of historiography is that history tends to be written by the victors. The present conventional wisdom concerning the Act seems to confirm this: there is probably a consensus now among political leaders, businessmen and trade unionists that the original opponents of the legislation were correct when they argued that it would never work because it flew in the face of industrial reality. One of the chief arguments of this book is to the contrary: the failure of the legislation, far from being inevitable, was the fortuitous outcome of power politics and particular circumstance. If the Act's defeat was the Conservative Government's Waterloo, it was, as Wellington said of the original battle, 'the nearest run thing you ever saw in your life'.

THE ORGANISATION OF THE BOOK

The organisation of this book is very simple. In telling the story of the legislation I have tried to follow the excellent advice of the King in *Alice in Wonderland*: 'begin at the beginning and go on till you come to the end: then stop.' Thus the core of the study consists of chapters 4–8 where the conception, birth and short turbulent life of the Act is unfolded. But since the opening three chapters do not directly deal with the Act some explanation of their purpose is necessary. The first chapter has a number of aims. It is partly designed simply to give any reader who may be unfamiliar with industrial relations some of the relevant historical information. A more important purpose is to illustrate the chief historical forces which shaped both the problems the Act was designed to tackle and the reception it received. This also accounts for the organisation of the chapter: the opening section traces briefly some institutional features of the place of unions in industrial relations; the second section examines the historical relationship between unions and the state and suggests that the legacy of this experience had an important effect on the fate of the Act; while the final section looks at the relationship between the unions and the Conservative Party, and argues again that the historical legacy was important in shaping the behaviour of both the Tory Party and trade unionists. The final aim of the opening chapter is perhaps most important of all: it is intended to give some analytical shape to the study. In this respect the final section – 'three traditions in industrial relations' – is important, since it is argued that debates about the reform of industrial relations are best understood as a dialogue between these traditions.

The point of the second chapter is much simpler: it discusses briefly some of the main developments in industrial relations which in the 1960s gave rise to the feeling that something was wrong with the system. Chapter three starts from the proposition that policy is a response not just to the past but also to the present. It is only possible to understand what was special about the policy of the Conservative Party by being aware of the alternative views which were developed in the years before 1970, when the Tories were laying the foundations of the Act. This third chapter thus examines the views put forward by key groups such as the trade unions and the employers. This is followed by a study of the evolution of Conservative policy to 1970.

These chapters may seem a long preamble to a discussion of the legislation itself – which occupies chapters 5–7 – but one of the many interesting features of the Act was the length of time it was in preparation. The Conservatives began to rethink their attitude towards the trade unions immediately after their election defeat in October 1964. By the time they were returned to office in June 1970 their industrial relations policies were worked out in detail. The period before 1970 thus merits close attention as one when many difficult arguments were voiced and – to some extent – settled.

Most case studies of the politics of legislation end at the point when a bill becomes a law, but since the most striking feature of this Act was the widespread defiance it aroused the politics of resistance are examined in chapter eight. Finally, the concluding chapter looks at some of the wider issues raised by the failure of the legislation, and examines some of its implications for the future.

1 The Historical Legacy

Although unions existed in embryonic form at least as long ago as the sixteenth century, modern British trade unionism is essentially a creation of the Industrial Revolution. The beginnings may be dated from the development of 'New Model' unions, especially the Amalgamated Society of Engineers founded in 1851.[1] These early unions had three characteristic features. First, they were occupationally sectarian. They normally organised highly skilled artisans and attempted to protect the interests of their members by restricting the labour supply through, for instance, control of apprenticeship schemes.[2] Second, though national organisations and a degree of central financial control marked out the unions as 'new model', they were still highly decentralised. They had often been formed from an amalgamation of local or regional organisations, and most substantive bargaining between workers and employers seems still to have taken place at district rather than national level.[3] Finally, the national leadership of these unions was constitutionalist in politics and conservative so far as industrial policy was concerned. Strikes were discouraged except under extreme circumstances, and while many leaders were on the radical wing of Liberalism the national leadership acted largely as a pressure group seeking piecemeal, restricted concessions through Parliamentary lobbying.[4] As a symbol of this the main TUC body, the Parliamentary Committee, was not replaced by a General Council until 1920.[5]

In the half century after 1875 these three characteristics changed in important ways. The social exclusiveness of unionism was breached after 1889 by the spread of general unions organising semi-skilled and unskilled workers. The full development of this trend was marked in the 1920s by the foundation of the Transport and General Workers Union (TGWU) and the National Union of General and Municipal Workers (GMWU).[6] The national leadership of trade unionism was also strengthened at the expense of lower levels by the emergence of a truly national system of industrial relations: pay and conditions over large sections of the economy were increasingly determined by industry-wide agreements negotiated between national representatives of employers and unions. This occurred as part of a gradual movement before 1914 – thus a national federation of engineering employers was formed in 1897[7] – but the First World War accelerated

the process. Government intervention in the economy, growing concentration of ownership, the central regulation of production, and wage
and price restrictions all helped effectively to 'nationalise' the system of
industrial relations.[8]

Finally, the period after 1875 saw a change in the political colour of
trade unions. Industrial militancy increased, reaching peaks between 1911
and 1914 and after the First World War. The unions detached themselves
from Liberalism, setting up their own party because of a desire to lobby
Parliament more effectively and because of socialist influences coming
mainly from the general unions established after 1889. By the mid-1920s
the national leadership, though still deeply attached to Parliamentarianism, had flirted briefly with syndicalism and was supporting in Labour a
party that was socialist in language at least.[9]

The defeat suffered by the unions in the 1926 General Strike changed
the direction of the movement.[10] The national leadership turned to a
policy of conciliation with employers and government, inaugurated by the
Mond-Turner talks in 1928. This was continued during the 1930s in the
efforts of Ernest Bevin and Walter Citrine to have the TUC accepted in
Whitehall as the legitimate spokesman for labour.[11] Partly because of
demoralisation after the General Strike, and partly because mass unemployment weakened the strength of workers against employers, strikes
became relatively rare until the late 'thirties. The shop steward movement
and worker militancy, which had both flourished in the acute labour
shortage during the Great War, subsided when the brief post-war boom
collapsed. Industry-wide bargaining continued to determine pay and
conditions during the inter-war years.[12]

The sharp decline in unemployment associated with rearmament and
war at the close of the 'thirties began the process of undermining this
national system. The severe shortage of labour during the war led
employers, often desperate to recruit workers, to offer rates of pay well
above those agreed nationally. This phenomenon, usually known as 'wage
drift', can be traced as far back as 1938.[13] The boom produced by the
Second World War also resulted in another important change. As a
reflection of the new assertiveness of workers, shop stewards – the unpaid
spokesmen of workers on the shop floor – began to appear in large
numbers.[14] The continuation of full employment after 1945 accentuated
these trends. By the middle of the 1960s wage levels for manual workers in a
key industry like engineering were to a very great extent determined by
negotiations within the workplace; while shop stewards, having at best an
ambivalent and at worst a hostile relationship with official trade unionism,
had in many cases replaced the official union machinery as the representative of the rank and file in the workplace. The implications of this
widespread undermining of the national system of collective bargaining
are examined in the next chapter.

TRADE UNIONS AND THE STATE

a) The role of law

British labour law before 1971 was notable, compared with that in other
countries, for the extent to which it abstained from intervention in
industrial relations. Most countries have explicit laws governing the right
to strike, the right to organise in trade unions, the regulation of the internal
affairs of those unions, the conditions under which collectively negotiated
agreements become legally enforceable, and even covering such substantive matters as levels of pay. In Britain, on the other hand, there was
before 1971 no positive legal right to strike; legislation ensured only that
legal intervention to curb or facilitate industrial action was severely
limited. The law was silent on the question of the recognition of trade
unions, though public policy tended to encourage union growth. As to
internal organisation, the law insisted on little more than that unions act in
accordance with their rule books, and concerned itself little with the
substance of these rules (although like much else, this was altered in the
1960s). Collective agreements between a union and an employer were, in
the opinion of most experts, legally unenforceable, while legally binding
agreements between unions and employers' associations – the institutions
at the centre of the national system of industrial relations – were explicitly
proscribed by the 1871 Trade Union Act. Finally, though there existed a
mass of legislation governing physical conditions of work – providing a
'floor of rights' in Wedderburn's phrase – pay and conditions were still in
the main determined by autonomous collective bargaining. Even the
Wages Councils, which covered industries where trade union organisation
was weak, and which could in certain circumstances produce legally
binding recommendations on pay, nevertheless operated within an
essentially voluntary framework.[15] The reasons for the comparatively
insignificant role of law are complex, but perhaps the most satisfactory
explanation runs as follows. Britain was unique in experiencing its
Industrial Revolution before any other country, and consequently it also
developed trade unions very early. In particular, by contrast with other
countries the rise of strong unions preceded the enfranchisement of the
mass of workers and the appearance of a strong working class political
party. Whereas in other countries – the United States in the 'thirties is a
good example – working-class voting power was translated into laws
facilitating the extension of trade unionism, in Britain the unions had
secured legal protection before significant numbers of manual workers
were enfranchised.[16]

Both trade unionism and strikes were banned by criminal law before
1824, though both in fact existed in spasmodic and local form. The repeal
of the Combination Acts in that year was engineered by a group of
Benthamite radicals, whose chief motive was to discredit trade unionism
by showing that when it was allowed to operate it failed to improve the

conditions of workers.[17] Repeal ushered in a half century when unions were in a legal limbo: they were not actually forbidden to organise but were subject to decisions of judges which threatened their funds and made involvement in strikes a criminal conspiracy punishable by imprisonment.[18] An Act passed in 1859 which was intended to clarify and settle their legal position, was rapidly nullified by judicial decisions;[19] but the 1871 Trade Union Act and the 1875 Conspiracy and Protection of Property Act finally laid down the legal framework within which unions were to operate until 1971.[20] The 1871 Act was partly concerned to establish that strikes were not crimes, but its most enduring contribution was to lay down the rules governing the internal organisation of trade unions. The abstentionist character of this legislation was to influence heavily the relations between unions, their members and the law for a century. It saw unions as akin to clubs, reflecting an essentially laissez-faire view of their nature and functions:[21] they could not be sued by their members, and agreements between unions were not to be legally binding; registration was optional and carried with it only some relatively minor advantages; and even registration obliged a union to do little more than have a constitution and act in accordance with it. The content of its internal rules was almost entirely its own affair.

If the 1871 Act was the very loose framework within which the internal affairs of unions were ordered for a century, the 1875 Act, passed by Disraeli's Government, was the 'golden formula'[22] which attempted to settle the conditions under which industrial conflict could take place. A judicial decision of 1872 had threatened to nullify the attempt made the year before to ensure that strikes were not a criminal conspiracy, so the key section of the 1875 Act provided – as a modern commentator puts it – 'that two or more persons cannot be indicted for conspiracy if the act they agreed or combined to do or to procure would not in itself have been a crime . . . provided it was to be done in contemplation or furtherance of a trade dispute.'[23] A trade dispute was defined to include disputes about wages and conditions of work, about employment and dismissals, and about questions of job demarcation. Only strikes in a number of key industries such as gas and – more ambiguously – political strikes were left open to criminal prosecution. The Act was also designed to ensure that peaceful picketing would not be a criminal offence.

The 1875 Act all but removed the criminal law from industrial relations; but in the thirty years after 1875 – especially in the period after 1890 – the courts developed the idea that the civil law could be used to restrict both picketing and strikes.[24] This culminated in the Taff Vale judgement by the Law Lords in 1901. The Lords ruled that the Amalgamated Society of Railway Servants was liable to pay substantial damages to the Taff Vale Railway Company as a result of industrial action called by one of the Society's officials.[25] The possibility of a union being liable for civil damages as a result of a trade dispute opened up the prospect of unions being crippled by Court action, and seemed to many union leaders to breach the spirit of the 1875 'golden formula'. The Conservative Government then in office was unsympathetic to amending the law,[26] and it was left to the subsequent Liberal Administration to introduce, partly as a result of pressure from the unions and its own radical wing, the 1906 Trade Disputes Act. The Act gave sweeping immunities to trade unions, freeing them from the threat of prosecution for most acts done in furthering a trade dispute. The definition of such a dispute was in turn so widely drawn as to include any actions – except possibly a general strike – in which a union might be involved.[27]

By 1906 the structure of trade union law for the next sixty-five years had been erected. It rested on four pillars: the Acts repealing the Combination Laws, which thus gave unions freedom to organise; the 1871 legislation which laid down a very permissive framework for the internal regulation of their affairs; the 1875 Act which gave them freedom from criminal prosecution when they were engaged in industrial action; and the 1906 Act which gave similar protection from the possibility of civil action. The structure which these pillars supported was altered in later years, but the pillars remained until the Industrial Relations Act. Between 1915–1919 and 1940–1951 legislation of a more interventionist character was in force, the most notable feature of which was a largely unsuccessful attempt to ban strikes by providing for compulsory arbitration.[28] But these were temporary expedients associated with war and – after 1945 – the critical aftermath of war. By contrast, the only serious attempt to reopen the settlement between the unions and the law was not intended as a short-term measure; the 1927 Trade Disputes Act, passed after the General Strike, banned the closed shop and sympathy strikes, and placed a number of other restrictions on unions. But its provisions relating to industrial disputes had apparently never been invoked when it was repealed by the Labour Government in 1946.[29]

The pattern described here has three striking features: the extent, already remarked on, to which legislation has been designed to take the law as far as possible out of industrial disputes; the fact that this policy has had the support – indeed has usually been demanded by – the trade union movement; and finally the fact that legislation has so often been concerned with removing limits placed on unions by the judges. Britain was one of the first countries to give workers a negative freedom to join unions and organise strikes, but not until 1971 was there any positive right to do so. (The 1971 Act gave a right to organise, but the freedom to strike was still expressed in the language of immunities.) One explanation for this has already been mentioned: the fact that workers were already able to exercise significant industrial power before the vote gave them political influence. But there is another important reason for the unions' support for abstention: the behaviour of judges.

The role of judges in interpreting labour law gives no better example of the independent power of judicial interpretation in shaping the application of legislation. It is no exaggeration to say that with the exception of wartime laws and the 1927 Trade Disputes Act every significant statute bearing on industrial disputes passed in the century after 1870 was the result of judicial decisions which had nullified the intended effect of previous legislation. Judicial attitudes to trade unions up to at least the First World War were influenced by two things: a strong attachment to notions of economic laissez-faire and to individualism in general; and a hostility to the aims of trade unions and the social groups they represented.

Attachment to laissez-faire tends to result in hostility to trade unions because a union is a sort of labour cartel whose purpose is to rig the free market in labour and thus drive up its price. Before 1875 the concept of criminal conspiracy was the chief judicial weapon against unions; indeed the whole notion seems to have been developed after 1825 largely to restrict the freedom to strike.[30] Three separate attempts were made by Parliament to remove the threat of the criminal law – in 1859, 1871 and 1875 – and only at the last attempt did it succeed. But the courts' attacks on the unions were not confined to the matter of strikes. A judicial decision of 1867 held that since a union was acting in 'restraint of trade' – a notion suffused with laissez-faire influences – it was unlawful and its funds could not therefore be protected, in this particular case against embezzlement by an official.[31]

The almost complete removal of the criminal law from industrial relations in 1875 did not, however, curb the influence of the judiciary. The labour unrest accompanying the spread of unionism among unskilled and semi-skilled workers after 1889 resulted in the development of the idea that a strike was a civil conspiracy, making those who called it liable to damages. Growing judicial hostility to combined working-class industrial action was also reflected in a series of judgements during the 1890s which severely restricted the conditions under which picketing could take place. This campaign reached its height with the Taff Vale case.[32]

That judicial hostility to trade unions was a product of more than an intellectual attachment to laissez-faire ideas is shown by the very different behaviour of the courts towards employers in the 1890s. Unions which circulated blacklists of strike-breakers were held to be guilty of a conspiracy; but the circulation of blacklists of strikers by employers was not held to be unlawful because the judges considered employers to be defending their legitimate interests.[33] Similarly, while in 1891 a combination of employers in a price ring which injured the trade of a competitor was not deemed a conspiracy because the members were held to be defending their legitimate interests, the same principle was not applied to unions until 1942. Indeed only from the middle of the 1920s did the courts begin to produce judgements which consistently reflected the terms of the legislative settlement reached with the unions in 1906.[34]

These episodes are more than a historical curiosity because they left indelible marks on the unions and the law in Britain. As we have seen, the unions achieved their freedom to organise and strike not just inde- pendently of the law but to some extent in defiance of it; the judges often seemed to be the employers' last line of defence. The result has been a strong – though not invariable – hostility on the part of trade union leaders to the use of law in regulating industrial relations. Furthermore, what might have become only a union folk-memory of judicial hostility was intensified during the 1960s by the revival of the judges' suspicions of certain aspects of the trade union movement.[35] The other important consequence of the struggle between the unions and the courts arose from .the way the freedom of unions to organise and strike was expressed. In many other countries, unions advanced by gaining positive legal rights; in Britain, by contrast, they sought and obtained immunity from judicial intervention. The fact that the equivalent of rights in other countries was expressed in terms of 'immunities' and 'privileges' coloured the whole debate on the reform of industrial relations. As Wedderburn has suggested, it led certain groups – in particular those with a legal training – to view unions as 'overmighty subjects' with special privileges; and this in turn influenced the final shape of the Industrial Relations Act.[36]

The unions' contact with public authority was not limited to the field of law. Inextricably intertwined with the whole question of their legal position has been their role as a powerful interest group in the community.

b) Unions and the government
Unions were one of the first great interests in the community to operate as a formally organised pressure group but one of the last to be fully accepted by government as a legitimate object of consultation and negotiation. As long ago as the 1860s, when a national leadership first emerged, unions were at work trying to influence the deliberations of a Royal Commis- sion.[37] The first Trades Union Congress was held in 1868, and a Parliamentary Committee of national leaders was established in 1871 with the express purpose of influencing the legislation passed in that year.[38] The unions' original excursion into pressure group politics was highly tentative, and though the Committee survived it was relatively quiescent in succeeding years.[39] Only the increased militancy of the 'nineties, coupled with reinterpretations of the law, produced a renewed interest in exercising influence on public policy.

The story of the unions' disenchantment with Liberalism and their sponsorship of an independent group of Labour parliamentary candidates is too well known to need repeating here,[40] but two points are of special relevance. First, the disenchantment was gradual; the drift from Lib- eralism can only be said to have been complete by the outbreak of the First World War. Second, there was a fundamental continuity in tactics between the period of the Liberal alliance and the sponsorship of Labour MPs: the prime reason for the shift was the desire on the part of unions to exercise greater influence over the legislation passed by Parliament. Unions thus still focussed their political activity primarily on the parliamentary arena.

The development of Labour as a party with fully fledged parliamentary ambitions, marked by its 1918 constitution, seemed to commit the unions further to a strategy of effecting changes by parliamentary action. But paradoxically the apparent climax of the parliamentary strategy coincided with the unions turning to other methods. There was a sharp increase in industrial militancy; the TUC was reorganised, the replacement of the Parliamentary Committee by a General Council emphasising an increased concern with industrial action;[41] and in 1920 there was even a brief flirtation with direct action as a means of changing government policy.[42]

The climax of this period came with the General Strike. The General Council, having stumbled unwillingly into calling out a large section of the trade union movement, stressed that they were engaged in an 'industrial' not a 'political' dispute.[43] Since the object of the strike was to compel the Government to continue paying a subsidy to the coal industry to keep up miners' wages the distinction was a fine one. The importance of the claim is that the national leadership, even at this point of apparent commitment to mass action, were anxious neither to challenge nor to appear to challenge the constitution. The failure of the Strike, caused in part by this very desire not to defy political authority, had two important effects on the future role of unions in politics. The belief that the Strike had been a nightmarish failure turned the leaders of the movement away from any direct challenge to government for a generation; a very genuine attachment to constitutionalism was reinforced by a conviction that in any struggle with government the unions were bound to lose.

A more immediate result was that in the aftermath of 1926 the leaders of the General Council turned to other means of influencing public policy. The unions had enjoyed direct access to Whitehall during the First World War: union leaders had entered the Cabinet, while nominees of the movement had sat on key government committees. This close relationship was not maintained when the war ended,[44] but after the General Strike it was to Whitehall rather than to Parliament that the General Council looked to rebuild its influence. Led by Ernest Bevin, the dominating figure in the movement for the remainder of the inter-war years, and Walter Citrine, the General Secretary of Congress, the TUC made a determined attempt to establish the right to be consulted in Whitehall on any matter affecting trade unionists.[45] A conscious attempt was thus made to have the trade union movement act as an orthodox Whitehall-focussed pressure group of the protectional type.

This policy enjoyed limited but steady success in the 'thirties,[46] but it was the Second World War that transformed the unions' position. Full employment and the need for maximum production meant that trade union cooperation was required. The process of incorporating the unions into government machinery began as early as 1938 but was considerably accelerated by the appointment of Bevin as Minister of Labour in 1940.[47] Trade unionists were now recruited into all levels of the government machine. Something like this, though on a less extensive scale, had happened during the First World War, but the difference now was that after 1945 the very close relationship was maintained. The election of a Labour Government, the existence of full employment and the need for union cooperation to tackle problems such as wage inflation all meant that the unions' role was almost as vital as in wartime. The TUC thus remained represented on numerous Whitehall advisory committees and was consulted by government over a whole range of questions.[48] The return of the Conservatives in 1951 did little to change the relationship; if anything, the result seemed to be to strengthen the link between the TUC and Whitehall.[49] The conversion of the Conservative leadership to planning in the early 1960s gave the TUC an additional importance as the 'voice of labour' on such bodies as the National Economic Development Council. Indeed during the 'sixties the tri-partite relationship between government, the TUC and Confederation of British Industry seemed to have become an integral part of the constitution.

By the end of the 1960s several important features marked the relationship between the unions and the government. First, there was on the part of the trade union leadership a long standing aversion – strengthened by memories of the General Strike – to 'unconstitutional' political pressure, which was usually taken to mean attempts to influence public policy by strike action. Second, though the unions sponsored a large number of Labour MPs they rarely used Parliament in their attempts to exercise influence on government.[50] In the classic manner of pressure groups with direct access to Whitehall they turned to MPs, if at all, only as a last resort when direct influence on the executive was of no avail. This neglect of Parliament reflected the access to Whitehall which the unions had sought since the 'twenties and enjoyed since 1940. The chief beneficiary of this trend was the TUC, which was strengthened by the desire of successive governments to negotiate with a single spokesman of labour.[51] Precisely how much influence all this access gave the TUC is a matter of dispute, but these various strands in the relationship between unions and government were to prove critical to the reception given the Industrial Relations Act.

TRADE UNIONS AND THE CONSERVATIVE PARTY

Conservatives have developed their own interpretation of the relationship between their party and the trade unions. It runs as follows.[52] In the nineteenth century – especially from the period of Disraeli's ascendancy –

Conservatives were the paternalistic defenders of the people against a Liberal elite of industrialists whose aim was to minimise the role of the state in order to maximise the exploitation of labour. The fact that a Conservative Government passed the legislation in 1875 which largely freed unions from the threat of criminal prosecution was thus no accident; it symbolised an enduring Tory approval of the trade union movement.

As a party myth this version doubtless serves useful purposes; as history it leaves much to be desired. It may be the case that some sort of rapprochement with the unions was a part – though hardly a clearly defined part – of Disraelian Conservatism. But 1875, when a Tory Home Secretary received a vote of thanks from the TUC,[53] marked the zenith of this policy. In the last quarter of the century the character of the party changed.[54] It drew its electoral and activist strength increasingly from the urban middle class, and its parliamentary leadership increasingly from the ranks of industry. Associated with these social changes, the Disraelian emphases on social reform and conciliation with the unions as the representative of the working class became heavily muted. By 1902 the party which had taken the criminal law out of industrial relations was, in the wake of the Taff Vale judgement, refusing to do the same with respect to the civil law.

Conservative hostility to the unions arose from three sources: intellectual conviction; the economic interests of powerful groups in the party; and the institutional interests of the party itself. As to the first, an organisation as strongly attached to laissez-faire economic theories as was Conservatism by the turn of the century inevitably looked with suspicion at trade unions, whose purpose was to distort the workings of the free market in labour. This intellectual opposition was reinforced by opposition to the economic challenge of unions on the part of groups such as employers, who by the turn of the century were highly influential in the party. Finally, the unions' increasing involvement in parliamentary politics meant that the Conservatives' party opponents received financial and organisational support from the labour movement. Growing industrial militancy, the 1913 Trade Union Act which obliged union members to contract out of paying a political levy which was used to fund the Conservatives' opponents, and the position of the unions as an organic part of a mass socialist party all contributed to the maintenance of suspicion. The political levy, since it affected the institutional interests of Conservatism, was an object of special attack. During the early 'twenties a number of attempts were made by Tory backbenchers to replace contracting out by contracting in.[55] The General Strike provided the opportunity critics of the unions needed, and the 1927 Trade Disputes Act tried to deal comprehensively with Conservative objections to trade unionism. The closed shop, offensive to supporters of economic laissez-faire, was banned; the economic and constitutional challenge was met by banning sympathy and general strikes; while the institutional interests of the Party were defended by making it necessary for union members to contract into payment of the political levy.

Of course the story is not one of total hostility. Indeed Stanley Baldwin, the party's leader from 1922 to 1937, was one of the chief forces within the party resisting moves to discipline the unions by legislation before 1927, and was a supporter of conciliatory talks after 1928. But Baldwin's attitude to industrial affairs and to the trade union leadership was essentially Disraelian, based on a paternalistic concern for the conditions of workers and good personal relations with their leaders.[56] A more significant — because in the long run more influential — move to accommodate the unions is associated with what Harris calls 'corporatist' ideas in the party. Schemes associated with Alfred Mond — a founder of ICI and the initiator of the Mond-Turner talks — and with Harold Macmillan envisaged solving the problem of union power by giving the official leadership a place in the machinery of the state — through some form of functional representation — in return for the exercise of control over the rank and file.[57] The implications of this thinking were very different from those embodied in the 1927 Act: by contrast with the latter's libertarian approach the 'corporatists' were prepared to allow the closed shop both as an inducement to secure official trade union cooperation and as a weapon with which union leaders could control members. A division along these lines was to be one of the main features of the debate about reform in the 1960s and 'seventies.

Corporatist ideas exercised an important influence on Conservative economic policy in the 'thirties,[58] but their effect on the party's behaviour towards the trade unions was relatively small. Despite the efforts of Bevin and Citrine to secure acceptance in Whitehall, the memories of the General Strike, the fact that the 1927 Act remained on the statute book and above all the inability of government to end mass unemployment contributed to a soured relationship.

The rethinking of Conservative policy after the 1945 election defeat marked a profound change in the Party's attitude to the unions. Since the six years of opposition were to leave their mark on policy up to 1964 this period is worth looking at in some detail. Two background factors were especially important. First, there was a widespread belief in the party that defeat was due in part to unpopularity among trade unionists; hence attempts such as that mentioned earlier to produce a version of the past stressing Conservative support for unions. Second, the commitment to maintain full employment meant that — in Macmillan's words — 'the harsh and cruel discipline of the days of unemployment'[59] no longer restrained union demands; some sort of permanent accommodation was needed. The party met these problems in two ways, one in terms of organisation, the other in terms of ideology. The former, though of no great substantive importance, marked a significant symbolic change in attitude. Before the Second World War the party had organised 'Labour Advisory Com-

mittees' which were effectively instruments of anti-trade union propaganda. The Committees became defunct during the war and were not
revived.[60] Instead, they were replaced by a Trade Union Advisory
Committee, set up to advise the party on labour problems.[61] It was one of
only five sub-committees of the National Union. At constituency level
attempts were made to encourage trade unionists to play an active role.
Constituency associations were required to include a trade unionist in their
annual conference delegation; and conversely the party leadership
encouraged members to join and become active in their appropriate trade
union.[62]

The ideological response was more complex, since it went to the heart of
the problem of how to find an accommodation with the unions. The party
faced two immediate problems: what, if anything, to salvage from the
Trades Disputes Act which Labour had repealed in 1946; and how to
respond to collective bargaining in a situation of full employment. The first
solution to the former appeared in the *Industrial Charter*, published in May
1947, and it represented a muted variation on a traditional theme. It
promised to legislate on three matters: to ban the closed shop in public
employment since it 'takes away a man's liberty'; to forbid civil service
unions to support political parties; and to revert to contracting in to the
political levy.[63] The problem of collective bargaining was tackled by the
development of a highly modified version of laissez-faire. The Labour
Government was accused of dominating the unions. The party argued that
union leaders, responsive to the wishes of government rather than to the
needs of their members, became remote from the rank and file, and that
this in turn led to unofficial strikes.[64] There were particularly scathing
attacks on the way union leaders cooperated in the Labour Government's
wage freeze after 1948. Labour, argued the party's spokesman on labour
affairs, was reducing the wage setting role of the unions 'and that is exactly
our complaint. . . . Their job is to look after wages and hours and
conditions, not to play politics and ignore the troubles of their own men
and women.'[65]

This approach did two things: it took the unions out of politics; and
equally it took the state out of collective bargaining, since it implied that
unions not only had no obligation, but even no right, to subordinate their
policies to the desires of government. In the three years after 1947 the
Conservative commitment to non-intervention in collective bargaining
was strengthened in a number of ways. In the search for peace with the
unions the commitments to legislation made in the *Industrial Charter* were
first modified and then dropped: in 1949 they had become a promise to call
a 'round table conference' with the unions to discuss matters such as the
closed shop.[66] In the 1950 election the party promised close consultation
with the unions before introducing legislation, and in 1951 the party
leadership, having first tried to avoid the matter, finally gave an explicit
promise to maintain the status quo.[67] The seal on this policy of abstention

was set by Churchill's appointment of Walter Monckton as Minister of Labour in 1951. Monckton was chosen because he had no clear party affiliation and was given the brief of ensuring good relations with the unions.[68]

By 1951 the essence of the Conservative response to the trade unions for the next thirteen years had been developed. It was dominated by an overwhelming desire for an amicable arrangement. After 1951 the TUC's position was, if anything, strengthened compared with the immediate post-war period. The contentious question of contracting out disappeared from official Conservative thinking, never to reappear. Above all, the party leadership strongly resisted any suggestions of legislative intervention in the questions of strikes or the closed shop. Indeed so sensitive were the leadership in this respect that any suggestion of intervention brought a sharp rebuke to the culprits. As late as the 1961 Party Conference the platform put up a senior Tory trade unionist to dismiss as 'shocking' a motion calling for an enquiry into the unions and legislation on the basis of the enquiry's recommendations;[69] in 1957 a Tory MP who called for a Royal Commission was rebuked in private by his Chief Whip — Edward Heath — for his 'unhelpful' attitude;[70] and in the autumn of 1959 Heath, now Minister of Labour, called in to his Ministry the two authors of an early day motion calling for a Royal Commission in a vain attempt to have the motion withdrawn.[71]

Official Conservative policy during the thirteen years after 1951 was very much of a piece, but it was nonetheless marked by significant nuances. The most important of these concerned the question of wage claims. The party came to office in 1951 espousing a modified version of economic laissez-faire. In pure laissez-faire theory the level of wages is determined by negotiations between the individual worker and employer, the level of pay being very much a function of the market situation of the former. The state fulfils a neutral role and the effect of combination — either in trade unions or employers' organisations — is to distort the workings of the market. The Conservative version in 1951 accepted the fact of worker combination and envisaged wages being determined by negotiation between unions and employers untramelled by state intervention.[72] But this version of 'collective' laissez-faire — where the bargaining units are not individuals but institutions — was accompanied by a fatal ambiguity about the role of the state. Formally government had been taken out of collective bargaining; but the 'background' role it was assigned included the maintenance of a high level of employment. Thus the state, by ensuring that labour was in short supply, had a significant effect on the operation of the labour market, allowing unions to use their institutional power to push up the rate of pay increases. The government could attempt to mitigate this indirectly through inducing unemployment through demand management, but given the electoral consequences of such a policy its freedom of manoeuvre was very limited.[73]

As a result of this ambiguity about the role of the state the behaviour of Conservative Governments over the matter of wage claims was – especially in the early 'fifties – schizophrenic in character. Successive Conservative Chancellors urged the unions to restrain their wage demands – in other words to subdue the function which they had been assigned by the party before the 1951 election – while Conservative Cabinets, and the Minister of Labour as their agent, conceded the unions' case in most instances. Thus in 1952 the Chancellor, as the custodian of sterling, was urging restraint on unions; while in the same year the Minister of Labour, as the custodian of friendship with the unions, was encouraging the engineering employers and the British Transport Commission to concede large pay claims.[74] This conflicting approach was probably exacerbated by the fact that Monckton's role in the Government was very specialised; he hardly considered himself a Conservative politician but rather a non-partisan minister for the preservation of industrial peace.[75] But the apogee of indecision was actually reached in 1957 when Iain Macleod was Minister of Labour and Harold Macmillan Prime Minister: the Government initially encouraged the engineering employers to resist a large wage claim, but having urged resistance the two, when it came to the critical point, exercised pressure on the employers to reach a settlement.[76]

The increasingly rickety state of the economy after 1960 clarified the Government's mind considerably.[77] The pay pause of 1961, and the setting up in 1962 of the National Incomes Commission with an explicit brief to work out a policy for pay increases, marked a significant incursion into wage regulation.[78] Though unaccompanied by legislative compulsion these moves represented the final discarding of the laissez-faire theory of wage determination with which the Conservatives had entered office at the beginning of the 'fifties. Government wage policy thus represented a significant variation on the theme of non-intervention in collective bargaining. Conservatives grew accustomed to intervention at least in this area of industrial relations.

An alteration of this magnitude could not, of course, be insulated from other aspects of policy and during the years of Conservative rule other significant shifts took place in the attitude of Conservative Ministers of Labour. Monckton's tenure of office – 1951 to 1956 – was marked by extreme quiescence: even the commitment to draw up a non-enforceable and rather vacuous 'workers charter' was dropped on the advice of both sides of industry, who felt that autonomous collective bargaining was best left untrammelled even by this minimal measure.[79] Monckton's chief contribution to Tory thinking was to state what became, with minor modifications, the apologia of successive Ministers of Labour in resisting calls for legislative intervention. Monckton saw industrial relations primarily as a matter of good 'human relations'. While government could create a favourable economic environment, industrial peace was mainly in the hands of management, who must display 'sympathetic handling of human relations.'[80] Workers were assigned a more subordinate role: they were to give 'the skill of their minds and of their hands to a common purpose which they understand and approve.'[81] These views represented a shift from the economic liberalism with which the Conservatives entered office. Industrial conflict was no longer a function of rational economic differences between workers and employers but a matter of human relations; and workers were no longer equal bargainers with employers in a free market but subordinates to be consulted and managed so that they gave of their best in a joint economic venture. The consequences for the state were, however, similar in both cases: economic liberalism decreed non-intervention lest the operation of market forces be undermined; 'human relations' theory led to non-intervention because such matters were held to be too delicate and complex for legal regulation.

Good industrial relations were thus a matter of careful management of subordinates. But this did not of necessity imply total quiescence on the part of government. Even Monckton, spurred by a rash of strikes in 1955, opened discussions with leaders of industry on how stoppages might be avoided;[82] and from the mid-'fifties on governments became increasingly concerned with the question of securing industrial peace. The desire to maintain good relations with the unions coupled with the 'human relations' theory meant, however, that they long avoided any suggestion of legislative intervention[83] in favour of two other approaches. The first centred on the individual worker. The 'human relations' theory stressed that the worker would not cooperate without sympathetic handling. From 1955 onwards, therefore, interest revived in ideas expressed in the *Workers' Charter* of 1947. In 1957 Macleod, faced with the worst year of industrial unrest since 1926, announced that he was to draw up a list of the best current employment practices in the hope that they would be more widely adopted.[84] The Conservatives were evidently not satisfied with the response, for by 1962 they had decided on legislative intervention: the Contracts of Employment Act, which became law in 1963, entitled workers to, among other things, a period of notice commensurate with their length of service, and was designed to remove some of the fears of redundancy. But this small carrot of security was accompanied by a stick: workers who engaged in unconstitutional industrial action would be deemed to have broken their continuity of employment and to have thus forfeited their rights under the Act. ('Unconstitutional' industrial action takes place in defiance of agreed procedures for settling disputes; 'unofficial' action occurs without the express permission of the union body which has the authority to call for such action.)

Workers might be consulted and every attempt made to give then a feeling of security, but official Tory policy recognised clear limits to the extent to which this could produce industrial peace. Workers were not to be entirely trusted because, as Mr Macleod put it in rejecting a call for compulsory secret ballots before strikes, 'the idea . . . that workers are less militant than their leaders . . . is not my experience, nor is it the experience of any Minister of Labour.'[85] It followed that the other way to industrial peace was through the moderating influence of the official union leadership. This was to be achieved by getting the trade union leadership together with leaders of industry to discuss the causes of strikes, as Monckton did in 1955. By 1960 the greater urgency of the problem was reflected in more specific action. During his brief tenure as Minister of Labour Heath convened the Joint Consultative Council of the NJAC and gave them a programme of discussion to improve industrial relations,[86] while his successor, John Hare, initiated talks between unions and employers in the strike-troubled motor industry. Yet the attitude was still abstentionist. Hare advised both sides: 'Get on with your studies of the unofficial strike problem. Immediately you are ready, please start talks with one another. If you want any help from me, I shall be available.'[87]

But a more critical note soon began to appear. Since, as Hare put it, strikes were 'a breakdown of loyalty and discipline',[88] there was a need for responsible trade union leaders to control militant members. The existence of unofficial strikes demonstrated that the official leadership was not doing its job properly. But the Government's role was still held to be to encourage the unions to reform themselves: in 1964, for instance, the Government refused to sponsor legislation to remove legal disabilities hampering trade union amalgamations, but ensured time for a Private Member's Bill to that effect.[89] But as the union leadership apparently failed to solve the problems of 'loyalty and discipline' the Government began to lose patience. In 1961 Hare, while launching a strong defence of voluntary reform, yet remarked that if change did not come by these means then legislative intervention – the content of which he did not specify – would have to be considered.[90]

Just over a year later, in introducing the Second Reading of the Contracts of Employment Bill – which he presented as an explicit break with the voluntary tradition – he indicated a sharp break with the dominant policies of the post-war years. Speaking of unofficial strikes he suggested:

> The most satisfactory way of dealing with all this is for the unions to put their house in order. By an assertion of responsibility and leadership they should see that the agreements which they conclude are honoured . . . the TUC decided last autumn to review the structure and purpose of the trade union movement . . . that review must be carried out quickly and must lead to reform. If it fails, then the situation will be serious and we must ask ourselves whether we can afford to let things go on as at present. My view is that we cannot . . . there is a strong body of opinion, by no means based on party political lines, which is demanding that the government should introduce new legislation to protect the public interest.[91]

The Contracts of Employment Bill is thus a watershed in policy. It signalled the Government's impatience with voluntary reform in three ways: impatience with the slow progress made by industry in giving the worker security; impatience with the individual worker, as indicated by the 'penalty' clauses against unconstitutional strikers; and impatience with the official union leadership, as indicated by Hare's remarks in the House of Commons. When it is recalled that by this time the Government had also explicitly abandoned its policy of non-intervention in the business of wage determination, it will be clear that the abstentionist model of the state's role in industrial relations had been modified in important ways.

By the early 'sixties, then, certain features marked the relationship between the trade unions and the Conservatives: a lingering suspicion which was a legacy of the events before 1939; the relatively amicable relationship painstakingly established in the late 'forties and 'fifties; and by the 1960s the growing impatience with what seemed – in the eyes of Conservative Ministers of Labour – to be the failure of union leaders to control their members in the national interest.

THREE TRADITIONS IN INDUSTRIAL RELATIONS

The changes described here are complex, but at the risk of oversimplification it is possible to distinguish three distinct historical traditions in the development of industrial relations, specially as far as the state's role is concerned. These traditions are important in two ways. First, their influence on past behaviour influenced the later attitudes of participants: the historical role of the judiciary, for instance, goes some way towards explaining trade union hostility to legal regulation. Second, these traditions represented part of the stock of ideas about industrial relations. When people began seriously to consider reform in the mid-'sixties these traditions were a common source of many of the most important proposals. The identifiable traditions may be discussed in terms of three categories: liberalism; voluntary collectivism; and compulsory collectivism.[92]

Liberalism was the dominant tradition in industrial relations for much of the nineteenth century. Though the liberal tradition could accommodate trade unions, it was characterised by an instinctive hostility towards them. This is accounted for by two separate, though related, impulses behind liberalism, market and moral. Market liberalism, in pure form, was hostile to any combination in the market place as tending to distort the workings of supply and demand. Of course few people were consistently opposed to combination, but in a vulgarised form of attachment to private enterprise and individual initiative market liberalism was very influential in, for instance, the Conservative Party before 1914. Market liberalism could be modified – as it was by the Tories after 1945 – to take account of unions, but it has never been dead as a source of suspicion of trade unionism. In the Conservative Party in particular there has always existed a substantial core who were thoroughgoing market liberals. Perhaps even more important, most Tory politicians have been receptive in some degree to arguments about allowing market forces to operate freely. Market liberalism enjoyed a revival in the party after 1964 and was to exercise a strong influence on the remaking of industrial relations policy.

Market liberalism is partly an empirical theory about the way economic forces operate, but it is equally fuelled by a moral concern for the freedom and integrity of the individual. Moral liberalism does not entail automatic hostility to unions, but it does produce a fear that they may coerce their own members or the rest of the community. Hostility to unions on this basis is largely a response to the contemporary growth of union power, but it also existed in the nineteenth century. It lies behind the insistence of the 1871 Trade Union Act in treating unions as akin to voluntary friendly societies and refusing them any legal powers over their members.[93]

In recent years the main custodian of moral liberalism has been the judiciary. In the 1950s and 'sixties a whole series of judicial decisions tried to limit the rights of unions to expel members, to compel unions to observe the dictates of natural justice in framing their rules and to limit the effect of strike action on the community.[94] The Conservatives also, despite their rapprochement with the unions after 1945, were influenced by such ideas. Attachment to them is best indicated by an enduring hostility to the closed shop on the grounds that it 'takes away a man's liberty.'

Liberalism has been an important but subordinate tradition in industrial relations in the twentieth century. Voluntary collectivism, on the other hand, virtually defines the system which existed, with two short breaks, from 1906 until the mid-1960s. Its key feature was the role assigned the state, which may best be described as one of benevolent neutrality. The state encouraged organisation by both workers and employers and even, through such devices as the Fair Trading Resolutions,[95] used its own economic power to assist the growth of unions. After 1945, in addition, it attempted to manage the economy so as to provide a background of full employment, which was itself advantageous to the unions. But the state largely refrained from intervention – especially intervention backed by legislation – in the regulation of industrial disputes and the substantive regulation of working conditions. The general tradition could coexist with a wide variety of opinions. In the case of the closed shop, for instance, Labour welcomed it while the Conservatives did no more than encourage workers to join unions. The common link – at least after 1945 – was that legislative intervention was thought inappropriate.

Voluntary collectivism was the dominant tradition for most of the twentieth century because it coincided with the interests of certain powerful institutions. It suited the unions, already comparatively well organised by the turn of the century, since it took out of the industrial struggle institutions such as the judiciary which they believed to be prejudiced in favour of employers; it suited individual employers since it allowed them freedom to accommodate themselves to their employees;[96] it suited employers' associations since under a system of industry-wide collective bargaining it gave them a key role; and after 1945 it suited the Conservative Party's desire to reach an accommodation with the unions. On a number of occasions, however, the tradition was challenged by the alternative of compulsory collectivism.

Compulsory collectivism in relatively pure form is really a hallmark of Communist and Fascist autocracies. Under it unions become incorporated into the decision-making machinery of the state and as the price of this become agents of state policy. Their bargaining functions are replaced by legal regulation, and recruitment is enforced by a legally compulsory closed shop. In this extreme form compulsory collectivism has never existed in Britain, but under the stress of two World Wars some of its elements appeared in diluted form: unions were coopted into the decision-making machinery, membership was encouraged by government, strong pressure was exerted on the official leadership to exercise discipline over the rank and file, and a system of compulsory arbitration was introduced which had the effect of making strikes illegal.[97] In practice unions were never so docile as a purely legal description might suggest, but equally the tradition of compulsory collectivism has not been confined to wartime. In the Tory Party during the 1930s some envisaged the integration of trade unions and employers' associations into government in return for the exercise of control over members.[98] As we shall see, this tradition was very much alive in the Conservative Party and among employers during the 'sixties. In the Labour Party, what may be termed a Fabian outlook has long been receptive to such notions; indeed the Webbs hoped to see voluntary collective bargaining eventually replaced by the method of 'legal enactment'.[99] Not surprisingly, then, the tenure of the Labour Governments between 1964 and 1970 coincided with a revival of compulsory collectivism and the development of large-scale intervention in collective bargaining. The most important instance – the Prices and Incomes legislation of 1966 – was admittedly intended as a temporary measure but others, such as the 1965 Redundancy Payments Act, the 1968 Race Relations Act and the 1970 Equal Pay Act signalled a steady growth. The most spectacular attempt at intervention occurred with Labour's abortive proposals in *In Place of Strife*, which would have given state financial support to unions; provided legislative backing for the extension of union membership and the closed shop; and would have involved Ministers, the Commission on Industrial Relations and the TUC in disciplinary action against certain strikers.

The traditions described here are not, of course, readily compatible. To someone influenced by moral and market liberalism certain aspects of voluntary collectivism are distasteful, while compulsory collectivism is wholly abhorrent. But one of the most striking features of the debate about the reform of industrial relations was the extent to which the different traditions mingled in the making of policy. No institution consistently spoke for one tradition and in some cases – the Tory Party being the most outstanding example – policy became a complex mixture of all three.

Nor do the traditions correspond to any easily recognisable grouping in British politics. The liberalism described here, for instance, conforms to the nineteenth-century notion of liberalism as individualism. Politicians conventionally described as 'liberal' – such as Mr Roy Jenkins – are collectivists as far as industrial relations are concerned. Nor does the liberal tradition imply a laissez-faire, passive role for the state. Though representatives of liberalism oppose state intervention when it takes the form of statutory wages policy, they tend to support other forms of intervention by the state as a means of restoring market forces and protecting the individual against the incursions of collectivism. The real supporters of laissez-faire in industrial relations in the post-war years have been the defenders of voluntary collectivism; liberals and compulsory collectivists were both in favour of positive state action, though on very different grounds and with very different ends in mind.

The various proposals put forward for the reform of industrial relations in the second half of the 1960s are best seen as responses to the crisis of voluntary collectivism. This crisis was a product of the ambiguous role assigned to the state: government, while formally neutral, maintained full employment, thus tilting the balance in the industrial struggle in favour of employees. This in the long run undermined the system and threatened the interests of powerful institutions. Before we examine their responses it is useful to look briefly at how in fact voluntary collectivism was weakened. This is the purpose of the next chapter.

2 The Crisis of Industrial Relations

The twenty-five years after 1945 were marked by a paradox: intense dissatisfaction with Britain's economic performance was accompanied by unprecedented economic success. For the first time in the country's history, full employment was maintained for more than a few years; the economy grew at a rate which compared favourably with its performance at the height of the Industrial Revolution;[1] and the benefits of expansion were distributed – albeit very unevenly – throughout all sections of society. Poverty still existed, but it would be difficult to find any group whose material lot had failed to improve in the quarter century after the end of the Second World War.

The sources of dissatisfaction in the face of such success are complicated, but the most immediate arose from a comparison of the country's economic performance with that of its chief competitors. The success of the British economy was based on the post-war boom in world trade, but relative to other countries we experienced a marked decline. In most of the tables of economic growth in industrial nations, Britain came at or near the bottom, while the historical decline in the country's share of world trade – which began as far back as 1870 – continued after 1945.[2] The general decline was dramatised by the well-publicised problems of such traditional industries as shipbuilding, and by recurrent balance of payments crises.

Nobody knows why this decline took place: it may reflect a 'natural' process of catching up by other countries who experienced their industrial revolution after Britain; it may be the result of markets lost during the two great wars; it may arise from the type and level of capital investment in the economy; it may be that certain characteristics of our social institutions inhibit enterprise and economic efficiency; or it may arise from a combination of all of these. The most common explanation for the shortcomings of the economy in the post-war years was essentially an institutional one. The institutions of British society, it was argued, were not adapted to the pursuit of rapid economic growth: the civil service lacked the expertise to manage the economy efficiently; the education system did not train people with the appropriate skills; while higher management lacked enterprise and efficiency, either because it was shackled by high rates of taxation or was not recruited by sufficiently meritocratic methods.[3] It is against this background of increasing dissatisfaction with the country's economic performance and increasing criticism of the main institutions of British society that the criticisms of the system of industrial relations must be viewed. The particular content of these criticisms was affected by the nature of the problems facing voluntary collectivism in the 1960s, and by the way in which these problems affected the interests of different institutions.

THE DECLINE OF THE NATIONAL SYSTEM

By the end of the 1930s a national system of industrial relations was widely established in Britain. Working conditions and, in the last analysis, procedural questions were settled by means of industry-wide negotiations between the representatives of trade unions and employers. By the middle of the 1960s these national institutions still remained, but in many industries – most notably engineering – they were in decline. Pay and conditions were increasingly determined by the direct action of groups of workers on the shop floor; disputes about working conditions or about the application or interpretation of agreements were increasingly settled after unofficial strike action by workers; and shop-floor institutions – such as shop stewards and joint shop steward committees – were increasingly replacing the formal union machinery as the representatives of workers.[4]

The main reason for the decline of the national system was the end of mass unemployment at the end of the 'thirties. The acute labour shortage during the war began the process of employers offering rates of pay well above those agreed nationally. By 1967 wage drift was so far advanced that the Donovan Commission calculated that it accounted for more than half of the average wage packet in engineering. Wage drift created problems for both governments and employers. The former became increasingly committed to restraining wage demands but found that drift severely restricted their capacity to do so, especially by voluntary means: there was little point in making agreements about wage norms with national spokesmen for unions and employers since they had a decreasing influence on rates of pay.[5] Wage drift was, it is true, limited to certain industries, and probably only existed in a really developed form in engineering. But, given the extent to which pay demands are affected by comparisons, industries in which drift occurred tended to act as pacemakers for the rest, thus complicating the task of securing general restraint.[6]

For the individual employer, wage drift created equally acute problems. In some cases the existence of drift signalled the almost complete loss of control over wage costs. Wages were frequently determined by a highly complicated series of ad hoc agreements, often negotiated with quite small groups of workers. Relative pay levels between different grades were highly unstable, allowing ample scope for 'leapfrogging' wage demands. Not only could one group of workers play off another against a common employer; it was also possible to extract wage concessions from one highly profitable concern and then use this as a lever to gain comparable increases elsewhere.[7] In the boom conditions of war and the expanding international economy of the early 'fifties, escalating labour costs could be borne, but increasingly fierce foreign competition in the late 'fifties and 'sixties both at home and abroad meant that export industries in particular were caught in a pincers movement: on the one side increasingly competitive foreign goods, on the other wage costs that were very difficult to control.[8]

Wage drift, though important, was only part of a wider phenomenon. The thirty years after 1940 saw a massive de facto expansion of workers' control in key areas of British industry. A whole series of decisions traditionally thought of as the prerogative of management – concerning speed of work, rates to be paid for particular types of work and the amount of overtime to be worked – were in many cases made jointly by management and workers, or even by workers alone. It was again in engineering that this development was most pronounced.[9]

The assertiveness of workers was best symbolised by the rise of the shop steward. At the end of the 'thirties there had been relatively few stewards, and those who did exist were marginal figures in industrial relations. With full employment the number of stewards rose rapidly: in engineering, for instance, the figure rose by over fifty per cent between 1947 and 1961. By 1967 the Donovan Commission estimated that there were over 175,000 in all.[10] This rise in numbers accompanied a transformation of the steward's role from that of a relatively unimportant auxiliary to that of a key figure in industrial relations in many industries. It was the steward – or a group of stewards – who negotiated the payments additional to national rates that accounted for wage drift; and it was largely through their stewards that workers began to exercise increasing control over their jobs. In addition, few union members attended meetings; their contact with the union was largely through their stewards.[11] By the 1960s shop-steward organisations in many cases rivalled, and in a few cases had virtually supplanted, official union organisation in the workplace.

The rise of the shop steward is most immediately accounted for by the end of mass unemployment, but there were other contributory factors. Management in many industries had a traditional preference for domestic bargaining within the workplace, which led them to turn to representatives of their own workers rather than to outside union officials.[12] It is also probable that the organisation of the trade union movement was a contributory factor. British unions are among the least bureaucratised in the world; they have, for instance, fewer full-time officers per member than unions in most comparable countries.[13] As a result, official union machinery found it very difficult to cope with the pressures arising from bargaining under full employment. Managers found themselves faced with demands from workers who realised that shortage of labour gave them a strong bargaining position; union officials could not cope quickly enough; and as a result management turned to the immediate representatives of the employees – the stewards – for quick solutions.[14]

In the decades after 1940 the national system was thus undermined in three related ways: by the appearance of wage drift; by the increased extent to which workers on the shop floor regulated day-to-day operations; and by the rise of the shop steward as a power to be reckoned with. These changes were accompanied by a fourth of equal importance. The national system had been one in which conditions of work were relatively clearly documented: written agreements tended to specify rates of pay, hours of work and the procedures to be used in settling disputes. But the extension of the domestic system of industrial relations was largely accomplished by the development of 'custom and practice';[15] that is, agreements became to a very great extent informal, arising not so much from explicit bargains formally struck as from the gradual development of certain practices over time.[16] For instance, lower management, often pressed by superiors to complete production schedules, would acquiesce in certain practices or make verbal agreements unknown to superiors. This was aided by the fact that few companies had developed coherent personnel policies.[17] It was this which led the Donovan Commission to dub the system of domestic bargaining an 'informal' one; and it was this absence of a clearly definable frontier of management power that provided one of the strongest motivations for reform.

Summing up the situation in the late 'sixties the Donovan Report argued that there were two systems of industrial relations in Britain:[18] a 'formal' national one which had declined dramatically in importance; and an 'informal' domestic one which was replacing it. It might be more appropriate to speak of three systems. There was, first, an established and effective national system of industrial relations, in which national negotiations really did largely determine conditions of work. It covered most public employment, including workers in nationalised industries. Nor was this system in retreat; during the 'sixties it had been extended to the coal industry, replacing a system in which domestic bargaining had played an important role.[19] The second system corresponded to Donovan's 'formal' model. The most extreme example of its breakdown occurred in the engineering industry where national agreements established minimum rates of pay that bore little relation to earnings; where wage drift occurred by a largely informal process of domestic bargaining; and where the national disputes procedure dealt with only a small proportion of all disputes, the remainder being settled domestically, often under pressure of unofficial and unconstitutional industrial action. This was the third, 'informal' system.

Arguments about the reform of industrial relations were to a very great extent arguments about the respective roles of the second and third of these systems. But the language of the systems was used mainly in expert circles. More generally, as a sort of short-hand, the issues were presented in terms of the country's strike record. Any discussion of the background to the Industrial Relations Act would be incomplete without an examination of this issue.

STRIKES AND INDUSTRIAL RELATIONS

Establishing an agreed interpretation of Britain's strike record is virtually impossible, and is certainly out of the question in the space available here. There are two reasons for this: the way the facts are gathered; and the differing interpretations that can be placed upon different sets of figures. The available figures are an imperfect indicator of the extent of industrial conflict for two reasons: short stoppages involving small numbers of workers do not have to be notified;[20] and the fact that the recording of strikes depends on their being notified by employers means that there is scope for variation in the extent to which disputes are recorded. This means that official statistics are rough and ready indicators which have to be treated with caution, and which are most useful for identifying long-term changes and particularly large variations.

The interpretation of these inexact statistics also presents problems. There are four common indicators of national strike activity: the number of strikes; the number of workers involved; the number of days lost; and, as a standardised measure, the number of days lost through strikes as a proportion of workers. Each of these indicators suggests different conclusions. As far as the number of strikes is concerned, most commentators would probably agree that the end of mass unemployment at the close of the 1930s marked a decisive break: the number of disputes jumped sharply, and has remained high ever since, with a marked acceleration in the late 1960s.[21] But these aggregate figures conceal important variations. Until the beginning of the 'sixties, strikes in the coal industry accounted for a large proportion of all disputes. During the 'fifties, the number of coal strikes rose while the aggregate figures remained stable; there was thus an overall decline in this period for the rest of the economy.[22] During the 'sixties, on the other hand, strikes in the coal industry fell steadily in number. In the light of this, it seems that during the decade the rest of the economy became steadily more strike-prone, while the acceleration from the late 'sixties is even more dramatic than the aggregate figures suggest.

But, even taking coal into account, the total figures by no means tell the whole story. In particular the impression they convey of a rising wave of strikes engulfing the economy is misleading. During the decade most sections of the economy became more strike-prone,[23] but the variations were still very great: to take an extreme example, between 1960 and 1970 the number of strikes in vehicles rose by two hundred and sixty per cent; in shipbuilding the comparable figure was only fifty per cent. As a corollary, the contribution of various industries to the strike totals varied enormously: between 1965 and 1970, for instance, engineering accounted for over forty per cent of all strikes.[24] Even within engineering, strikes were distributed very unevenly: research carried out for the Donovan Commission suggested that between 1960 and 1966 only nine per cent of members of the Engineering Employers' Federation experience an unconstitutional strike;[25] another investigation of the same industry found that, of 432 establishments looked at, only thirty per cent had ever had a stoppage, and three of these accounted for forty-one per cent of all strikes.[26]

At the risk of oversimplification, two sets of conclusions can be suggested. First, the overall number of strikes rose with the end of mass unemployment; remained on a high plateau outside the coal industry until the beginning of the 'sixties; and rose again in the 'sixties, accelerating sharply after 1966. Second, though strikes became more common throughout the whole economy in the 'sixties, the figures suggest a picture of intense conflict in a limited number of industries – and even firms – rather than a really widespread struggle.

Establishing an agreed interpretation of the next two sets of figures – for days lost and number of workers involved – is even more difficult. This is because a single big strike can enormously inflate the figures: in 1962, for instance, there were over two hundred fewer strikes than in the previous year but because of a large engineering dispute the figures for number of workers involved rose fivefold, and the number of days lost almost doubled.[27] Because of this it is difficult to discern a trend, beyond the not very surprising rise in the figures with the end of mass unemployment and a very clear leap after 1967. The final indicator – days lost in strikes per thousand workers – is in principle the most useful figure, since it is a standardised measure which takes account of differences in size of workforce. But this measure can also be enormously inflated by a single large strike – as happened in 1957 and 1962 – and consequently it is difficult to extract any significant figures beyond the two now familiar: a rise with the advent of full employment, and a further increase in the late 'sixties.[28]

These bald figures mean very little in themselves. The arguments about the reform of industrial relations usually referred to two other features of strike activity: the extent to which disputes were unofficial and unconstitutional; and the way Britain's strike record compared with that of other countries. The importance to be assigned to figures for unofficial strikes varies with the measure used. During the 'sixties over ninety per cent of all strikes were unofficial, and this marked a great change from the 'thirties when such disputes seem to have been virtually unknown.[29] The rise of the unofficial dispute is indeed the most striking symptom of the development of the 'domestic' system. But though the great majority of strikes were unofficial the contribution of such stoppages to the other figures, though impressive, varied greatly. During the 'sixties the percentage of all days lost in unofficial actions, for instance, varied from just over eighty-five (in 1967) to sixty-two (in 1961). This is of course because the unofficial strike, though more common than the official stoppage, tends to be shorter.[30]

The significance of these figures is far from clear. An unofficial strike is not necessarily one which is in defiance of union authority. Strikes may be unauthorised for a variety of reasons: some are so short that they are over before the appropriate union body has time to consider them; or, since to authorise a strike may involve strike pay, a union may elect to save money by not declaring a strike official.[31] The level of unofficial stoppages indicates the extent to which initiative had passed to the shop floor, but it is not necessarily evidence of widespread defiance of union authority. In some unions, indeed, officials seem to have adopted a complaisant attitude to unofficial disputes. A study of a section of the engineering industry, which has been especially prone to unofficial action, argues that union officials, far from disapproving of them, had accepted the unofficial dispute as an integral part of their strategy.[32] It seems, then, that the boundary between authorised and unauthorised stoppages is not as clear as might appear at first sight.

There is a problem also in estimating the impact of unofficial strikes. One of the most common diagnoses in the late 'sixties was that Britain was suffering from a rash of short, unpredictable unofficial stoppages which interrupted production and undermined business confidence. But it was argued against this that the situation was more complex: that employers had built up means of defence against unofficial strikes; that 'lost' production was very often quickly made up; and that strikes were frequently used as a safety valve by workers who, if they did not strike, took time off in other ways.[33] An instance of the last effect seems to have occurred in the coal industry, where the decline in unofficial stoppages was accompanied by a rise in absenteeism.[34]

When attention is turned to international comparisons, the picture is even more clouded. Most available figures are quite meaningless for the purposes of comparison: to talk of number of strikes, or days lost, is pointless unless allowance is at least made for differences in size of workforce. Only a standardised measure is of any use. But even this can tell us very little, since there are wide international variations in the definition of a strike and in the way statistics are collected and assembled.[35] As a result, only the crudest variations can be detected. However, the figures for the mid-'sixties which showed Britain about mid-way in the international league table can probably be relied on,[36] and it is probably also the case that the country's relative strike-proneness increased during the late 'sixties, though this must be seen in the context of a general international rise in strike levels.[37]

A summary of the strike record in the years before the passage of the

Industrial Relations Act could run as follows. Full employment produced a clear rise in all the strike indicators, and the figures remained high in the 'forties and 'fifties. From the beginning of the 1960s the number of strikes outside coal mining began to rise, though the other measures showed no clear tendency to do so. By then the characteristic British strike had been established: it was short, unofficial, involved relatively few workers and was concentrated disproportionately in the engineering industry. The Donovan Report communicated this picture of the strike situation widely, but at the very time the Commission was carrying out its investigations conditions were changing in such a way as to render its description a historical record. From 1966 onwards the number of strikes rose sharply; and from 1967 there was a sharp increase in other figures, such as the number of days lost. Strikes also became more overtly economic in origin: about a half related to wage claims, compared to about a third in the 'pre-Donovan' era.[38]

As we shall see, the fact that there was an intensification of industrial conflict in the years immediately before the election of a Conservative Government in 1970 exerted a significant influence on the legislation which was finally produced. But the widespread belief that reform of industrial relations was necessary developed before this sharp rise in industrial disputes and – at least at the level of discussion in the news media – was related to the alleged existence of a 'strike problem'. Yet if the preceding discussion does nothing more, it suggests that no simple conclusions can be drawn about strikes in Britain before the late 'sixties: the figures are unreliable; different indicators suggest different conclusions; and the exact political and economic significance of certain sorts of strikes is not at all clear. Why, then, did so much of the argument focus on the matter of industrial disputes? Part of the answer probably lies in the fact that the mass media concentrate on strikes because of their inherently dramatic quality, whereas loss of production through other causes such as sickness cannot be so dramatised. An additional reason in the case of newspapers is that they face highly militant printing unions who have used their strategic position to extract very high wages. As a result, the newspaper industry has a very direct economic interest in attacking industrial militancy.[39] But these cannot be the only reasons, for concentration on the strike 'problem' occurred not only in the media. Most politicians also justified demands for reform in such terms. Part of the reason for this lies in the anecdotal quality of much of the evidence politicians use to support an argument. One of the most common features of the speeches of politicians is the way in which a small amount of systematic evidence – in the form, for instance, of statistics about strikes – is padded out with anecdote: a single spectacular dispute, however atypical, will receive more attention than a volume of statistics.

But there are also more substantial reasons for the widespread definition of the problems of industrial relations in terms of strikes. One of the most important arose from the state of the British economy. Whatever may be the truth about the actual economic effect of strikes, it is undoubtedly the case that by the late 1960s a great many people in positions of influence believed that they harmed the economy, and believed also that the underlying weakness of the British economy made the country especially vulnerable to the harmful effects of stoppages. (Much the same remark can be made about the general decline of national collective bargaining institutions: it may well have been the case that the decentralisation of bargaining had actually occurred only over a limited part of the economy, most notably engineering, but political decision-makers undoubtedly believed that Donovan's picture of the decline of national bargaining was a general phenomenon.) Given the beliefs about the weakness of the economy, all the effort expended to show that we had a better strike record than the Australians or the Americans was beside the point; the implicit argument was that the country's position was so weak that it could not afford even a moderately poor strike performance.

A final and important reason for the concentration on strikes arises from the dramatic quality of an industrial dispute. Industrial action takes many forms other than strikes: go-slows, overtime bans and – on piecework – refusal to work a job or working at a day work pace. These are, from the point of view of the politician or the newspaperman, invisible and unrecorded, whereas the strike is highly visible, usually recorded and frequently dramatic. The rise of domestic bargaining and workplace militancy constituted a threat to powerful institutions in industrial relations. Unfortunately it was often difficult to express the force of this threat in simple terms. An employer may plausibly argue that it is wrong for workers rather than managers to control such matters as overtime rosters and the speed of assembly lines, but this is a difficult and subtle argument. The general question of where power should lie in industry is similarly very complicated, and cannot be convincingly solved in a few short sentences. Strikes on the other hand – especially unconstitutional ones – which were a symptom of the power struggles in the workplace did have a dramatic quality which allowed argument in relatively simple terms: immediate effects could be identified, and particular individuals could be demonised or sanctified.

The fact that strikes were used as a form of shorthand for the struggles within industry had important consequences for the debate about reform. The first of these was that the arguments tended to be conducted on two levels: a public discussion which concentrated on strikes, and a debate among more esoteric circles which frankly recognised that strikes were not the most important underlying problem. The evidence of important groups to the Donovan Commission and the discussions within the Conservative Party after 1964 come into the latter category. A second consequence was that much of the effort devoted to prove or disprove the contention that Britain had a strike problem was beside the point, since strikes were merely a symptom of more important struggles.

This sketch of some problems of industrial relations in the post-war years leads naturally to a discussion of the ways in which the main interested parties responded to them. This forms the subject of the next chapter.

3 The Collectivist Hour

The policies advanced by prominent groups in the 1960s are relevant to the present discussion in a number of ways. By comparing their views with what the Conservative Party stood for after 1964 we can see what was distinctive about Tory attitudes. By looking at the views of important groups, we can also examine some significant influences on the Conservatives, who were, for instance, heavily influenced by the behaviour of the judges. Finally, we can identify some important negative influences on the making of Tory policy: at the end of the 'sixties, for instance, some important aspects of Conservative thinking can only be understood in terms of the party's need to differentiate its product from that offered by its Labour rival.

A great many people and a wide range of groups were interested in the problems of industrial relations, but four sets of institutions were especially important: the judges, the employers, the Labour Movement and a range of public bodies encompassing the civil service, the National Board for Prices and Incomes (PIB) and the Royal Commission on Trade Unions and Employers' Associations (the Donovan Commission). The most important point which will emerge from this discussion will be the attachment – with some important exceptions – of most of these institutions to collectivism in industrial relations.

THE JUDGES

Since judges were an important catalyst in the movement for reform, it is appropriate to begin with an examination of their views. One qualification is, however, necessary: since the judiciary is not a formally organised pressure group and is not primarily concerned with industrial relations, its views can only be gauged by examining separate judgements delivered at sporadic intervals. To speak of judicial 'policy' is a misnomer; nevertheless, the different judgements do show a consistent pattern.

By the close of the Second World War, judges had finally accepted the settlement between the unions and the state embodied in the Acts of 1871, 1875 and 1906, the main point of which had been to reduce to a minimum the role of law in industrial relations. From the middle of the 1950s, however, a number of judicial decisions implicitly questioned two aspects of this settlement: the abstention of the law from the regulation of the internal affairs of unions and from industrial disputes. The 1871 Act, in treating the unions as essentially private bodies, had said little about their internal regulation. By the late 1950s, a large body of legal opinion was worried by what it considered to be the possibilities for the abuse of power over union members implied by this permissive approach. At first this attitude insisted on no more than that unions observe their own rule books in their relations with members,[1] but by 1962 – possibly under the impact of a ballot rigging case in the ETU – a prominent judge suggested that the courts should be able to insist that union rules – especially those concerning expulsion of a member – be framed in accordance with criteria of natural justice.[2]

The courts' increasing interest in their rule books was a minor irritant for the unions, but the judges' interest in industrial disputes caused them serious alarm.[3] A number of decisions seemed to narrow the definition of a trade dispute so as to exclude from the protection of the 1906 Act strikes caused by inter-union disputes and strikes whose aim was to induce breaches of commercial contract.[4] The most significant case of all, that of Rookes v. Barnard, came to a head in 1964. Its precise legal implications were – and still are – unclear, but the trade-union leadership believed that it virtually nullified the protection given to unions by the 1906 Act.[5] The political implications of the case were threefold. First, it gave an opening to those in the Conservative Party who were demanding a radical change in the traditional role of law. Second, in an indirect way it led to the setting up of the Donovan Commission, which in turn stimulated so much of the argument about reform. Finally, it contributed to an increase in the hostility with which the unions regarded the courts.

THE LABOUR MOVEMENT

The Labour Movement's responses to the problems created by the rise of the domestic system were very diverse, but two are especially important: those of the Labour Government after 1964 and those of the national leadership of the trade union movement. Since these were very different, they need to be discussed separately.

a) The Labour Government 1964–1970.
Labour entered office committed to solving the problems of the economy and to embarking on a large programme of social reform without raising taxation. Both implied the general aim of increasing the rate of economic growth. The unions and their members were to make a number of contributions: they were to restrain wage demands; to abstain from unofficial strikes generally; and to reject, in particular, action designed to defend restrictive practices which hindered improvements in productivity. The last were defined as one of the key problems of industrial relations. The

Prime Minister's speeches on the matter developed a familiar pattern: 'wildcat' strikes could not be afforded; demarcation disputes were 'scandalous'; while 'hoarding of labour and work-sharing must be scheduled as practices totally inimical to our national recovery.'[6] He was echoed in more apocalyptic style by his Minister of Labour.[7] The nub of the problem was thought to be a lack of discipline, and it was to be solved by an assertion of authority on the part of the official union leadership.

In attempting to bring about this result, the Labour Government at first worked within the prevailing tradition of voluntary collectivism. Wage restraint, for instance, was to be achieved by a voluntary 'Declaration of Intent' signed with the TUC and the CBI in December 1964.[8] As to restrictive practices, the problem was said to be one for action by management and the official union leadership.[9] But this policy of abstention was soon breached in a number of important ways. To begin with, early in the life of the Government the threat of legislation was used to spur managers and unions into action. Thus in September 1965 Ray Gunter, the Minister of Labour, was threatening a legislative solution to the problems of the motor industry if the two sides failed to solve the strike problem;[10] later on in the same month Harold Wilson was declaring that 'we must outlaw those on either side of industry who bring about unofficial disputes';[11] and a short time later Gunter was telling the TUC that unless 'discipline was forthcoming on a voluntary basis . . . then the only solution lies in more fundamental means.'[12]

Within a year the economic situation had forced the Government to intervene in the wages market. The significance of the 1966 Prices and Incomes Act should not be overestimated: it was intended as a temporary measure; the legislative backing for its provisions was only used after a union had successfully challenged the Act in the courts; and every attempt was made to confine the use of facilities for compulsion to a last resort.[13] Nevertheless the legislation represented a considerable increase in government regulation of collective bargaining: apart from freezing wages for a short period, Ministers had the power to refer wage demands to a public body, the Prices and Incomes Board; they could give legislative force to the recommendations of the PIB; and in the last resort workers could even be fined if they struck in defiance of a ministerial order. In addition the PIB was given a wide-ranging brief to investigate, and recommend reforms in, industrial relations, although as we shall see its industrial-relations advisers were sceptical of the usefulness of legislative intervention.[14]

In other respects, too, the years after 1964 saw a decline in the Labour Government's attachment to voluntary collectivism: the 1965 Redundancy Payments Act, the 1968 Race Relations Act and the 1970 Equal Pay Act all involved measures of government intervention in industrial relations.[15] This trend reached its height with the appearance of the White Paper, *In Place of Strife*, in 1969. The Government had appointed the

Donovan Commission in 1965 to conduct an investigation of the state of industrial relations. There is little doubt of its disappointment when the majority of the Commission rejected legislative intervention as a cure for unconstitutional strikes (Gunter had told the Commission at the beginning that he wanted a tough report).[16] *In Place of Strife* argued that legislation could have some relevance, and proposed that the Secretary of State should have power to enforce by fines the recommendations of a public body, the Commission on Industrial Relations, in cases of inter-union disputes; to impose a cooling-off period in the case of some unconstitutional strikes; and to order a ballot of workers in some disputes.[17]

Most public arguments were focussed on these particular clauses, but these provisions were only part of a larger package which marked a sharp break with the tradition of voluntary collectivism: unions would be required to register under pain of a fine; certain types of collective agreements were eventually to be forcibly registered; the CIR was to have power to recommend the recognition of certain unions by employers; the state was to provide finance for the modernisation and professionalisation of unions; and there was constant stress on the intimate cooperation which was to take place between the Secretary of State, the CIR and the peak associations of employers and unions.[18]

The Labour Government's definition of the problems of industrial relations between 1964 and 1970 was relatively straightforward: the productivity of labour was thought to be too low, and this was believed to be due in part to a loss of authority by the official union organisations. The initial response was to try to cajole the unions into reasserting themselves, and when this failed the Government turned unwillingly to the state as a disciplinary instrument. The story is thus one of a gradual shift from voluntary to compulsory collectivism. The liberal tradition, which was to so influence the Tory proposals, was hardly discernible. *In Place of Strife* did contain some proposals for safeguarding workers' rights against unions, but on the closed shop Ray Gunter's response was typical: he suggested that it might be granted to unions in the motor industry in return for their disciplining workers who took part in unconstitutional strikes.[19]

The story of the defeat of *In Place of Strife* – and of the more limited package of measures which the Government sought to introduce as a matter of urgency in the summer of 1969 – has been well told by Peter Jenkins.[20] The opposition of the TUC communicated itself to the Labour backbenches, and the Government was forced to withdraw the measures to which the unions took objection for fear that they would fail to secure a parliamentary majority. These events mark an important turning point in the history of industrial relations in the post-war years. As we shall see, the Tories concluded from the affair that a spineless Labour leadership had capitulated to trade-union pressure, and determined that they would behave very differently when they achieved office. This in turn intimately affected the way the Conservatives treated the unions during the passage of the Industrial Relations Act, and had an important effect on the eventual fate of the legislation.

Despite the Tory view of the events, the defeat of *In Place of Strife* was not in any simple sense a surrender to the TUC. The proposals were dropped because trade-union objections were having such an effect on an already demoralised PLP that the Government's parliamentary majority was in danger of destruction. The distinction between these two interpretations of what happened is admittedly a subtle one, but it is nevertheless important. When it came to the point, Labour backbenchers were unwilling to let their leaders drive them further down the road of compulsory collectivism in the face of union opposition. The consequence was that the Government rationalised its failure to have its proposals accepted in the language of voluntary collectivism: the episode was claimed to have had the beneficial effect of pushing the TUC into voluntary reform of its own procedures for settling inter-union disputes.[21] By the end of its term of office in 1970, Labour was essentially back to the point where it had begun in 1964, rejecting both liberalism and compulsory collectivism in favour of voluntary reform. The trade unions had also reached this point by 1970, but they travelled by a different route.

b) The Trade Unions.
The leaders of the Labour Party judged industrial relations from the point of view of national economic policy, and the effect that this would have on the electoral fortunes of the party; but for the leaders of the unions these could be only part of a wide range of considerations. Three important factors affected the unions' behaviour: the problem of the authority of the official union leadership over workers on the shop floor; the institutional interests of individual unions, especially so far as membership was concerned; and the question of the state's role in industrial relations. To complicate matters, these three sets of considerations tended to push different unions in different directions.

The main effect of the wartime and post-war changes in the system of industrial relations had been to create problems of power and authority for a number of large unions: the rise of domestic bargaining in the workplace lessened the importance of national negotiations; the increasing assertiveness of shop stewards challenged the authority of national leaders over the rank and file; and the inability of national leaders to control their members reduced the leaders' credibility in making bargains with governments. One of the most common responses to this situation was to try to assert the authority of national institutions. We can see this most clearly in the case of the TUC in the early 'sixties, when the General Council was dominated by a group of union leaders especially worried about the loss of their authority. In 1960, at the instigation of one of these leaders,[22] the General Council set up a Committee to consider the problem of unconstitutional strikes, and adopted a number of its suggestions. It recommended, for instance, the expulsion of strike-leaders where unofficial action was 'taken or prolonged contrary to general policy and specific advice'. If those expelled simply joined another union then, the report suggested, the Bridlington rules might have to be changed to prevent this. Shop stewards were assigned a limited role within factories, but joint committees of stewards were frowned on, while national steward organisations were held to be 'contrary to the obligations of union membership.' Stewards who defied their Executive were to be condemned, and Executives which failed to assert their authority were 'not carrying out their responsibilities to affiliated unions.'[23] This essentially hierarchical picture of unions is epitomised by a remark of one union leader during the debate on the report: 'the trade union movement . . . is an extremely powerful machine and it can be driven only by experts.'[24] Defence of the authority of national institutions was also reflected in the evidence of the TUC to the Donovan Commission, in which Congress argued in favour of national bargaining with plant bargaining as an adjunct.[25] This attitude was reflected also in the rejection by the TUC of the Donovan analysis of the decline of the national system of industrial relations.[26]

This concern with maintaining the authority of the national leadership was related to the question of institutional stability and expansion, especially as reflected in membership figures. These are long-standing concerns: the Bridlington rules, established in 1939, are designed to ensure stability by preventing TUC affiliates poaching members from each other.[27] The unions' main response to the question of reform in the 'sixties was shaped by these institutional interests. At the 1962 Congress, the General Council was instructed to examine the structure and functions of the movement, and of the TUC in particular. The decision was hailed as the unions' contribution to the reform of industrial relations – during the debate George Woodcock posed his famous question, 'What are we here for?'[28] – but the subsequent examination gave no hint that fundamental questions about industrial relations were ever raised. Instead the exercise turned into a series of discussions on union amalgamations. The General Council, dominated by the large unions, reflected their expansionist ambitions in pressing for amalgamations; while smaller unions, fearful for their identity, resisted takeovers.[29]

The question of the role of the state in industrial relations – the third element in the unions' behaviour – was increasingly posed as the debate about reform started by the Donovan Commission got under way. The unions were divided in the answers they gave. The TUC, in its main evidence to Donovan, put forward a purist case for keeping the state in its traditional place: 'we think collective bargaining is between industry and trade unions. . . . Our idea of the state in general would be that its function is to try and create an economic situation in which industries and unions could conduct their bargains.'[30] Indeed so complete was this attachment to non-intervention that the TUC even opposed legislation which would benefit unions, such as that enforcing union recognition.[31] The state, remarked one union leader, should hold the ring, not jump into it.[32]

But under the pressure of challenges to their authority and to the institutional interests of their organisations the leaderships of some individual unions were less chary of government intervention. The GMWU, at that time the third largest member of the TUC, announced that while it defended what it called 'voluntaryism' its approach to state intervention was 'selective and functional'. Though it opposed the introduction of legally enforceable procedure agreements, it was prepared to support compulsorily imposed conciliation pauses – 'cooling-off periods' – in certain cases, and even to argue that anyone who tried to apply 'pressure or coercion' during such pauses should be fined.[33] The manner in which a desire for institutional security could breach an attachment to voluntarism is nicely illustrated by the case of another large union, the Amalgamated Engineering Union. Having initially put forward to Donovan many of the usual arguments against attempts by the state to enforce certain sorts of collective agreements, in a supplementary memorandum the union suggested that in return for the closed shop and the check-off, the automatic deduction of union subscriptions from pay, unions might be willing to 'outlaw' unofficial strikes.[34] Pressed on the matter, the AEU President offered, though in very vague terms, a possible bargain: the unions, though opposed to legislation, might cooperate if offered the security of the closed shop.[35]

It was rare for trade union leaders to contemplate legislative intervention even in such speculative terms, but as the matter of incomes policy was to show there were divisions within the movement. Most major unions gave formal assent to the Declaration of Intent of December 1964. When this voluntary policy was replaced in July 1966 by a statutory freeze, a majority in support could still be found on the General Council. This was partly a matter of reluctant acquiescence in short-term measures because of the economic crisis; but it also reflected a desire to bring under official control those developments which threatened the authority of national leadership. In moving the official General Council motion supporting the Government's freeze, Bill Carron of the AEU argued that a prices and incomes policy was essential; that there was a long-term problem of wages exceeding output; and that Governments had behaved 'like Micawbers' while the economy had become 'chaotic'.[36]

During the passage of the Industrial Relations Bill, it was sometimes argued that the unions had always been united in opposition to legislative intervention. But, as the preceding discussion suggests, matters were rather more complicated than this. There was certainly widespread suspicion of the courts. There were also some union leaders who were purists in their opposition to any state intervention. But there were others who were prepared to accept some measures – such as the 1966 statutory wage freeze – in a crisis, and others – including some of the most powerful members of the General Council – who were led by a concern for authority and institutional stability to contemplate state help in restoring discipline.

In order to work out a policy which could take account of these divisions, and to meet the challenge of the Labour Government's increasingly étatiste inclinations, the unions responded by strengthening the role of the TUC, offering centralised control by Congress as an alternative to centralised control by the state. Thus in December 1965 the General Council established an Incomes Policy Committee to make 'observations' – the Council's own word – on trade-union wage claims.[37] Similarly, the unions responded to the proposals contained in *In Place of Strife* by giving the General Council power to intervene in inter-union disputes, and to order affiliates to discipline members. The effect of these commitments on industrial relations is unclear, but there is little doubt that the TUC leaders believed that they were making significant concessions.[38]

Between the middle and the end of the 1960s most of the important groups concerned with industrial relations – such as the employers – became increasingly disenchanted with the tradition of voluntarism. In the case of the unions, however, the reverse happened. In 1964 the TUC actually welcomed an investigation into industrial relations. The General Council believed there was a 'strong case for a general enquiry', though they demanded and got as their price for cooperation legislation nullifying the effects of the Rookes v. Barnard decision.[39] Many union leaders were worried about the threat of shop-floor power, and a few important individuals were ready to contemplate a legislative solution to their problems. It was at this point that the unions would have been least hostile to legislation. But in the succeeding years the character of the leadership changed significantly. The most dramatic shift occurred in the Engineers' union. In 1967 Bill Carron – the union leader perhaps most receptive to legislation – was succeeded as President by Hugh Scanlon, who quickly became the leading opponent of legal intervention. This change of personalities marked the rise of a coalition of Communists and other left-wingers in the AEU, and in turn signified a change in the balance of power on the General Council.

At the same time, the official leaderships of many unions were trying to accommodate unofficial trade unionism. Thus at the end of the decade the TGWU – the largest TUC affiliate – began to reorganise itself internally to take account of shop-steward organisation.[40] The General Council's remarks on the role of stewards at the end of the decade, contrasting sharply as they do with those quoted earlier, indicate clearly the way in which attitudes changed. While the General Council admitted the possibility of differences over policy between unions and their stewards, it was stressed that the latter 'have authority and responsibility and cannot be excluded from consultation in the formulation of policy and bargaining . . . [In] particular bargaining situations the authority and responsibility (of joint shop stewards' committees) is complementary to the responsibility and authority of executive committees.'[41]

Between 1964 and 1970 there was, therefore, a change in the attitude of the unions towards legislation. When the Conservatives left office, there were a number of important leaders who were highly receptive to arguments about the need to restore official union authority, and even to the possibility of doing this by legislation. By the time the Tories came to introduce their proposals six years later, attitudes had changed: the political complexion of the General Council had altered, and there was an increased willingness to meet the challenge of shop-floor leaders by integration and cooperation rather than by the assertion of authority. Thus after a brief flirtation on the part of some leaders with the tradition of compulsory collectivism, by the close of the decade voluntary collectivism had been strongly reasserted.

If the trade-union response can be viewed as a dialogue between these two traditions, the third – that of liberalism – was almost totally absent. The unions shared none of the liberal objections to the closed shop, a fact which is hardly surprising in view of its considerable benefits in terms of membership stability and discipline. But even limited proposals – such as the idea of some public surveillance of the content of union rules – were also rejected.[42] The unions have been virtually united in the view that coercion and maladministration are not problems, an entirely predictable view since to admit otherwise would have been to open the door to external regulation. The only significant proposal has been the suggestion of the TUC that rule books should be revised to keep them up to date.[43] In their lack of sympathy with the liberal tradition the unions bear a marked, and perhaps surprising, resemblance to the outlook of the chief spokesmen for employers. The latter's analysis of the problems of industrial relations also amounted to a debate between voluntary and compulsory collectivism, but in their case the outcome was a very different set of proposals from those supported by the unions.

THE EMPLOYERS

For most of the post-war years it could hardly be said that there was any recognisably consistent response by employers to the rise of shop-floor power. Challenges from unions and workers were met in an improvised fashion. As the very rise of the domestic system and the spread of custom and practice indicate, the most common reaction was to submit to the challenge of workers, though this reaction was occasionally punctuated by determined attempts to reverse the process.[44] As the Donovan Report argued, one of the most common characteristics of British employers was their lack of attention to personnel policies: many main boards of companies did not include a personnel director, and the pattern of industrial relations was set by the mass of informal agreements and practices on the shop floor.[45]

The establishment of the Donovan Commission forced the national spokesmen for the employers to consider a more systematic response, the most important of which came from the CBI. The Confederation had been formed late in 1964 by the amalgamation of three employers' groups. One of these, the British Employers' Confederation, exercised great influence over CBI industrial-relations policy: the Labour Relations Department of the CBI was virtually taken over in its entirety from the BEC, and what had originally been a BEC working party drafted the CBI evidence to Donovan. The BEC in turn, a relatively small organisation, was heavily dominated by the engineering employers. It thus transpired that the CBI's diagnosis of the ills of industrial relations – and in part the suggested cure – was heavily influenced by the special problems of the engineering industry. It was in engineering that wage drift, unconstitutional action and other manifestations of the rise of the domestic system were at their most extreme.

The initial CBI evidence to Donovan, published in November 1965, identified three key problems: unconstitutional strikes; inflationary wage increases which outran rises in productivity; and restrictive practices which prevented the use of machines and men with the maximum of efficiency. The central problem was the high unit cost of labour.[46] Unconstitutional strikes were deplored chiefly 'because of their effect on work practices; they create inflationary wage drift and perpetuate restrictive practices and inefficient manning scales'.[47] The implication was that arguments about whether or not the country was especially strike prone compared with other countries were irrelevant; indeed a 'good' strike record might be a bad sign if it were bought at an inflationary price.

This diagnosis of the problem remained essentially unaltered during the years ahead, as did the proposed remedy: this amounted to the maintenance and if possible the strengthening of the national system of industrial relations at the expense of the domestic system. Both in its initial evidence to Donovan, and in its response to the final report, the CBI rejected the view that plant agreements should be anything other than a supplement to national bargaining.[48] Similarly, while accepting that productivity agreements could promote the more efficient use of labour, the Confederation argued that all too often wage increases secured in one plant were rapidly transmitted throughout an industry without corresponding concessions on productivity.[49]

The methods originally proposed by the CBI to strengthen national institutions were, with one important exception, compatible with the tradition of voluntary collectivism. A large number of proposals were concerned with improving existing machinery and developing voluntary methods of conciliation. The possibility of legally enforcing collective bargains was rejected as attractive but impractical. An amendment to the

1906 Act was proposed so as to give employers the opportunity of taking civil action in the courts against those who took part in sympathy and unconstitutional strikes, and against those who struck without being members of registered unions.[50]

It was on the question of registration that the CBI departed clearly from the tradition of voluntarism. Under the legislation existing at the time, registration had little to do with the conduct of industrial relations. It was quite voluntary, and entailed only minor advantages and commitments in the internal conduct of a union's affairs. The CBI proposed that registration should effectively become a state licence to operate as a union, and only registration would entitle an organisation to the sort of legal rights normally associated with trade unionism. The intention was that any union not granted the licence of registration would find it difficult to operate; it followed that the threat of de-registration could be used by the state to control the activities of unions. It was precisely this calculation which was to make registration so contentious a point in subsequent arguments about changes in the law.

While registration would have remained voluntary under the proposals put forward by the CBI, only strikes by registered unions would have attracted the protection of the 1906 Act. More important, the threat of de-registration would have been used to encourage unions to penalise unconstitutional strikers.[51] The CBI also suggested other measures to increase the disciplinary effectiveness of unions: an increase in the number of full-time officers; a better salary structure to attract more competent officers; and the reorganisation of unions so as to integrate plant unionism into the official structure.[52] The advantages of this approach were candidly admitted: it was unrealistic to expect an individual employer to discipline strikers, since this would force the union to support them; much better, from the employer's viewpoint, for the union, prodded by the state in the person of the Registrar, to take on this difficult task.[53]

The 'strong Registrar' solution remained the core of the CBI's proposals in the years after 1965. In 1970 it set up an internal working party under Leonard Neal to review its policy.[54] The working party recommended a strong Registrar with power to 'take action against trade unions whose members persistently flouted agreements.'[55] But in the intervening years the CBI had moved ever further from the voluntary tradition. In 1965 it argued that its proposals were within the prevailing framework of voluntarism, and that legislative regulation should be kept to a minimum. In particular it rejected as impractical the idea that certain sorts of collective agreements – in particular those covering procedure – should be made legally enforceable.[56] By the end of 1967, however, the organisation had concluded that the arguments against enforcement 'no longer weighed so heavily with the membership.'[57] In 1970 the Neal Report advanced even further. It argued that the Registrar ought to have power to impose a legally binding procedure agreement on certain industries.[58]

There were two main reasons for this change. First, the problems themselves – such as strike-proneness – increased in severity. Second, there were internal changes in the CBI. John Davies, the Director General, who in the early days of the argument had been concerned with establishing the Confederation, began to turn his attention increasingly to industrial relations, and his views leant towards legislative intervention. More important, perhaps, there were those within the organisation itself who had from the very beginning favoured legislation. The influence of the engineering employers was particularly important. There were close connections between the CBI and the Engineering Employers' Federation.[59] and the latter were mounting considerable pressure in favour of drastic intervention. In its desire to strengthen national institutions, and its reliance on the Registrar, the EEF followed the CBI closely in its evidence to Donovan;[60] but in the case of the EEF the Registrar's teeth were meant to be even sharper. The threat of de-registration could be used to induce unions to fine members who broke agreements. The Registrar was also to have power to impose penalties directly.[61] A number of means were proposed to strengthen the hand of the official union machinery. There was implicit support for the closed shop, since the fact that workers 'do not necessarily require to remain members to get another job . . . contributes to a general lack of discipline and responsibility in their actions'.[62] The practice of electing union officials was frowned on, since this made them too responsive to the wishes of the rank and file.

The Federation also wanted the state to play a direct role in tackling industrial relations problems. It proposed a tribunal, presided over by a High Court judge, with power to impose fines on unconstitutional strikers. There would also be a tribunal which would hear complaints of unjustified restrictive practices, and in certain cases make orders to workers to desist from them.[63] These proposals raised the question of enforceability. What if workers refused to pay fines, or struck against them? The Federation offered two replies: in the last analysis it had to be assumed that the law would be obeyed; and since in the first instance the union would be the disciplinary agent this apparently was felt to raise the prospects for success.[64]

The responses offered by the CBI and the EEF to the problems of industrial relations, which laid most emphasis on wage inflation and the restoration of the authority of national bargaining institutions, flowed from their position as national organisations of employers. It was partly a matter of institutional self-interest: national organisations were unlikely to view favourably the development of a domestic system which undermined their functions. In the CBI's case, it was also a matter of commitment to certain national economic objectives: in their view an incomes policy could not work without strong central institutions for collective bargaining. In the case of the EEF, its function as an employers' association was to try – unsuccessfully as it turned out – to keep wage rates at a level which could be met by its more economically marginal members.[65] Its opposition to the domestic system was based on the belief that special rates negotiated in particularly profitable plants were then transmitted throughout the rest of industry.

This commitment to the national system led to policies whose aim was to produce a workforce more subject to the discipline of national institutions. But if employers were to try to exercise discipline directly, opposition would be provoked, so the official union machinery and the state were to do the job. The CBI initially leant on the former, but gradually came to share the étatiste inclinations of the EEF. The years under discussion can thus be seen as a period when the tradition of compulsory collectivism was in the ascendant. The EEF was in the vanguard because the problems were at their most acute in engineering.

One of the most striking features of the employers' response – as in the case of the unions' – was the absence of any significant influence from the tradition of liberalism. But for a passing reference to the Registrar's role in overseeing union rules,[66] the CBI ignored the question of the coercion of individuals in unions. On the closed shop, its attitude in the 'sixties was largely agnostic,[67] since its own members were split. But both the CBI and the EEF wanted to strengthen, not weaken, the hold of the official union movement over the individual member; and both opposed the idea of a free market in wages in favour of negotiations between strong central institutions. Their ideal system of industrial relations involved a trade-union movement staffed by a powerful bureaucracy making agreements on behalf of a well-disciplined rank and file.

Other organisations of employers echoed this rejection of liberalism in even more emphatic terms. As early as 1965, the motor manufacturers had proposed legislative sanctions against unconstitutional strikes in their industry, and had offered the unions the prospect of a closed shop in return.[68] Their views ran the whole gamut of compulsion: a strong Registrar; legally enforceable procedure agreements; a public body to enforce the negotiating rights of a single union in a plant; what amounted to a closed shop in return for the unions disciplining unconstitutional strikers; a system of courts; and enforcement by the deduction of fines from pay.[69] Employers' organisations in the building and shipbuilding industries, more restrained, echoed the CBI's call for a strong Registrar and for strengthening the capacity of national unions to discipline their members.[70] The local authority employers, on the other hand, embraced compulsory collectivism: they advocated a closed shop for unions; legal enforceability of all collective agreements throughout the economy; and penalties against both workers who struck in breach of contract and employers who paid above nationally agreed rates.[71]

But the response of the national institutions was not the sum of the responses of individual employers. National associations were concerned to defend national bargaining, partly out of institutional self interest and partly to keep earnings at a level which could be borne by inefficient and less profitable members. There were several splits in the employers' ranks. One concerned compulsory membership of unions. National associations, dominated often by large employers, were frequently prepared to concede some form of closed shop in return for unions disciplining workers, while the chief organisation representing smaller companies condemned any such arrangements.[72] The extent to which individual companies were willing to strengthen the national system of industrial relations – the essence of the remedy offered by the employers' associations – also varied enormously. In practice, of course, the majority of companies were quite unprepared to defend the national system: the very growth of domestic bargaining indicated that. For highly profitable firms, or for firms in capital intensive industries, observance of nationally agreed rates had no attraction.[73] A profitable and efficient employer, faced with a labour shortage, found that the most obvious way to solve it was to pay more than his rivals. In industries where labour costs were a relatively small proportion of total costs – such as oil refining – it also made sense to negotiate 'productivity' deals, which either genuinely increased the efficiency with which equipment was used, or bought off the threat of a strike which would have left expensive equipment lying idle. Employers' associations occasionally tried to discipline firms who 'poached' workers by offering high rates, but the available sanctions proved quite ineffective.[74] In asking for a strengthened national bargaining system policed by the unions and the state, national associations were thus asking not only for increased control over workers, but also for increased control over individual employers.

THE PUBLIC INSTITUTIONS

Apart from the judiciary, three public institutions were closely concerned with industrial relations in the period before 1970: the civil service, especially the Ministry of Labour; the Prices and Incomes Board; and the Donovan Commission.

In formal terms, senior civil servants have no partisan views on policy; in practice, as is well known, both individuals and departments frequently develop very strong views on policy. The problem for the outside observer is that the constitutional fiction of impartiality makes it difficult to discover what these views are. What follows is therefore based partly on published evidence, but relies also on information gathered by less formal means. Despite this qualification, there seems little doubt that during the 'fifties and early 'sixties acceptance of the prevailing tradition of voluntary collectivism was widespread among senior civil servants. It seems that Joseph Godber, the last Tory Minister of Labour, was still getting advice opposing legislation in any drastic form right up to the general election of

1964. The Ministry of Labour evidence to Donovan, published in 1965, though a carefully balanced document, exuded an air of scepticism about legislative solutions. On strikes, for instance, it argued that their causes were very complex and that 'most of the changes in the law commonly suggested to solve the strike problem are unrealistic and unacceptable'.[75] It reviewed in highly sceptical fashion the various possibilities, concluding that some changes in the civil law were a possibility. It also mooted the possibility of legally enforceable procedure agreements, though without commending them.[76] The Department of Economic Affairs, more directly concerned with the problem of implementing an incomes policy, argued in favour of stronger central institutions, in particular for a strengthening of the influence of the TUC and CBI. But the Department was unclear how this could be done, and explicitly rules out legislation as a method.[77]

By 1969 this situation had changed, and many senior officials in the Department of Employment in particular were in favour of intervention. The change is symbolised by the fact that Sir Denis Barnes, who drafted the 1965 evidence to Donovan and was Permanent Secretary during the passage of the Act, also played a key role in drafting *In Place of Strife*. The reasons for the change are twofold. It is, first, not difficult to imagine increasing disenchantment with the voluntary system as the strike statistics climbed steeply after 1966. The civil servants, after all, were better placed than most to observe the figures. But a second reason, according to a senior member of the Department at the time, was the transfer of responsibility for incomes policy to the Department in 1968: 'As long as the prime responsibility for . . . incomes policy was outside the Ministry . . . it was possible for the Ministry to continue with its traditional role. The distinction between industrial relations and incomes policy could therefore be maintained. When . . . the Ministry became the Department of Employment and Productivity with prime responsibility for the prices and incomes policy there had to be a significant change in attitudes towards intervention.'[78]

If senior civil servants became increasingly inclined to legislative intervention in the late 'sixties, the same could not be said of the two other public bodies mentioned. The Prices and Incomes Board had no unified voice on industrial relations. According to the official historian of the Board, its industrial relations branch was predisposed towards the voluntary tradition.[79] The Board's individual reports and recommendations certainly showed it to be no friend of the national system. It was, for instance, one of the chief apostles of productivity bargaining, rejecting the employers' thesis that it produced an inflationary effect throughout the economy.[80] On the other hand the Board's Chairman, Aubrey Jones, argued before the Donovan Commission for a strengthening of national bargaining institutions, backed by legislative sanctions: power, he suggested, should be shifted to the centre by giving to the Board powers akin to those of the Monopolies Commission; in enforcing the recommendations of the Board Ministers would consult the TUC and the CBI; and, if a recalcitrant resisted the Board, the Minister and the peak associations, then legal compulsion could be used. In this way the state and the leading interest groups would form an alliance: 'reserve legal powers would help to increase the influence of the CBI and the TUC over their members and, on the other side, the opinion of the CBI or the TUC would underpin the legal power.' There would be no return, Jones remarked, to 'free' collective bargaining.[81]

Given that the Board employed a large number of well-informed people with strong opinions of their own, a lack of unanimity is hardly surprising. This same feature is evident in the case of the Royal Commission on Trade Unions and Employers' Associations, which reported in 1968. The Commission's origins are obscure. As we shall see, the Tories favoured a more limited and briefer enquiry which would have concentrated on the state of law in the wake of the Rookes v. Barnard decision, but the Labour Government transformed this into a Royal Commission under the chairmanship of Lord Donovan in 1965. The probable reasons are twofold: it is clear that the Government believed reform was necessary, and it hoped that setting up the Commission would buy time for a voluntary approach to be tried; also, in view of Gunter's reported remark that he expected a tough report[82] it seems probable that the Government hoped that if it did decide to legislate it could use the Report's recommendations to justify its measures in any conflict with the unions. In this second expectation it was to be disappointed.

There is little doubt that the Donovan Commission was generally thought of as an investigation of trade unions, with the reference to employers' associations added merely for the sake of balance. But the final Report laid the main blame for the problems of industrial relations at the door of management, and of employers' associations in particular. The core of the Donovan Report was an exposition of what has since become a standard critique of the British system of industrial relations. National agreements, it was argued, were increasingly being eroded by domestic regulation. The domestic system had grown in a haphazard fashion: it was 'largely informal, largely fragmented and largely autonomous.' This in turn led to unconstitutional strikes and a 'Persian Market' system of piecework which upset wage relativities and caused tensions and conflicts.[83]

Part of the blame for this was put on full employment, but the Report argued that a more important consideration was the failure of management and employers' associations to adapt to the decentralisation of collective bargaining. In a famous phrase, the Report spoke of two systems of collective bargaining, 'the national and the local.' The former was largely an empty formality, but it still exerted an influence over men's minds.[84] Management still hesitated explicitly to negotiate terms at variance with national agreements, but the realities of shop-floor power pushed it – or its subordinates – into making wholesale informal concessions. Employers' associations, desiring to maintain wage rates at levels which could be met by all their members, opposed individual agreements in general and productivity deals in particular. The Report argued that in future the associations would have to drop their insistence on comprehensive national agreements; the domestic system would have to be formalised by the negotiation of plant and factory agreements; and there would have to be an extension of productivity bargaining.[85] It reviewed sceptically the main proposals for introducing more law into the system – secret ballots, cooling off periods and legal enforcement of collective agreements – and concluded that they were all inappropriate.[86]

'One person with a belief', J. S. Mill once remarked, 'is a social power equal to ninety-nine who have only interests.'[87] The Report illustrates the dictum nicely. The powerful groups with interests at stake – the TUC, the employers' associations and the civil service – strongly favoured strengthening the national system. The Report rejected such views, and in this it was heavily influenced by one man, Allan Flanders, a Fellow of Nuffield College in Oxford. Flanders' influence was felt in two ways. First, the Report rested heavily on his evidence for its identification of the central problems of industrial relations, and also its recommendation that the solution was to formalise the domestic system.[88] Second, a number of those who played a key part in drafting the Report were strongly influenced by Flanders as a writer, colleague and teacher. The Commission's Research Director was a former pupil of Flanders, while Hugh Clegg, the author of the decisive draft of the central chapters, was a colleague and friend.

As is the case with most Royal Commissions, the Donovan Report was treated by the politicians – when it suited them – as an authoritative and impartial statement of the problems and solutions. It was nothing of the sort, and was in fact as much a 'political' document as *In Place of Strife* or *Fair Deal At Work*. A minority of the Commissioners were from the beginning opposed to a legislative solution to the problems of industrial relations. This group managed after long debate to transform itself into a majority by gaining the support of a number of waverers.[89] Nor did the commitment to voluntary reform flow simply from an acquaintance with facts: Flanders, who influenced the Report so greatly, was as much a social philosopher as a social scientist, and his commitment to reform in the workplace stemmed from a strong sympathy with the labour movement and a belief that management should share authority with workers.[90]

Because writing the Report involved political bargaining and compromise, the final product contained features which appear strange if viewed simply in terms of intellectual consistency. A key section rejected the use of law as a means of reform, yet the Report also recommended that certain immunities offered by the 1906 Trade Disputes Act be restricted.[91] The explanation for this apparent contradiction is that a majority could be found for this particular piece of legal intervention even though the Report as a whole was sceptical of such measures. The thoroughgoing voluntarists were thus reduced to inserting a note of disagreement.[92] In addition to this, there were a number of dissenting notes on various aspects of the Report, and a note of reservation which virtually amounted to a Minority Report by one Commissioner, Andrew Shonfield, who rejected the whole thrust of the voluntarist argument. His case constituted an assertion of the tradition of liberalism: the main Report, he argued, 'barely concerns itself with the long term problem of accommodating bodies with the kind of concentrated power which is possessed by trade unions . . . the deliberate abstention of the law from the activities of mighty subjects tends to diminish the liberty of the ordinary citizen'.[93] He recommended making strikes which endangered life and health illegal, and ending the immunity in the 1906 Trade Disputes Act for workers who refused to drop certain restrictive practices.[94]

Faced with an issue that poses critical problems for powerful interest groups, British politicians commonly respond by setting up a Royal Commission to take the heat out of the situation by producing 'impartial' recommendations. Thus the intended function of the Donovan Commission was, in Ray Gunter's words, to give 'the guiding lights . . . that will enable the country to decide what should be the legislation necessary.'[95] It certainly produced guiding lights, but they did not all guide in the same direction. The Commission reflected instead the deep disagreements about reform: there was the voluntarist core of the Report; alongside this was a nagging doubt about the voluntarists' case which surfaced occasionally, as in the proposals to amend the 1906 Act; and finally there was Shonfield's more robust assault on the premises of voluntarism. The disparate character of the final document meant that Donovan's intended function was not fulfilled: it could not be taken as the clear recommendation on policy which would have allowed Labour to legislate and thus pre-empt the Tory proposals. The Commission's influence was more indirect. The necessity of giving evidence concentrated the minds of a great many people concerned with industrial relations. Though it exercised little direct influence on Conservative policy – by the time it reported, the Conservatives' *Fair Deal At Work* had already appeared – the evidence published by the various groups did, as we shall see, influence the evolution of Tory thinking. The Tories used the Report for a variety of purposes. Before 1970 party spokesmen, anxious to emphasise the distinctiveness of their policies, concentrated on Donovan's defence of voluntary collectivism: it was denounced as 'a report to forget' and as 'a mouse of a report'.[96] But by the time the Industrial Relations Bill was published, the Conservatives were anxious to mobilise consent for the legislation, and it was now asserted that their measures rested on 'the heartland of Donovan'.[97] The change of emphasis is only partly a matter of selective quotation; it also reflects the diverse nature of the Report's recommendations. Thus stimulation and legitimation, rather than policy-making, were Donovan's functions.

THE COLLECTIVIST HOUR

'The regulation of industrial relations is really the attempt to regulate the class struggle,' writes a leading Labour politician interested in the matter.[98] The different views of industrial relations expressed by the interested parties lend some support to this remark. There is a conflict between labour and capital, and it was reflected in the different ways unions and employers responded to the problems of industrial relations. Yet this is far from the whole story. There were some remarkable similarities between the views of employers' spokesmen and many trade-union leaders. They were united, in particular, on the defence of national bargaining institutions against the challenge of the domestic system: one of the chief points of agreement between the TUC and the CBI in commenting on the Donovan Report was that its description of the decline of the national system was overstated and its recommendations for strengthening domestic bargaining unwise.[99] A corresponding alliance – expressed in actions rather than words – in defence of the domestic system may also be observed: just as there were groups in the labour movement, such as shop-steward organisations, which resisted national authority, so there were individual employers who wanted only to be free to deal with their own employees, unhampered either by employers' associations or public bodies. Aubrey Jones described the situation as follows: 'what we are really concerned with is not management versus unions, but more organised forms of power as against less organised forms of power.'[100] This is only half the picture: there was and is a conflict between management and unions, but cutting across this there certainly was a battle between more and less organised forms of power, between on the one hand national bargaining institutions and on the other the supporters of the domestic system.

Support for organised forms of power did not of necessity imply a movement to compulsory, as distinct from voluntary, collectivism: leaders of the Labour Movement in the mid-'sixties, for instance, tended to argue that a strengthened TUC could do the job in a voluntary setting. But the apparent intractability of the problems produced disillusion with volun-tarism: employers' organisations, the civil service and the Labour Government until the climacteric of June 1969 all turned increasingly to the state to bolster up national institutions. Only the trade-union leadership, engaged in the late 'sixties in reaching an uneasy peace with workplace unionism, retained faith in voluntarism. The two ad hoc bodies set up to pronounce authoritatively and impartially on the problems of industrial relations – the Donovan Commission and the Prices and

Incomes Board – did not do so because of their internal divisions. This is ironic but unsurprising: as bodies intended to make authoritative pronouncements, they had to include as members the representatives of the main interest groups; as a result, they necessarily reflected the divisions between these groups.

The story before 1970 was, then, the familiar one of a dialogue between two traditions of collectivism. Liberalism was only weakly represented, with the exception of Shonfield's contribution and spasmodic intervention by the judiciary. The institutional interests of both the unions and the big employers' associations were threatened by many of the policies suggested by liberalism. In addition, the commitment of many groups – including the civil service and the CBI – to a national incomes policy made them sceptical of any moves which seemed to devolve power away from national bargaining institutions to the workplace. For a vigorous assertion of liberalism – though one mingled with other, often contradictory influences – we have to turn to the Conservative Party.

4 The Problems of Liberalism

By 1963 the Conservative Party was in an ambivalent state with regard to its commitment to voluntary collectivism. This was reflected in the Contracts of Employment Act, the last attempt by a Conservative Government before 1970 to deal with the problems of industrial relations. It showed in particular in the provisions denying the benefits of the legislation to unconstitutional strikers. The party had not resolved its ambivalence by the time of the October 1964 general election: during the campaign it pledged itself to no more than a short enquiry into the implications of the Rookes v. Barnard decision.[1] But after the Conservative defeat events moved quickly: nine months after the election the party leadership had privately committed itself to fundamental changes in policy, and in September 1965 the commitment was made public in a policy document, *Putting Britain Right Ahead*. Though later altered and extended, the industrial relations policies outlined in this document laid the foundations of the Industrial Relations Act. It contained three key proposals: the setting up of a powerful Registrar to regulate the internal affairs of unions; legal enforceability of certain sorts of collective agreements; and 'a range of industrial courts' to hear claims on a wide range of disputes covering dismissals, disputes between unions and appeals against the decisions of the Registrar.

At first sight, the speed of change seems astonishing: a settlement with the unions painstakingly arrived at and maintained over a long period of time was discarded in less than a year. The obvious questions to answer are: how and why did the change occur? Part of the answer is that the speed is more apparent than real. Well before 1965, official party policy contained portents of change. 'Moncktonism' – the desire to avoid antagonising the unions at virtually any cost – only existed in pure form during the halcyon years of rapidly expanding trade and production between 1951 and 1954. During the next decade, as the problems of the economy became more severe, the party leadership edged away from voluntarism: by 1963 the abstentionism of the early 'fifties in respect of wages and strikes had been breached.

The leadership's unease was reinforced by pressures coming from within the party. Four groups were pressing for reform: the constituency

associations; back-bench MPs; party pressure groups such as the Bow
Group; and officials in the party organisation.

It is difficult to estimate with any accuracy the contribution of local
activists to the change in policy. From 1954 onwards the tone of resolutions
discussed at party conferences certainly became increasingly critical of the
unions,[2] and in 1961 there was a heated debate over a call for a Royal
Commission.[3] It seems likely that for some years before the change of
policy took place there was a widespread belief among activists that
'something should be done' about the unions; but the fact that it never got
beyond spasmodic complaints and nagging on occasions such as the annual
party conference probably meant that the direct influence of activists was
small. But it is not so easy to discount the notion that pressure from this
quarter may have been influential in more subtle ways. There was
undoubtedly a body of activists that was intensely critical of the existing
Tory approach to the unions. The cumulative effect of this group's
arguments over a number of years at selection conferences, party meetings
and informal contacts with party leaders is impossible to estimate but was
potentially very significant.

Whatever the precise effect of grass-roots opinion in the party, it did not,
as we have said, play any direct role in the changing of policy. To observe
the direct agents of change we have to look further up the party hierarchy,
in the first place at back-bench MPs. During the years of office between
1951 and 1964, MPs rarely dissented in public from the views of the
leadership: criticism was largely confined to early day motions from a
couple of iconoclastic backbenchers.[4] But the drift of opinion among those
MPs who interested themselves in labour affairs may be gathered from a
speech to a Conservative summer school in 1956 by the vice-chairman of
the back-bench Labour Committee, Charles Fletcher-Cooke. Among
other things, he suggested reviving that section of the 1927 Trade Disputes
Act which made sympathy strikes illegal; more stringent laws on picketing;
compulsory registration of trade unions and extensive regulation of their
internal rules; and the enforcement of these measures by withdrawing the
immunities of the 1906 Trade Disputes Act from unions who attempted
defiance.[5] But proposals such as these—which contain the kernel of the
Industrial Relations Act—never surfaced as part of persistent back-bench
demands. The next coherent proposal from this quarter did not appear
until July 1964 when Ronald Bell, an MP on the liberal right of the party,
presented a Private Member's Bill to establish a body to regulate the
internal affairs of unions.[6] In the same year Conservative legislation
against restrictive practices in the retail trades produced demands in the
1922 Committee for similar legislation on unions.[7] There is, then, some
evidence of back-bench dissatisfaction with prevailing policy, but none of
any serious attempt to alter it before the 1964 general election.

Individual backbenchers could—and did—contribute to the debate
about policy outside the parliamentary arena, through their membership

of internal party groups which mounted critiques of party policy. The mos
detailed of these contributions came from the Inns of Court Conservative
and Unionist Society – effectively a society of Tory barristers – who i
June 1958 published a long pamphlet entitled *A Giant's Strength* suggesting
changes in the law. The authors identified the key problem of industria
relations as the disproportionate growth of union power over the
community at large and over individual union members.[8] They proposed
to tackle the former by setting up tribunals of enquiry before strikes took
place, and by withdrawing legal immunities from industrial action taken
before the tribunals sat; by withdrawing legal protection from unofficia
strikes, and making a general strike a criminal offence; and by curbing
restrictive practices by requiring unions to justify them before a Restrictive
Practices Court.[9] Union power over the individual trade unionist they
proposed to tackle chiefly through an attack on the closed shop which,
though not to be made illegal, was to be rigorously controlled by the device
of registration.[10] *A Giant's Strength* has often been presented as the
intellectual ancestor of the Industrial Relations Act,[11] and there are
certainly numerous points at which it corresponds with the final legislation. But the reason for this is not that the Conservatives relied on the
pamphlet in framing their legislation, but rather that the Tory lawyers
were expressing typical Conservative responses to the regulation of
industrial relations. There is hardly an idea in *A Giant's Strength* which did
not exist in previous Tory thinking.[12] The pamphlet did not shape the final
Act; rather, it reflected Conservative concerns – over strikes, the closed
shop and the constitutional position of unions – which were also to be
found in the 1971 legislation.

The pamphlet is significant in two other respects. First, it reflected the
views of a group of Conservatives who, though they had little direct
influence on policy at the end of the 1950s, were to do so at a later date. The
most important of these was Geoffrey Howe who, though not one of the
authors of *A Giant's Strength*, took a close interest in the finished product and
publicised it in *Crossbow*, the Bow Group journal with which he had close
connections. Under Howe's influence *Crossbow* was to return frequently to
the question of trade union reform.[13] The second sense in which *A Giant's
Strength* is significant is that it was the most comprehensive Tory statement
of the case for reform before the party officially committed itself in 1965. As
a result, it exemplifies many of the themes that later came to characterise
Tory thinking. The pamphlet's starting point – suspicion of trade-union
power – was squarely within the liberal tradition. Many of its
recommendations – such as increased restrictions on the closed shop – also
reflected the tradition. But it anticipated future debates in allowing its
liberalism to be modified by a second set of considerations, defined as the
collective needs of the nation as a whole in the face of foreign competition.
Thus liberalism was not extended to balloting union members before a
strike, since this might have shown widespread support for industrial

action.[14] Similarly, though the closed shop was attacked, competition between unions for members was felt to be economically harmful, and the freedom of a worker to change unions was to be limited by increasing the authority of the TUC under Bridlington rules to expel unions found guilty of poaching.[15] This tension between liberalism and collectivism was to be a recurrent feature of the recasting of policy after 1964.

The final important group interested in reform was the party bureaucracy. In the period up to the 1964 election, publications from the party organisation contained a steady stream of criticism of trade unions, concerning in particular the closed shop, the political levy and restrictive practices.[16] Following the election, one official played an especially important part. Stephen Abbott was secretary to every one of the main working parties on industrial relations set up after 1964; he acted as a kind of civil servant to Tory front benchers between 1964 and 1970; wrote the initial draft of *Fair Deal At Work*; and was a senior adviser to Robert Carr at the Department of Employment between 1970 and 1972. Abbott's background is especially interesting in the light of the final content of the Tory legislation. He joined Conservative Central Office in 1960, taking on responsibility for industrial relations among other things. With the exception of the war years he had spent all his working life as an executive with Metal Box, a large engineering group, and he spent most of the 1950s managing a Metal Box subsidiary in the West Indies. The latter experience was important in two ways: from his West Indian base Abbott travelled widely throughout the United States and Canada, observing a system of industrial relations in which the law played a very prominent part; and in the West Indies he gained experience of working under a system where legally binding agreements were a common feature of collective bargaining.

By the time he began to work for the Conservative Party, Abbott seems to have been highly sceptical of the established party policy of abstention from legal intervention. But in 1960—when he first went to work for the Tories—a Conservative Minister of Labour was much closer to his civil servants – who favoured abstention from legal intervention – than to party officials. It took three sets of external events to open up the leadership not only to Abbott but to others who wanted a change of policy. The first we have already encountered: the general worsening of the economic situation in the early 'sixties, which began to undermine the confidence of the party leadership in prevailing policies. Faced with the problem of how to respond they turned to, among others, the party officials. In May 1962 R. A. Butler, as head of the party's Advisory Committee on Policy, set up an internal working group to advise on future legislation on industrial relations. This included representatives of Conservative trade unionists, backbenchers and leaders of the National Union, with Abbott as secretary. The working group circulated a private report among party leaders,[17] the gist of which was subsequently published.[18] At least one of the group's proposals—that unconstitutional strikers forfeit the right to service—related redundancy notices—found its way into the Contracts of Employment Act. Other parts of the Report bore fruit in 1965, including its proposals for increased regulation of unions by the Registrar, and for labour courts which would hear cases of unfair dismissal.[19]

The second external event concerned the case of Rookes v. Barnard. It had a twofold significance. First, it arose out of a closed shop, and thus aroused all the liberal suspicions of the excessive use of trade-union power. Rookes, a draughtsman with an airline company, had resigned from his union; the union forced the company to sack him, and he embarked on a legal battle for compensation lasting over eight years. The case aroused considerable sympathy in Conservative circles: Geoffrey Howe, for instance, who was then writing on labour law for the *Sunday Telegraph*, was one of the first to comment on its implications, and helped arrange publication of Rookes's own story. The second sense in which the case was significant was even more important. The substance of the House of Lords decision in 1964, which had little direct bearing on the closed shop, threw into confusion the law relating to strikes and produced an urgent need for clarification. The effect was to open up the whole matter of the status of the 1906 settlement with the unions, and to intensify the questioning of traditional Conservative attitudes. One symptom of the Government's decreasing confidence in this respect was the increasing ease with which Abbott gained access to Joseph Godber, the last Tory Minister of Labour: by 1964 he was seeing him regularly, and had virtually established himself as a sort of unofficial political adviser.

Godber's response to Rookes v. Barnard was to propose the setting up of a small committee which would report quickly on any necessary changes in the law.[20] Godber initially proposed to wait until after the 1964 election before establishing the committee, in the rather forlorn hope that this would remove the issue from political controversy; but under pressure from the TUC, and probably from his own civil servants, he had begun consulting with unions and employers on its composition by September 1964.[21]

At this point, the third external event intervened: the Conservatives narrowly lost the October 1964 general election. This was the most important single event in the genesis of the 1971 Act. It is possible to make an intelligent guess as to what would have happened had the Conservatives not been defeated. There would have been no Royal Commission. A small committee would have been set up with the limited brief of reporting quickly on the state of the law in the wake of the Rookes v. Barnard judgement. An Act would have been passed substantially restoring the legal position existing before the Lords' decision. But the definition of the immunities enjoyed by workers in a trade dispute would have been narrowed, while the Registrar would probably have been given increased authority to prevent abuses of power by individual unions over their members. In short, the changes would have been important but not fundamental. The election defeat, however, precipitated a root-and-branch re-examination of policy.

Less than a week after the defeat, Edward Heath replaced R. A. Butler as head of the party's Advisory Committee on Policy, with a brief to review the whole range of Conservative attitudes to important issues. Heath's response was to set up nineteen study groups covering the major areas in which the party was interested.[22] Given the state of the law, and the state of opinion within the party, it is not surprising that one of these was called 'Trade Union Law and Practice'; it was, as one of those closely involved with the whole process put it, a nap selection. Because of delays in recruiting members, this group did not effectively begin work until early in 1965, but once the job was started it moved very quickly. By August it had produced proposals which were incorporated into *Putting Britain Right Ahead*.[23] Between 1964 and 1970 there were actually three separate groups, though the membership overlapped considerably: the group which produced the initial proposals; a second which worked under Sir Keith Joseph, who succeeded Godber as front-bench spokesman after Heath's election to the party leadership in 1965; and a third which worked to produce *Fair Deal At Work* under Robert Carr, who succeeded Joseph in 1967. After *Fair Deal* appeared, the group remained in being but it met relatively infrequently and much of the work was done by Abbott, Carr and Howe.

The details of how the groups worked are of little concern here, but some features of their work do need remarking on, since they show how determined the Tories were to make a clean break with the past. Abbott, who was critical of the policies of the 1951–1964 period and was associated with proposals contained in the 1962 report, was appointed secretary. It is clear that throughout he behaved more like a senior adviser than a mere recorder and circulator of minutes: he played a part in recruiting members of the group, and was a source of position papers and drafts of the proposals from which the various groups worked. The composition of the working parties also showed the desire for reform. The first group soon gathered a number of individuals who were associated with a desire for change, including members of the 1962 working party such as Ray Mawby, a trade unionist and Tory MP, and Sir Max Bemrose from the National Union.[24] Early in 1965 Howe, by now quite well known as a critic of the unions, was also recruited. The final indication that the group was intended to produce a break with the past is provided by a decision about its chairmanship. The normal practice with the various groups was, where appropriate, for the relevant front-bench spokesman to chair meetings. The practice was also followed in the case of trade union law after Joseph's appointment in 1965. Before this, however, Godber, though leading for the Tories in the Commons, was simply an ordinary member of the study group. The chairmanship went to an outside businessman whose name has remained secret. The reason is clear: as the last Tory Minister of Labour Godber was too closely associated with established policies to be given a key role in their alteration. His replacement as front-bench spokesman by Joseph was part of the first batch of changes made by Heath as leader of the Party, and was followed soon after by the appointment of Howe as a junior member of Joseph's team.

Two final features of the remaking of policy after 1964 had an important influence on the fate of the legislation which the Conservatives produced after 1970. The first was that policy was largely a party product. During the years of office before 1964, Conservative policy reflected the pressures on the leadership coming from the civil service and powerful interest groups such as the TUC.[25] The election defeat removed the influence of the civil service, and the groups which worked out policy were dominated by back-bench MPs, members of the shadow cabinet, representatives of the National Union and figures drawn from the party organisation. Since many of these had contacts outside the Party – with the business community in particular – this did not mean that policy was made in isolation from groups outside the party. It did mean, however, that the process was very different from the close consultation and negotiation with key interest groups which had characterised the making of policy when the Tories were in power.

This was accentuated by a second practice. On Heath's instructions, the various groups were treated as if they were cabinet committees: their proceedings were kept confidential, the circulation of minutes was highly restricted, and their membership was not divulged, reportedly on the grounds that Heath did not want members bothered by the press.[26] This, of course, restricted further the possibility that policy would be made in the context of a dialogue with the main interest groups. There was, of course, not a complete hiatus: the group working on industrial relations law had access to the steady stream of evidence which was being produced for the Donovan Commission; Abbott and his chairmen spent a great deal of time going round firms talking to individual trade unionists and employers; and the proposals the Tories published at various intervals themselves elicited comments from the interested parties. But this was very different from the sort of influence on official policy exercised by the powerful interest groups during the years when the party was in office. After 1969, when the Tories became worried about enforcing their proposals, more serious attempts were made at consultation: there was increased contact with the CBI; some private meetings were held with a number of trade-union leaders; and Abbott had a long session at Congress House with Vic Feather, General Secretary of the TUC. This attempt to sell a policy which had already been effectively decided on was, however, very different from the practice of working it out in the first place in consultation with various groups. The fact that policy was made in this way, combined with the unwillingness of the Conservatives seriously to modify their proposals when they were in office after 1970, was to have a very great effect on the final fate of the 1971 legislation.

This account of the making of Conservative policy disposes of one accusation that has been levelled against the Tories: that their proposals were an expression of class interest, and that the Act was an employers' Act.[27] On the contrary, the most striking feature of the whole process was the extent to which policy-making in the party was insulated from the main interest groups in industrial relations. As we shall see, this institutional isolation was to be reflected in the proposals the Conservatives developed; for, far from being employers' legislation, the final Act was very far from what employers wanted. Indeed, if the Act had been class legislation in the narrow sense of its being in tune with the interests of business, it would have stood a far better chance of success since one of the reasons for its eventual failure was the reluctance of employers to operate its provisions.

However, an alternative account of the origins of the Tory proposals does throw some light on why the party was receptive to new ideas after 1964. It is commonly suggested that pressure of public opinion, and the desire to curry favour with the electorate, led the Conservatives to manufacture proposals which would seem to be 'doing something about the unions'.[28] The state of public opinion – and more important the Tories' perceptions of the popular mood – was indeed important, but in a rather subtle way.

There is little doubt that the publication of detailed proposals in *Fair Deal At Work* in 1968 was prompted by the fact that the Conservatives believed that they were onto an electoral winner, and were anxious not to allow the Labour Government to pre-empt their position by passing legislation in the wake of the Donovan Report. But the first important commitments made in 1965 cannot be explained in such terms. The party leadership always claimed that it took up the matter of trade union reform before it was thought to be an electorally useful issue.[29] The Conservatives' own reflections on the causes of their 1964 defeat support the view that the new policies on industrial relations were an indirect rather than a direct product of electoral calculation. The relevance of public opinion seems to be as follows. One of the most common responses to defeat among British political parties is for them to attempt to return to traditional ideas and traditional sources of support. After October 1964 the Tories accordingly tended to argue that they lost the election because of the defection to Labour of important groups in the upper working and lower middle classes. The way to recapture this support, it was argued, was to pursue policies which were less collectivist in character and more sensitive to individual enterprise and initiative.[30] The new policies on industrial relations were a reflection of this new emphasis on competition and efficiency,[31] and their electoral relevance was that they were part of a package of measures which would attract the support of what Iain

Macleod called the 'salariat', who expected to benefit from a more competitive atmosphere. The changed line on industrial relations thus sprang from something more complicated than a desire on the part of the Tories to be seen to be curbing the power of the unions. It reflected, rather, a wider resurgence of liberalism, especially market liberalism, in the party.[32] The development of this new liberalism, and the conflicts between it and other strands in Conservatism, were to be important features of the arguments over how to reform the trade unions which went on in the party during the years of opposition.

TWO FACES OF TORYISM

The development of Conservative policy up to and after 1970 can best be interpreted as an attempt to answer two sets of questions: what was the most desirable way to solve the problems of industrial relations; and which solutions would be most likely to gain acceptance by interested parties such as unions and employers? The fact that the two questions often suggested different answers – that intellectually desirable solutions might not gain acceptance – helps explain the arguments that went on in the Party and also throws light on the twists and turns of policy after 1965. It is crude but essentially accurate to say that during the years in question the Conservatives never managed to decide whether their policies ought to be collectivist or liberal. On the one hand, trade unions could be accepted completely, given a whole range of privileges and be expected in turn to control their members, all of which implied a centrally controlled system of collective bargaining. On the other hand, the unions could be bypassed, their legal privileges reduced, collective bargaining decentralised and a determined attempt made to introduce the disciplines of the market into industrial relations. Only a few in the party believed the choice to be as clear as this; but the changing balance between the two accounts for much that happened after 1965. This tension was made more acute by the problem of securing the acceptance by employers and unions of the party's policies. In their hearts Tories wanted liberal or individualist policies in industrial relations; but liberalism foundered on the rock of enforceability, for it was plausibly argued that, however desirable such policies might be in principle, the reality was that collectivism was so strongly impressed on industrial relations that any solution which failed to take account of this collectivism would be stymied by the main institutions such as the unions. Much of the argument had to be couched in these terms because liberalism was extremely influential immediately after 1964.

The liberal tradition was reflected not only in the industrial relations policies presented in public in September 1965, but also in the way the party hoped to sell its policies to those involved in industrial relations. One of the first casualties of the new liberalism was the commitment of the previous Conservative Government to direct intervention in the wages market. The regulation of incomes and the efficient use of labour through elimination of restrictive practices were now held to be matters for independent management initiative. As Keith Joseph put it in presenting the new proposals, the purpose of public policy would be to ensure competition: anti-monopoly policy, changes in taxation and other measures would produce a 'leap in productivity'.[33] A more competitive economic atmosphere, and one in which rewards for efficiency were great, would encourage management to tackle restrictive practices. At the same time, proposals for better retraining schemes for workers, wage-related unemployment benefits and help in house removals were designed to encourage workers to cooperate in removing inefficient practices. The function of public policy was thus to stimulate the labour market into operating with maximum efficiency.[34]

The moral dimension of liberalism was also in evidence after 1964. 'A new and powerful Registrar' was proposed: registration would be an effective condition of enjoying the traditional trade-union immunities, and would depend on a union's satisfying the Registrar on its rules such as those governing admission and expulsion of members, and union disciplinary procedures.[25] A third set of proposals concerned the legal enforceability of collective agreements. As we have seen, the Contracts of Employment Act had withdrawn its benefits from individual workers who were in breach of procedure, but this had proved totally ineffective. It was now proposed that 'certain sorts of agreements, especially those dealing with procedure' should be made legally enforceable. Since penalising individual workers had apparently had no effect, it was proposed that unions should do the enforcing, if necessary by expelling members. Failure to do so would involve fines on unions.[36] Associated with these measures was a proposal for a 'range of Industrial Courts' to deal with breaches of procedure, and to hear appeals from the decisions of the Registrar.[37] These proposals were, in effect, very much an elaborated version of the courts suggested by the group to which Abbott had been secretary in 1962.

The proposals presented in September 1965 reflected in some degree the influence of all three of the main traditions in industrial relations. There was much that still reflected voluntary collectivism, such as the 'background' role assigned to the state in such areas as the retraining of workers. But the party's policies were now also suffused with the language, and some of the substance, of liberalism: the excessive power of unions over their own members, and their capacity to hinder the efficient workings of the market in labour were to be tackled by legislation. Voluntary collectivism and liberalism could to some extent complement each other, but the influence, in addition, of compulsory collectivism introduced contradictory elements. Thus, while the commitment to make procedure agreements legally enforceable could be justified in the language of liberalism – in terms of the honouring of bargains[38] – the means chosen for enforcement implied something very different. If unions were to be compelled to police agreements, then they clearly needed some sanctions against their own members. The Conservatives proposed the most obvious sanction: expulsion.[39] But this was only likely to be effective if it involved some deprivation, such as the loss of employment. This implied a situation in which the state – through the Court or the Registrar – licensed a closed shop, in return for the policing of procedures. On the other hand, the whole weight of the liberal tradition was against compulsory trade unionism. Given these implicit contradictions, it is hardly surprising that the 1965 proposals were vague on the question of the closed shop; but the attempts to work out these contradictions were to be an important feature of later developments in policy.

The implied contradiction between a liberal and a collectivist solution to the problems of industrial relations was made explicit in an open disagreement at the 1965 party conference between members of the policy group. The extent of disagreement may be gauged from the fact that it spilled over into public argument between Aidan Crawley, a back-bench MP who was a member of the group, and Keith Joseph, the newly appointed shadow spokesman. Crawley, in sharp contrast to Joseph, demanded the introduction of a military-like discipline among workers. The present situation, he argued, resembled one where a soldier refused to use a new weapon, and was exempted from discipline because he was involved in a trade dispute. He demanded that all collective agreements, not just those related to procedure, be made enforceable, and attacked as a 'major weakness' the economic liberalism of the party's proposals on restrictive practices, which relied on the independent initiative of management as a means of attack.[40]

The party after 1965 was thus engaged in attempting to strike a balance between liberalism and collectivism, and also in attempting to frame its proposals so as to secure consent from the official union leadership and from workers on the shop floor. An added complication was that differences of opinion on these issues corresponded to no easily identifiable divisions in the party. It might be thought that collectivist opinion on industrial relations represented that wing of the Conservative Party which was in close touch with business, especially big business. It is true that business pressure groups were at this time proposing solutions which entailed much more state intervention, and much higher levels of compulsion, than were envisaged by the Tories. In addition, the liberalism, moral and economic, which was central to Conservative thinking, did find little place in the views put forward by employers' groups. Even apparently similarly proposals could arise from very different intentions. Thus both the CBI and the Tories wanted a strong Registrar; but, whereas the CBI saw him as a means of securing a compliant workforce, for the Tories he was a means of safeguarding the individual against what they considered to be the excessive use of union power.

The notion of such a division between individualists and collectivists has been best put by Wedderburn, who speaks of the Tory proposals as representing two sets of opinions: those of the organisation man concerned with order, and those of the 'Conservative lawyer imbued above all else with doctrines of individual rights, often without regard to the shop floor problems of collective bargaining.'[41] As a metaphor for the conflicting emotions which beat in the Tory breast this is suggestive, but as a description of the lines of division in the party it is quite inaccurate. The liberals in the party were by no means confined to the lawyers, nor were the lawyers remarkably liberal compared with others. As we saw earlier, *A Giant's Strength*, far from being the quintessence of individualism, reflected the tensions between the liberal and collectivist traditions, and the Tory lawyers' evidence to Donovan reflects the same contradictions. Nor were those in the party with business contacts or experience particularly averse to liberalism in industrial relations. Among its strongest supporters were Joseph, who had close contacts with the building industry; Nicholas Ridley, a director of several engineering firms;[42] and Abbott, whose years with Metal Box still appear to have left him with a liberal opposition to the closed shop. Indeed, the most extreme statement of the liberal tradition in these years came from Conservative trade unionists in their evidence to the Donovan Commission: they opposed the closed shop; argued that unions should only be allowed to register if their rules met the standards of natural justice; expressed worry about the implications of deducting union subscriptions from pay; favoured the extension of plant bargaining; and were suspicious of the implications for individual liberty of the formation of big pressure groups such as the CBI.[43]

The point being made here is important since it modifies considerably a common picture which represents the liberal parts of the Industrial Relations Act as having been foisted on the Conservatives by lawyers with no experience of industrial relations.[44] The truth is that the split between liberalism and collectivism did not correspond neatly to differences between groups within the party. Though certain individuals could be identified with one or other tradition, most Tories had within them Wedderburn's 'organisation man' and also his libertarian lawyer. Party policy reflected faithfully the conflicts between the two.

The conflicts were particularly important in three areas between 1965 and 1970: the matter of enforcing collective agreements; the question of the closed shop; and the role of the state in tackling restrictive practices. The first of these raised three problems: what sort of agreements should be enforceable; how were unions to be brought to sign agreements; and what was to happen when members broke an agreement? The answers in 1965 had been: procedure agreements alone to be automatically enforceable, and unions to do the enforcing under pain of being fined. Despite dissent within the policy group and from others in the Party[45] the proposal to restrict enforceability to procedure agreements was maintained by the

group that drew up proposals for the 1966 general election. But it had
apparently now been concluded that it was not sufficient to rely on unions
to police agreements. The party returned to the direct pressure on workers
first used in the Contracts of Employment Act, but in a more drastic form:
it adopted a proposal for fines on workers who broke procedures, to be
collected by direct attachment from wages. There were thus to be two
stages to enforcement; unions would in the first instance discipline their
members, and if this failed direct legal sanctions would be imposed.[46]

This of course left undecided the argument about the range of
agreements to be made legally enforceable, and this was tackled by the
group which produced *Fair Deal* in 1968. Its solution has all the marks of a
compromise between the conflicting views. The 1966 proposals for
guarding against breaches of agreement were retained, and the principle
that all agreements should be legally enforceable was conceded. But,
whereas previously procedure agreements were to be automatically
enforceable, it was now proposed that all collective agreements be put
'on a par with any other type of contract – no more, no less'. Hence all
agreements would be presumed to be legally enforceable in the absence of
an explicit statement to the contrary.[47] Though later modified, this
essentially was the formula used in the 1971 Act.

All these rather complex changes were a response to the basic problem of
enforceability: what laws could management and workers be persuaded to
operate? In Conservative eyes, much that was wrong with industrial
relations sprang from the failure of workers to honour agreements, a failure
indicated by the high level of unconstitutional strikes. Part of the Tory
solution involved strengthening the hand of management by making
agreements legally binding. But this would be opposed by workers, and the
changes in policy represented a continuing search for an enforceable
formula. Those who believed the problem of unconstitutional action to be
really severe favoured making all agreements legally binding; on the other
hand, the idea of restricting legal enforceability to procedure agreements
was supported as a compromise measure which would strengthen
management while limiting the area of potential conflict with the unions.
Combined with this question of the range of agreements to be legally
enforced was the matter of what deterrents would support the law. In this
case, the main alternatives were either to force the unions to discipline their
own members or to penalise workers directly by means of, for instance,
fines. The difficulty of the first of these was that it was not certain that the
unions would cooperate; even if they did, the sort of powers they would
need were unpalatable to Tory liberalism. But any attempt to fine workers
raised the spectre of mass defiance of the law. In debating enforceability
the Conservatives were thus wriggling on the horns of several uncomfortable dilemmas, but the fact that they did ponder the problems at some
length reinforces an important point about the final Act: contrary to many
suggestions, it was not a hasty, ill-thought-out measure. The Tories were

fully aware of the dangers they ran in trying to change the law, and they quite consciously took risks which they believed necessary in order to reform collective bargaining.

The question of the closed shop posed fewer explicit problems for the party. The closed shop was offensive to both moral and market liberalism: to moral liberalism because it was thought to restrict individual liberty and to give rise to the abuse of union power; to market liberalism because it distorted the workings of the free market in labour. But banning the closed shop raised problems long recognised by Conservatives: how to enforce a ban; how to reconcile the liberty of the individual with the existence of unions strong enough to police collective agreements; and how to avoid industrial unrest if unions had to compete for members.[48] Most employers' organisations, noting these problems, came down broadly in favour of the closed shop. The party found things more difficult. The 1965 proposals, without mentioning the matter explicitly, seemed to imply that one condition of registration might be a promise not to operate a closed shop. An explicit commitment had, however, to await the publication of *Fair Deal*. The pamphlet tried to solve the various problems by outlawing pre-entry closed shops but by allowing agency shops under certain stringent conditions. What the Tories understood by an agency shop was a form of post-entry closed shop – where workers were required to join a union after they were hired – with generous grounds for conscientious objection to membership. The aim of this provision was to reconcile libertarian considerations with the stabilising effect of the closed shop and the desire of management to hire whom it pleased and deploy labour as it thought fit.[49]

This last consideration was linked to the question of restrictive practices, the third great problem which concerned the Conservatives during the years of opposition. The 1965 solution had been heavily influenced by the revival of market liberalism in the party: market forces were to be strengthened and management given special incentives to tackle practices which restricted the most efficient use of labour.[50] The big doubt was whether employers would be willing to take the opportunity if doing so involved conflict with unions. The frequent claims by party spokesmen that the prime responsibility in industrial relations lay with management, and that present problems represented a failure by both sides of industry, were more than rhetoric. They indicated a strong suspicion that an economically liberal solution would founder on the unwillingness of employers to stand up to worker power.[51]

The suspicions can hardly have been allayed by the fact that the CBI's proposals involved handing to the state – in the person of the Registrar – the messy job of identifying and eliminating restrictive practices. One solution to this problem was to prod management into action by raising the rewards for the efficient, through taxation policy, and by penalising the inefficient, by compelling companies to publish their yields on capital.[52] For managements who were prepared to act resolutely various forms of assistance would also be made available. Since a largely irrational fear of redundancy was thought to be the cause of most restrictive practices,[53] the fears of workers were to be allayed by a government economic policy aimed at expansion, and by a whole set of proposals on retraining and redundancy payments.[54]

These measures, all compatible with a basically liberal approach, were contained in the 1965 programme. Unease about their adequacy resulted in two separate developments: further attempts were made to strengthen the hand of managements who took independent action; and, by contrast, there was increased resort to the direct intervention of the state. The initial response to criticism was the proposal, made in 1966, that strikes to defend restrictive practices would not attract the traditional immunities enjoyed by those engaged in industrial disputes.[55] This was compatible with liberalism, since it left to the individual employer the decision as to whether or not to sue. But it was coupled with a proposal that the Prices and Incomes Board be used independently to identify 'flagrant' restrictive practices; that it hear arguments on the matter; that it invite the parties 'to mend their ways within a given time'; and that if they failed to do so it could seek damages through the Industrial Relations Court.[56]

These proposals were, even at the time, apparently felt to be unsatisfactory, for it was promised that they were 'not our last word.'[57] Sure enough, they were extended considerably in *Fair Deal*. The hand of management was strengthened by narrowing drastically the range of industrial disputes which would be immune from civil prosecution. Among those no longer protected were strikes called to enforce a closed shop or to prosecute inter-union disputes, and those intended to prevent management hiring certain types of labour.[58] In addition, the decision to replace the pre-entry closed shop by agency shops was partly motivated by the view that, while the former increased employee control over 'production methods, job allocation and general conditions of work', under a union shop 'the pressures on management are less powerful because it retains greater authority in the engagement of labour'.[59] A more direct attempt to use the state to tackle restrictive practices was contained in the proposal that, for a union to register, it would have to satisfy the Registrar that its rules did not 'contain restrictive provisions which were contrary to the public interest'.[60] The earlier proposal that the PIB should be able to take to court those engaged in unacceptable restrictive practices was, however, dropped, and was replaced by the idea of a 'Productivity Board' which would merely investigate, persuade and publicise.[61]

The problems faced by the Conservative Party in tackling restrictive practices are especially illuminating because they go to the heart of questions about managerial power. They explain some of the other problems over the closed shop and the enforceability of agreements, and they also affected the final big issue discussed during the years of opposition: the question, which also severely vexed the TUC and the CBI, of how far the formal national system of industrial relations should be decentralised. The liberal rhetoric of Tory proposals, with its emphasis on competition and encouraging management to tackle restrictive practices independently, implied a high degree of decentralisation. *Fair Deal* saw the plant- and factory-based productivity bargain as a key weapon in the attack on inefficient labour practices, and envisaged a Donovan-like extension and formalisation of the domestic system.[62] Yet *Fair Deal* also saw an expanded role for employers' associations in negotiating and policing legally enforceable agreements.[63] This ambiguity reflected a division within the party. On the one hand, there were some who wanted the rhetoric of market liberalism to be fully realised: the shop steward should be recognised as 'the moment of truth' in the bargaining process, in place of the sham negotiations on a national scale; public policy should be concerned with exalting the former at the expense of the latter.[64] Another liberal likewise argued that *Fair Deal* was inadequate because of its failure to 'break the power of the central bargain.'[65] Against this, some in the party were echoing the views of the employers' associations in arguing that decentralisation of bargaining increased wage inflation, and simply allowed unions to pick off employers separately.[66] Small wonder, then, that *Fair Deal* dispensed bromides when it came to sum up its position: 'We . . . welcome the growing trend towards local bargaining . . . at the same time we see a continuing role for national bargaining.'[67]

Arguments about the extent to which bargaining should be decentralised were important because they affected a key question: what was the main problem in industrial relations? Tory arguments in 1965 identified it as the inefficient use of labour. The problem of strikes was important, but mainly as a reflection of the ability of labour to hinder the authority of management. Indeed in Keith Joseph's view it was 'the strikes that do not take place' that were often most serious, since they indicated that industrial peace was being bought at an unacceptable price.[68] But by the time *Fair Deal* was published, the emphasis had changed. Restrictive practices were still seen as a great problem; but the direct and indirect effect of unconstitutional strikes was now thought to be an independent problem, apart from any implications it may have had for the efficient use of labour.[69] The language of Tory leaders underwent a corresponding change. Joseph tended to set the strike problem in the context of restrictive practices; Carr saw unconstitutional strikes as 'the British disease', and stressed their independent effect in disrupting production.[70] Part of the explanation for this may be that Joseph was a much more thoroughgoing economic liberal than Carr. An additional reason can be found in the strike figures themselves: Carr's assumption of responsibility in 1967 coincided with a very sharp rise in the level of militancy, and the change of emphasis may thus be seen as a response to the objective seriousness of the situation.

The shift in emphasis had implications in turn for the extent to which collective bargaining could be decentralised. Market liberals saw unofficial strikes as the product of misguided attempts to impose national authority: 'strikes are unofficial because the union has to some extent been suborned and used against the workers.' The solution was to go back to 'the bargain being negotiated between the employer and his men.'[71] Official policy accepted part of this analysis: the condemnation of statutory incomes policy rested in part on the belief that by undermining the main function of the union, government policy merely created shop-floor militancy.[72] But increasing concern with the 'disease' of unconstitutional strikes brought a concern to impose national 'discipline' on individuals. From 1967 onwards there was a constant stress on the need to strengthen official trade-union leaders. *Fair Deal* proposed, as we have seen, that unions and employers' associations be able to make legally binding agreements on behalf of their members, and proposed also that they be able to sue their own members to recover damages imposed as a result of a breach of agreement. The state was also given direct powers. *Fair Deal* considered, and rejected, compulsory arbitration, but it suggested following the model of American legislation in allowing a minister to set up an enquiry into certain strikes, to apply to the Industrial Relations Court for a cooling-off period, and to apply to the Court for a secret ballot on the terms of an offer.[73]

This discussion illustrates the varying strands in Tory attempts to identify and settle the problems of industrial relations before 1970. But this was only half the difficulty: once solutions had been found they had to be made workable. The problem of securing consent led to important developments in the substance of the Conservatives' proposals.

THE PROBLEM OF CONSENT

The party needed consent from a large number of groups, but two were especially important. From rank-and-file workers it wanted observance of collective agreements, and submission to legal penalities when agreements were broken; and from the official leadership of the trade-union movement it wanted a willingness to operate any new laws – by, for instance, signing legally binding agreements – and assistance in policing procedures.

The initial response to the first problem was to opt for indirect enforceability: the 1965 proposals suggested that unions be given the task of ensuring rank-and-file compliance. In addition, since the obstructiveness of workers was believed to spring from a sense of insecurity, the expanding and prosperous economy which party policy was designed to produce would result in a cooperative work force. The first of these approaches encountered the problem of how to give unions sanctions over workers. The 1966 response was to allow direct fines on workers who broke agreements, but *Fair Deal* in 1968 returned to the notion of enforceability through unions. They would be given additional powers over members through the agency shop, and through being allowed to sue members who brought damages on the union by breaking agreements.[74] Fines collected by attachment from wages were still thought feasible;[75] but by 1969 Carr, faced with a similar proposal put forward by the Labour Government, dismissed direct sanctions as 'sterile and contentious'.[76]

All this was aimed at minimising the chances that workers would defy the law in large numbers. There was a long-standing belief – dating at least from the affair of the jailed miners at Betteshanger colliery in 1942[77] – that, if the law became seriously embroiled in a conflict with a substantial number of workers, then the law was likely to come off second best. Schemes such as attachment from wages and enforcement through unions were designed to avoid the symbolically inflammatory situation in which workers were imprisoned for defiance. Similarly, the constant stress in Conservative arguments on the use of civil rather than criminal sanctions was again designed to reduce further the chances of a direct clash between the worker and the state.[78] In the last analysis, however, it was admitted that, even under civil law, workers who were determined on defiance could end up in prison. The Conservatives were fully aware of the dangers they were running, but they never really got beyond the hopeful assertion that in the last analysis the law would be obeyed.

The problem of securing obedience from the individual worker was linked to that of obtaining the consent and cooperation of official trade unionism. The Conservatives were torn by contradictory impulses: on the one hand, their fear of a direct clash between the law and workers led them to turn to unions as policing agents; but on the other hand their liberalism blanched at the sort of concessions to organised trade unionism which would be necessary if unions were seriously to carry out this function. Indeed, members of the policy group strongly criticised the corporatist implications of the Labour Government's attempt in 1969 to rely on TUC and CBI cooperation in enforcing some of the proposals contained in *In Place of Strife*.[79] The initial Tory proposals of 1965 tried to solve the problem by making the unions the enforcement agents, but offering them almost nothing in return. Unions might derive a very cold comfort from the fact that there would be a limitation on the amounts they could be fined for failing to control their members,[80] and there was the hardly enticing recommendation – apparently not to be backed with legislation – that where a union had already established itself in a firm it ought to be recognised if a majority of workers desired this.[81] In addition, it was proposed that the new Industrial Courts be able to hear appeals in cases of unjust dismissal, though the key questions of what criteria would guide its judgements, and what redress would be available, were not spelt out.[82] The chief carrot offered the unions was not directly concerned with industrial relations at all, but echoed the liberalism of the late 1940s: an economy freed from excessive state intervention would prosper, and unions would be able to harvest appropriate rewards for their members.[83] The increasingly étatiste character of the Labour Government's economic and industrial relations policies after 1965 encouraged the Conservatives to develop this theme. In the years up to 1970 the unions were repeatedly offered the return of free collective bargaining in return for accepting a new framework of law. Carr has confirmed that such an explicit bargain was part of Conservative calculations.[84]

But a bargain based on market liberalism was evidently felt to be insufficient, for the years after 1965 were also marked by the development of proposals designed to encourage compliance in other ways. These consisted in part in a fleshing out of existing proposals: by 1966, for instance, there was a firm commitment that the Industrial Relations Court could award damages in cases of unfair dismissal.[85] But it was with *Fair Deal* that the strategy of enticing the official union leadership was most highly developed. Procedures for appeals against dismissals were further elaborated, and employers were to be compelled to recognise and negotiate with a union where workers indicated such a desire in a secret ballot. In addition there were proposals which would increase the disciplinary power of the official leadership and provide a degree of membership stability. The proviso that unions could sue their own members to recover damages incurred for breaches of procedure agreements was perhaps a bit far-fetched, but the proposals for agency shops, albeit under stringent conditions, represented in Conservative eyes a considerable concession.[86]

All this was tied in with the question of registration. The idea of the registration of trade unions as analogous to the registration of commercial companies – providing a legal licence to operate – was long established in Conservative thinking, but the 1965 proposals used the device sparingly: the purpose of the Registrar was chiefly to ensure that union rules did not infringe libertarian principles. By 1968 registration had become the coping stone of the Conservatives' proposals. The Registrar was to be used as a weapon against restrictive practices and the pre-entry closed shop; registration was to be a condition of obtaining an agency shop; and the provisions for obtaining recognition could only be activated for a registered organisation.[87] The importance of registration increased still further in 1969, when the party unveiled proposals for settling recognition disputes by secret ballots, since only registered unions were to be eligible to contest such ballots.[88] The growth in the significance of registration after 1965 was an indication of the increased extent to which the party was trying to solve the problems of industrial relations with the consent and cooperation of official trade unionism. In 1965 the unions had been offered little more than general promises of prosperity, whereas four years later registration offered a complicated array of privileges and obligations. Registered unions were offered the possibility not only of winning concessions at the expense of employers, but also of gaining members at the expense of other unions. Conversely, the non-registered union would operate under a number of potentially severe disadvantages. These considerations were to become very important indeed when the Act became law.

THE POLITICS OF POLICY IN OPPOSITION

In the years after 1964 the Conservatives' proposals for the reform of industrial relations underwent – as we have seen – a complicated series of variations. Indeed so complex were the various changes that it may be wise to present a straightforward summary of what the Tories stood for by the time the process was nearing its end in 1970, before attempting a general analysis of the problems of policy-making in opposition. The party's commitments amounted to those outlined in *Fair Deal*, supplemented by a small number of other proposals made public in 1969.

Fair Deal suggested setting up a Registrar who would ensure that unions and employers' associations operated under rules which accorded with criteria of democracy, justice and the public interest. Only registration would confer on an organisation of workers the full legal status of a trade union. Unions would enjoy immunity from civil prosecution only when engaged in a lawful trade dispute, and the definition of the latter would be considerably narrowed so as to exclude strikes called to enforce a closed shop, intra-union and sympathy strikes, and stoppages called to prevent management hiring certain types of labour. Collective agreements would be presumed to be legally binding unless they contained a clause to the contrary. Registered unions would be able to obtain recognition from employers if the majority of employees supported such a demand, and they could obtain an agency shop under stringent conditions. There would be a legal right to join or refuse to join a union, and a right of appeal against either unjust dismissal by an employer or 'coercive action' by a union. Appeal would in the last resort be to an Industrial Court, composed of a legally qualified chairman and lay members from both sides of industry.

This Court would have three additional functions: it would hear requests from the Secretary of State to order a cooling-off period in certain important disputes; it could order a secret ballot to discover the wishes of those involved in such a dispute; and it could order arbitration in a dispute where the national interest was threatened. The Secretary of State, in addition to his power to refer disputes to the Court, could independently bring his department's conciliation procedures into play in certain cases. Finally, a Code of Practice was proposed to provide those involved in industrial relations with a standard at which to aim and be assessed by. In October 1969 these proposals were supplemented by a number of others. The Court was to be given power to order a ballot to resolve recognition disputes between unions; every employee was to have written statements of his rights and obligations at work; all companies above a certain size were to have elected councils; and companies above a certain size were to be obliged to give their employees as much information as they gave to shareholders.

The most striking intellectual feature of the policies developed by the Tories in opposition was their eclecticism. The other important groups interested in reform tended to be heavily influenced by a limited set of traditions: the judges were strongly under the sway of moral liberalism; the unions, the employers, the Labour Party and the civil service oscillated between voluntary and compulsory collectivism. The Conservatives, on the other hand, drew on the whole range of traditions, a fact which reflects both the richness of the party's ideological inheritance and its key role as the representative of a wide range of social and economic interests in British society. In 1965 the proposals were shot through with the language and substance of moral and market liberalism. During the succeeding years this liberalism remained very important, but for a number of reasons – the replacement of Keith Joseph by Robert Carr, the rise in the level of unconstitutional strikes, the problems of securing union consent – there was an increasing stress on the need to strengthen the institutions of collectivism, especially official trade unionism. The most indicative change in this respect concerned registration: in 1965 it was chiefly a device to safeguard individual liberty against the excessive use of union power; by 1970 this job remained, but it was harnessed to that of securing order and discipline in industrial relations. Elements of compulsory collectivism had been introduced, as the party moved to a position where unions would be licensed, and in return would gain state-backed powers over their members through such measures as those relating to agency shops and recognition by employers. But voluntary collectivism was not ignored: the Code of Conduct, for instance, was an echo of proposals first mooted in 1947 and was designed to provide a voluntary framework of good behaviour to which the collectivist institutions would conform.

The fact that it is possible to analyse in some detail the intellectual complexion of Tory policy on industrial relations is itself indicative of a quite novel feature of the Conservatives' behaviour before 1970. Traditionally, the Conservatives have appealed to the electorate for a doctor's mandate, avoiding any detailed commitment to policies in favour of general assurances of good government. But when Robert Carr became Secretary of State in June 1970 he possessed – in *Fair Deal* – the detailed draft of a Bill which only needed translation into appropriate legal language to stand as a legislative proposal; indeed this is largely what happened. There is a remarkable contrast here with what occurred in 1951, when the Conservatives had similarly returned to office after a long period in opposition. On that occasion Churchill and other leaders had deliberately made their proposals as vague as possible in order to allow maximum freedom to negotiate with the unions once they were in office.

One possible explanation for the change is that the two decades after 1951 saw an alteration in the character of Toryism, from Churchill's romantic and patrician view of government as an intuitive reconciling of the great interests in the community to Heath's bureaucratic manager-ialism with its concern with the nuts and bolts of policy. There is undoubtedly something in this view. When R. A. Butler took on the job of reshaping Conservative policy after the election defeat in 1945, he was content to outline the shape of the new Toryism in broad brush strokes;[89] but when Heath was chosen to do the same job in 1964, he inaugurated a frenzy of activity, setting up a complex array of committees on civil service lines which produced a deluge of research and working papers.

This account can only be a partial explanation of the Conservatives' behaviour, however, since their actual conduct of the 1970 election campaign did not represent a sharp break with the past. Indeed it was only in industrial relations that they entered the campaign with a really detailed set of public commitments. Electoral opportunism accounted in part for this detail: *Fair Deal* was published because the Tories believed the unions were unpopular and they calculated that the proposals would win votes. But there was also a more personal reason: in the years after 1964 a number of very able people – especially Stephen Abbott and Geoffrey Howe – became strongly convinced that reform of industrial relations was a vital matter. Abbott seems to have been especially important in this respect: his energy and commitment were a constant source of pressure to have policies set down and clarified in a detailed way. In Abbott the party had provided itself with the equivalent of a first-rate civil servant, and like any effective and forceful civil servant his energies were devoted to hammering out detailed proposals which could provide a more precise framework for action than is allowed for by the sort of vague aspirations so often used as election fodder.

The Conservatives' behaviour after 1964 means that we can observe something rather unusual in British politics: the working out of a detailed policy in opposition, with all the problems that this involves. The difficulties are not quite what one might expect: no doubt ignorance, haste and lack of foresight often afflict politicians out of office, but that is not what strikes one about the Conservatives' experience between 1964 and 1970. Indeed, the complicated variations in policy charted earlier arose from a quite subtle understanding of the problems of industrial relations and a keen awareness of the difficulties of enforcement. .

The Conservatives' problems arose from a different source. Parties which are expelled from government – especially those, like the Tories in 1964, who lose office after a long period in power – tend to turn in on themselves. The reasons are partly psychological, reflected in demands that the party return to its origins after the distractions of government; and they are partly institutional: the links the party leadership has with the great pressure groups while in office are weakened. Contact with one of the most important groups of all – the civil service – is virtually severed by loss of office while links with the representatives of labour and employers – institutionalised, for instance, in the National Economic Development Council – are severely weakened. Hence the phenomenon noted earlier that, after 1964, Conservative industrial relations policy was largely a party product. The Tories were of course quite aware of the problems of cooperation and enforcement, but their main attempt to secure the consent of interested parties was done by proxy – through unilateral developments in policy – rather than through the detailed negotiation and consultation which usually characterises the relationship between a governing party and the powerful interest groups.

This problem is especially acute as far as the Conservative Party is concerned. Labour in opposition at least has ties of sentiment and organisation with the trade unions; and, as the negotiations which produced the social contract after 1970 show, it is quite capable of capitalising on this advantage. The contacts between the Conservatives and the business community, on the other hand, though important, are much more informal: consider, for instance, how unlikely it is that the Tories would sit down with the CBI to work out a social contract on which to fight an election.

The essential problem of any party in attempting to develop policies while in opposition may be summarised as follows. The government of our society consists largely in managing the competing and conflicting demands of powerful interest groups. It thus demands sensitivity and sure handling of such groups. But opposition is a state which encourages a party to turn to its own ideas, concerns and resources, away from the immediate pressures of interest-group politics. When a party is returned to government, its capacity to manage the transition intimately affects the degree to which its policies secure the consent and cooperation of powerful groups. This was the great difficulty the Conservatives faced when they were quite unexpectedly elected to office in June 1970. How they coped with it is the concern of the next chapter.

5 The Politics of Consultation

The Conservatives fought the 1970 election on industrial relations policies which had been publicly stated in some detail by the end of the previous year; but events in the months immediately before the election were to influence the reception accorded the policies when they were turned into legislative proposals. The first of these was the effective ending of wage restraint by the Labour Government at the end of 1969. The result was that the liberal bargain which the Tories hoped to strike with the unions – ending wage controls in return for the acceptance of new laws – was no longer possible. The second was associated with this: the months before the election saw an unprecedented rise in the level of pay awards and a sharp increase in the level of strikes.[1] From a propagandist point of view this gave added point to the Tory critique of industrial relations; but the existence of severe wage inflation when the party took office meant that the bargain by which, in return for union consent to the new laws, government would engage in a self-denying ordinance with respect to wage determination was now very difficult to offer. After June the Government became more and more openly involved in a struggle over wage claims with the trade-union movement. Indeed the arguments between the unions and the Tories over the Industrial Relations Bill were only a part of a wider conflict. The unions' opposition to legislation coincided with a series of bitter clashes over pay between the Government and a number of unions in the public sector, notably the power workers and the post office workers. These did not concern the matter of legislation directly, but they certainly extended the range of conflict and made an already strained relationship even more difficult.

Finally, there was the Labour Government's defeat over *In Place of Strife*, which occurred in 1969 but which intimately affected Tory strategy when the party was returned to office. As with the wave of militancy, this could be turned to good propagandist effect, in the accusation that Labour had succumbed to sectional pressure, but as at least some of the Conservative leaders privately recognised the intensity of union opposition augured ill for the party's own policies. Largely for electoral reasons the Tories had

committed themselves in great detail on the question of industrial relation
reform, and this reduced their freedom of manoeuvre. They responded to
this problem in three ways. One was to temporise in the hope of increasing
the chances of obtaining union consent. Hardly anyone within the party
had publicly opposed the policies on the ground that they would
antagonise the unions,[2] but apparently within the shadow cabinet doubts
had been expressed over a number of years by Sir Edward Boyle, William
Whitelaw[3] and Quintin Hogg. These were, though, occasional reservations rather than serious opposition, and the main idea which seems
to have emerged from them was that of phasing the proposals so as not to
introduce too many controversial measures at once, a suggestion which
bears an interesting similarity to one coming from the CBI after the general
election.

A second response – and one which received serious consideration in the
months leading up to the election – involved meeting the unions head on
by introducing much more compulsion into the proposals. In particular,
the increasing likelihood that the unions would simply opt out of legally
enforceable agreements by insisting on exclusion clauses was met by
suggestions either that the state should impose legally binding agreements
in certain cases, or that it should allow one of the parties to any contract to
do so.[4] Howe and Abbott, after a long visit to the United States, produced
a discussion paper suggesting the latter, and suggesting also an increase in
the extent to which the official union organisation should be held
responsible for maintaining discipline in the work place.[5] This shift
towards further compulsion left its mark on the eventual legislation; but, as
we shall see, it was a third response – implementing the proposals to which
they were already publicly committed – which the Conservatives finally
adopted. It is, however, likely that even at the point of election victory the
party leaders were unclear as to how far they would advance along the
road to compulsion in order to meet the challenge of union opposition.

Apart from its effect on the substance of the party's proposals, the fear
that the unions would try to destroy any Conservative measure also
affected the strategy adopted by the leadership in putting forward policy.
We saw earlier that in opposition policy was very much a party product,
rather than the result of negotiations between the party leadership and the
affected interest groups. In the period before the election, the relevance of
the interest groups was further diminished because of an increasing
emphasis by the leadership on the importance of elections as a means of
deciding policy, and on the primacy of electoral mandates: if elected,
Heath emphasised, the proposals on industrial relations law would be
implemented, and there would be consultation only on the details.[6] This
was of course aimed at the trade unions and the Labour Government's
alleged subservience to them, but, as the CBI was shortly to discover, it
applied to employers also. The result was that after June the Conservatives
were to be divided not only from the unions but from employers'

spokesmen, and the divisions concerned not only the substance of policy but also the way it should be decided.

The events which affected the Conservatives also influenced other groups, notably the employers. The CBI's response in the aftermath of the TUC's victory over *In Place of Strife* was twofold: first, to try to come to an agreement with the TUC; and, second, to work out new policies of its own. At a weekend conference held in February 1970 the leaders of the two organisations produced an agreement that industrial relations should be left to both sides of industry without government intervention.[7] But this formula papered over very large divisions. The TUC meant that there should be no important changes in law. What the CBI meant emerged from the proposals of the working party it set up under Leonard Neal in the same month. The resulting report – the 'Neal Report' – which was adopted in draft form by the Council of the CBI in July 1970 essentially stated the CBI's position in later negotiations with the Government. Its three key proposals revived ideas current among employers when the Donovan Commission was at work: restriction of the immunities offered to unions involved in trade disputes; selective imposition of legally enforceable procedure agreements; and most important of all a new Registrar with much greater powers than at present.[8] What the CBI meant by keeping government out was – as the Director General Campbell Adamson put it – that the panoply of courts, binding agreements and injunctions should not be introduced.[9] The Registrar was to be someone with a high degree of administrative discretion who would apply the law selectively to, as Neal put it, strengthen and protect the existing parties to the system – unions and employers.[10]

The Conservatives and the CBI thus had very different ideas about the role of the law. What the Tories wanted was to extend the traditional remedies and procedures of the civil law to the problems of industrial relations: aggrieved parties would have the right to apply to the courts for remedies, and those courts would operate according to traditional legal principles of precedent and impartiality. This was reflected in the fact that the institutional heart of the Conservatives' proposals lay in the National Industrial Relations Court; the Registrar, the key administrative figure in the scheme, had a subordinate part to play. The CBI, on the other hand, wanted the law used in a very different manner, and this is reflected in the fact that in their proposals the Registrar was the most important figure. Instead of the law being administered openly and (the CBI would have said) rigidly by the Courts, the Registrar would have enjoyed a great deal of discretion. The phrase employers often used in private was to the effect that he would be a 'Robens figure': in other words, instead of being a judge restricted by the normal rules of judicial procedure he would be a quasi-political figure, a 'fixer' with freedom to deal with each case separately.

But the differences between the Tories and the employers concerned more than the content of policies; they also concerned the manner in which decisions should be made by government. The Conservatives, having stressed the importance of the electoral mandate during the pre-election period, moved to implement their programme on industrial relations immediately after their victory. Carr, the midwife of the new policies, was appointed Secretary of State for Employment; Howe was appointed Solicitor General, and immediately moved into the Department of Employment with the task of overseeing the drafting of the legislation; and Abbott was appointed a senior adviser to Carr. Shortly afterwards the Queen's Speech committed the Government to immediate legislation.[11] As if further to signal that the Conservatives were determined to go ahead with root-and-branch reform based on their election manifesto, the Government committed itself to publishing its proposals as a Consultative Document before engaging in any serious negotiations with the interested parties.[12]

The CBI, on the other hand, took the election pledges a good deal less seriously. Its behaviour during the period after the election suggests that it regarded the Conservative victory not as a prelude to the implementation of Conservative policies but as an opportunity to work out a new set of measures in consultations between Government, employers and unions. This flexibility extended to its own proposals. Even in the wake of the Neal Report, for instance, the CBI President argued that it would be a mistake 'to be at all specific on issues such as the legal enforceability of agreements and the registration of unions'. Any new legal framework would, he suggested, need to be worked out in consultation with the CBI and the TUC: 'at a moment like this the CBI does not wish to inflame the situation in any way. We want to keep the temperature down as much as possible.'[13] The final Neal Report contained what was essentially a substantial concession to the unions: it suggested that initial legislation be confined to the setting up of a strong Registrar, with the objectionable proposal for legally binding agreements to be postponed until it was clear how the Registrar was working.[14]

Differences about the relevance of election commitments occurred not only between the Conservatives and the employers. The reaction of the TUC was in this respect remarkably similar to that of the CBI. Though the TUC favoured different policies, many trade union leaders shared the belief that policy could only be worked out in three-sided negotiations. Before June 1970 some union leaders were apparently expressing private scepticism about the Conservatives' determination to press ahead with their measures when in office, and a particularly fierce speech by Heath was evidently designed to reassure them of Tory seriousness.[15] Heath did not wholly succeed, to judge from the TUC's relatively sanguine public statements after the Conservative victory. Vic Feather remarked that it was one thing to have policies in opposition, another to introduce legislation as a government. The Tories, he prophesied, would now 'take notice of reality. Responsibility is a great incentive to thought'.[16] Jack

Jones noted that governments come and go, but the TUC remains: 'it will be up to the new Government . . . to negotiate with the TUC.'[17] More important, since it represented some approximation to a general view, was the General Council's statement on the Conservative victory, which contained only a few words on industrial relations and which stressed the hope that the government would adhere 'to the democratic processes of joint consultation.'[18] This is not to imply that union leaders expected the Conservatives quietly to drop their proposals, but it does seem that they expected protracted consultation and argument leading at least to modification of the measures. As we shall see later, their response to the Consultative Document supports this interpretation. The TUC resembled the CBI in believing that the election was a prelude to decision-making, rather than a means of decision in itself. In remarking that 'whether you won the election last week or not, this trade union movement will be above that',[19] a prominent trade unionist was only putting into extreme form the widely held assumption that negotiations with interested parties, not election results, should determine policy.

The Conservative decision to issue a Consultative Document immediately meant that little detailed discussion on reform took place in the aftermath of the election. The TUC had no meeting with Carr to discuss the issue specifically, and, though in September Congress passed a resolution warning of opposition in general terms to the Conservative measures, the unions gave the impression of waiting on events.[20] The CBI was rather more active, if only because in the Neal Report it had a set of clear proposals to put to the Government. At two meetings in August CBI leaders stressed to Carr their scepticism about the idea of allowing unions to enter voluntarily into legally binding agreements, and pressed again for a strong Registrar with the power to police agreements rather than leaving employers to do so through the civil courts. These views represented a substantial dissent from the drift of Conservative thinking, though the CBI's general comments on the meetings stressed the amount of agreement which existed between employers and Government.[21]

If the months between June and October – when the Consultative Document appeared – were a period of calm on the legislative front, the same could not be said of industrial relations generally. The period immediately after the election was marked by a very high level of strike activity, including a key dispute among local authority workers and a State of Emergency declared because of a dock strike.[22] The local authority workers' dispute finally ended any hopes that the Conservatives might have had of reaching a liberal bargain with the unions involving the ending of government intervention in the wages market. Carr's refusal to allow his Department's conciliation service to mediate in the dispute convinced union leaders that the Government was adopting the role of contestant rather than referee in the wages battle.[23] By September the TUC, convinced that the Conservatives' opposition to statutory incomes

control meant, in effect, incomes restraint in the public sector, was trying
to coordinate union opposition to Government wages policy.[24]

The other plank of the Conservatives' by now rickety platform for doing
a general economic deal with the unions – involving an expanding
economy – also collapsed in October, when the Government's cuts in
public spending were strongly opposed by the TUC, which has always
been expansionist in this respect.[25] It was thus clear some time before the
appearance of the Consultative Document that any bargain with the
unions would have to be made solely in terms of the legislation.

Worsening relations between unions and the Government were a
reflection of a generally deteriorating industrial situation. Shortly after the
Conservative victory, the strike figures showed that the level of disputes
had risen to a new height.[26] Even more important from the employers'
point of view, the pressure of wage claims was high and climbing higher.[27]
In the same month as the TUC began trying to coordinate union resistance
to Government wages policy, the CBI called a conference of employers to
attempt to organise resistance to wage demands.[28] In the key engineering
industry, the EEF was complaining bitterly, both before and after the June
election, of the pressure of wage costs, and sought a special meeting with
Carr in July to discuss the situation.[29]

The high level of industrial militancy in this period decreased even
further the likelihood that some sort of negotiations might take place
between unions, employers and Government over the content of the
proposed legislation. But the strike pattern in these months also introduced
an additional complicating factor. Since 1967 the Conservatives had
identified the short, unconstitutional strike as the key problem of industrial
relations; and this, together with the importance of restoring authority and
discipline, remained the central theme of Carr's remarks on the strike
problem during the passage of the Bill. But at the very point when the
Conservatives were preparing their legislation, the strike pattern altered,
to one where disputes became longer.[30] One result was to deflect employers
away from attempts to change the law on industrial relations to a concern
with using the social security system as a weapon against strikers. Since
strikers could typically only claim benefits for their families after being off
work for two weeks, the withholding of social security benefits was
irrelevant in deterring the very short strike which the Tories had thought of
as the characteristic British dispute.[31] As strikes lengthened, and began to
pose a set of problems additional to those raised by short unconstitutional
disputes, the spokesmen for business began to press for the curtailment of
social security benefits. In fact the Conservatives did respond to these
pressures, but the response was separate from the Act, and the main
justification for the legislation was still expressed in terms of ending short,
unconstitutional disputes.

THE CONSULTATIVE DOCUMENT AND THE PROBLEM OF THE MANDATE

The most significant feature of the Consultative Document which appeared on 5 October 1970 was its fidelity to the Conservatives' pre-election proposals. The four 'general principles' on which the Government proposed to legislate – the right to join or to refuse to join a union, the right of workers to negotiate collectively, the right of workers to withdraw labour subject only to their individual contract of employment, and the necessity for all parties to have clearly 'defined rights and obligation' – could all be traced back to *Fair Deal*.[32] Similarly, two of the key institutions which were set up to operate the proposed Act were drawn from the 1968 proposals. A National Industrial Relations Court, equivalent to a branch of the High Court but staffed by lay members as well as a judge, was to be set up with power to hear claims on any breaches of the proposed Act. The Industrial Tribunals, first set up under the 1964 Industrial Training Act, were turned into lower divisions of the Court. The Court could exercise its power by awarding compensation and making orders, and would have the power to enforce its orders.[33]

The position and power of the second institution – the Registrar – similarly differed little from *Fair Deal*, though, as we shall, see the importance of registration had increased considerably. The Registrar remained essentially an ombudsman, with the job of ensuring that union rules and practices complied with the liberal principles of the legislation. Indeed in one important respect there had been a move away from CBI opinion, since the *Fair Deal* proposal that the Registrar be enpowered to refuse registration to unions that operated 'unacceptable' restrictive practices was now dropped.[34]

The major institutional innovation in the document concerned the Commission on Industrial Relations and this, though not in *Fair Deal*, had been anticipated in advance of the election.[35] The CIR, which had been originally set up by the previous Labour Government, was given increased powers of investigation. It was to be a key institution in two ways: it represented one of the Government's chief concessions to voluntary collectivism, since it was to be 'primarily concerned to assist employers and unions in the voluntary reform of industrial relations';[36] and it was central to the operation of the proposals on union recognition, the agency shop and the determination of bargaining units. Its importance for the Conservatives was finally established following the adoption of proposals on bargaining units and recognition which were produced by Howe and Abbott following visits to America early in 1970. It may best be conceived of as an equivalent of the American National Labor Relations Board.[37]

On the substance of the new laws, the Consultative Document also closely followed pre-election thinking. For the individual worker there was a legal right to refuse to belong to a union; but reflecting the Conservative fear, strengthened since *In Place of Strife*, that the unions would refuse to register, the corresponding right to join a union was restricted to registered organisations. It was to be an unfair industrial practice to strike, or to threaten to strike, to force an employer to discriminate in any way against a unionist or non-unionist.[38] The idea of an 'unfair industrial practice', an innovation since *Fair Deal*, may best be interpreted as yet another Conservative attempt to solve the problem of what to do about employers who refused to use the new laws. *Fair Deal* had tried to solve the problem of protecting individual rights by exposing those who induced strikes to the possibility of civil damages. This in turn relied on the willingness of employers to sue. The introduction of the unfair industrial practice – which Howe seems to have suggested after his American visit early in 1970 on the analogy of the 'unfair labour practices' in American legislation – increased the likelihood of legal intervention, since affected individuals or organisations could ask the Court to issue an order to desist. Not only did this increase the possibility of direct legal intervention, but it also brought the Court more directly into the field of enforcement, since a refusal to desist could constitute contempt. The unfair industrial practice was adopted as a common solution to this problem, and as a result there were numerous such practices referred to throughout the final Act.

Turning to the question of the legal immunities of unions in industrial disputes, the Document again closely reflected *Fair Deal*, especially in the matter of distinguishing between registered and unregistered unions. Only the former were to enjoy immunity from civil prosecution when taking industrial action, and the definition of a trade dispute was in turn narrowly defined to exclude such disputes as inter-union and sympathy strikes. Not only were unregistered unions excluded from immunity, but it was to be an unfair industrial practice for them to try to induce workers to strike in breach of their individual contracts of employment. Finally, while there would be an upper limit to damages which could be awarded against registered unions, unregistered organisations faced no such limit.[39]

This discrimination between registered and unregistered organisations was reinforced by the provisions relating to recognition and bargaining rights. Unregistered organisations could not request the Court to order the CIR to investigate the merits of a recognition dispute.[40] In this the proposals closely followed the party's pre-election thinking; but the elaboration of the details produced a variation. It had been objected – and was to be in the future – that the Conservative proposals to settle recognition disputes by means of secret ballots would lead to a proliferation of unions. Labour had tried to solve the problem in 1969 by only allowing for a ballot at the discretion of the CIR.[41] The Conservatives tried yet again a compromise between liberal principles and a concern with industrial peace: workers were to be allowed to vote in a recognition dispute; if a substantial proportion disliked the outcome, they could after a suitable period apply to the Court for a further ballot; but the CIR was used as a filter to prevent proliferation, since it would investigate the suitability – by reference to its support and resources – of any claimant for recognition, and in effect frame any question on a ballot paper.[42]

Related to the question of recognition was the matter of the closed shop. Here again the Consultative Document amounted to little more than an elaboration of *Fair Deal*: as in the latter, the pre-entry closed shop was to be void in law, and was to be replaced by an agency shop, which would be available only to registered unions. A disavowal of the pre-entry closed shop was also to be a condition of registration. The Document stiffened up the proposals by making any attempt to enforce the closed shop an unfair industrial practice, and specified that for an agency shop – which would contain substantial concessions to conscientious objectors – to be obtained, a majority of affected workers would. have to vote in its favour.[43]

We can turn finally to the question which had most vexed the Tories while in opposition, that of the enforceability of collective agreements. As we saw earlier, in the months before the election the party's leaders had contemplated an approach which would have involved a large degree of compulsion. Partly because such a solution represented too great a departure from liberal principles, and partly because of the inevitable conflict with the unions which would ensue, the Document finally adopted the *Fair Deal* solution: there would be a presumption of enforceability behind every written agreement unless it contained a clause expressly to the contrary. But this section of the Document did contain one substantial apparent concession to the CBI and other groups of employers. Where no legally enforceable procedure agreement existed, a registered union, an employer or the Secretary of State could apply to the Court for the matter to be referred to the CIR which in turn could, after investigating the matter, recommend the terms of a procedure agreement. If no voluntary acceptance was forthcoming, one of the three parties could apply to the Court for the recommended agreement to be imposed.[44] At first sight, this looked like a significant step in the direction of compulsory collectivism, since it seemed that a really determined Secretary of State could introduce legally binding procedure agreements over whole sections of the economy. As the employers were soon to discover, however, the provision was not all it seemed.

The Consultative Document is sound evidence, if further evidence were needed, of the Conservatives' determination not to be deflected from their pre-election course. It contained only one significant procedural addition to the party's public commitments – the unfair industrial practice – and the attractiveness of this had been established before the election. Similarly, the major institutional innovation – the use of the CIR as a sort of British National Labor Relations Board – was decided on before the return to office. The Document also reflects the extent to which Tory policy continued to be worked out independently of the main pressure groups. The CBI, the most active group at this stage, extracted only two significant concessions, one of which turned out to be illusory. The first was the decision to drop the Productivity Board, which *Fair Deal* had proposed as a means by which the state could supplement management's attacks on restrictive practices. This proposal was dropped after the CBI objected that the Board's functions were unclear. Even in this case the Board's demise can not be fully ascribed to the activities of an outside pressure group: the Cabinet argument which finally killed the PIB shortly after the June election augured badly for the new Board, since it was to be based on a reconstituted PIB.[45]

The second concession concerned, of course, the procedures by which the NIRC could impose – at the CIR's recommendation – legally binding procedure agreements. This looked like a very large step towards accepting the argument of the CBI – and other employers' organisations – that without this measure the unions would nullify the legislation by insisting on the inclusion of a 'non-enforceability' clause in all contracts. But in fact the Government had given something very different from what the employers wanted. On closer inspection it turned out that what the Document proposed was that agreements be imposed on individual undertakings – probably meaning firms – rather than on whole industries. This was unacceptable to the CBI, which had consistently defended the national system of collective bargaining, and to the EEF, which had an even more direct interest in retaining industry-wide agreements. On closer acquaintance, it turned out that the employers' organisations had got the worst of both worlds: they had failed to get a commitment that industry-wide enforceability could be imposed, while the possibility that such a course would be open to individual employers opened up the possibility that national non-enforceable procedure agreements would be deserted. None of this seems to have struck either the CBI or the EEF at first glance, but after the lapse of a few days the EEF in particular announced the new measure to be a major drawback. Federation officials were reported to have thought at first that the formula in the Document was the result of a drafting error, and to have been shocked on discovering that this was really the Government's intention,[46] a striking indication of how far the Government and the pressure groups were at cross-purposes. This question of enforceability was to prove one of the main points of difference between employers' organisations and the Government.

In responding to the Document, the employers' organisations were in a dilemma. Since union opposition was to be expected, it was important that those who generally thought legislation desirable should unite in public. The Document thus collected a number of public testimonials: newspapers close to business opinion, such as *The Times* and the *Financial Times*, which during the summer had been voicing the CBI view that any proposals would have to be the result of close consultations with both sides of industry,[47] now welcomed the Document despite the fact that the Tories had ignored the advice and stuck to their mandate.[48] Similarly, the CBI gave the proposals a public welcome despite the fact that the detailed doubts which it expressed – over the Registrar, legally binding agreements, and the whole strategy of implementing the proposals as a complete package[49] – amounted to a fundamental critique of them. The problem was that the employers' objections to the proposals were pragmatic, based on the belief that, though desirable, they would be impossible to implement because of union opposition. To have condemned the Document explicitly on these grounds would have been to hand a propaganda gift to the unions, and thus to make it even less likely that the proposals would succeed.

The most important response to the Consultative Document came, however, from the unions. Their initial reaction to the Conservative victory had been a compound of hope and belief that the pre-election proposals would not be implemented. Hugh Scanlon described the General Council's attitude as follows: 'We knew when we lost the election last June what was facing us but we said, "Do not do anything until we meet the Ministers." We met Ministers and got precisely nowhere. We said, "Do not do anything until we see what the Bill says".'[50] The behaviour of the TUC is consistent with this description. Though Congress in September passed a motion opposing legal intervention – singling out cooling-off periods and legally enforceable agreements – the possibility of negotiation was by no means ruled out. Indeed Vic Feather remarked a trifle wearily: 'It may be that we shall have to embark again on another tedious process of educating the politicians about industry.'[51] On 24 September the General Council sent the resolution passed by Congress to Carr, with a letter pointing out the reforms initiated by the TUC in the aftermath of the Donovan Report and *In Place of Strife*. The Council argued that the Government's role in industrial relations ought to be confined to the traditional one of providing information and such services as conciliation and arbitration, and offered to meet Carr to discuss 'how the Government could help both sides of industry to secure further improvements in the voluntary system.'[52]

The tone of this was in part deliberately disingenuous, but it also represented a real wish to strike a bargain. There was a substantial group within the General Council which, while opposed to the substance of the Conservative proposals, was not too unhappy about the threat of legislation, since it could be used to justify a tightening up of authority within the trade-union movement. The leadership of at least two large unions – the General and Municipal Workers, whose President was that year's Chairman of the General Council, and the Electricians and Plumbers – reflected the traditional anxieties about authority posed by the rise of shop-floor power. Thus, while the unions were largely united against the substance of the Government's proposals, a substantial and influential body of opinion lived in hope of negotiation. As a result, the initial reaction to the Consultative Document was subdued: Vic Feather's first response was to note its complexity and suggest that the length of time allowed for comments be extended. Four days after publication the Finance and General Purposes Committee of the General Council – its 'Cabinet' – considered the Document, and produced a long list of objections, most of which were to become familiar. The Committee also decided to send the objections to the Government, and again asked for an extension of the amount of time allowed for consultation.[53]

On 13 October a delegation of TUC leaders met Carr to discuss the Document. The meeting had a very important effect on the future of the legislation. The Secretary of State announced that the Government's proposals rested on eight 'pillars', which were irremovable. Any negotiation could only be about the detail of the pillars. The eight included all the provisions to which the General Council's Finance and General Purposes Committee had taken exception four days before: the right to join or not to join a union; registration of unions; the introduction of legally binding agreements; restriction of the existing legal immunities possessed by unions; provisions for ballots and cooling-off periods; machinery for laying down legally binding procedures; rights for union recognition; and machinery to define bargaining units and establish rights to representation.[54] The General Council responded by calling an emergency meeting two days later, which decided in effect to boycott all further consultations. The General Council 'were still willing to consult with the Government if they were given an assurance that the Government was open to persuasion on the merits of its central proposals but . . . if there were to be no further discussions the blame lay fairly and squarely on the Government.'[55] Since Carr's 13 October statement explicitly ruled out consideration of the 'central proposals' the General Council were breaking off discussion. The same meeting took a number of other decisions which were to shape the TUC's subsequent behaviour. It was decided to mount a campaign of mass publicity to persuade trade unionists and the general public that the proposed legislation was undesirable.[56] In fact, however, the General Council had now all but accepted the inevitability of an Act, as was shown by its other major decision, which was to call a Special Congress, not to organise opposition against either the Document or the Bill, but 'at a time when, if the proposals appeared likely to become an Act, the Movement would need to determine its attitude to such an Act.'[57] There really never was a serious TUC campaign against the proposed legislation as such. From 15 October the TUC's actions were premissed on the assumption that what had to be done was to discredit the workings of the impending Act and to ensure that the unions did not cooperate with it.

The events of 13–15 October are of the greatest importance in understanding the final fate of the 1971 Act. They mark the parting of the ways between the Government and the unions over the legislation; the realisation by the General Council that negotiation and compromise were not going to take place; and, as a result, the commitment by the TUC to a

policy of destroying the Act. If Carr had not insisted on the inde-
structibility of the eight pillars, a very different outcome could have
occurred. The unions would have negotiated, though reluctantly. The
final Act would still have been denounced by the TUC, but there is good
reason to suppose that after the initial protests it would have become an
accepted part of the industrial relations scene. Carr's insistence on the
eight pillars, and the General Council's reaction, thus contributed in
important ways to the final failure of the legislation. Because of the long-
term effect of these events, it is important to explain them. In the case of the
Conservatives, however, their behaviour is something of a mystery.

Tories would doubtless argue the Government's action in refusing to
negotiate about the principles of the legislation is easily explicable: the
Party had worked its policy out before it gained office; had warned the
unions that it would stick to its mandate if it received one; and, having won
the election, proceeded to do just that. This is precisely where the mystery
lies, for the Government's behaviour in this respect was completely
uncharacteristic – a totally un-Tory aberration. Traditionally the
Conservatives have disliked the idea of offering the electorate detailed
promises, as distinct from general assurances of good government. What
makes their behaviour all the more curious is that they were under pressure
from both of the main interest groups – the CBI and the TUC – to act in a
traditionally Tory manner: to forget their electoral promises and to work
out a deal with the chief affected parties. Of course the Conservatives had
already behaved in an unusual fashion in working out detailed policies
while in opposition, but this could be dismissed as an eccentricity induced
by electoral opportunism and the frustrations of being out of government.
The real problem lies in explaining why they persisted with the proposals
once in office. To have quietly dropped measures contained in a two-and-
a-half year old pamphlet – *Fair Deal* – might have been a little embarras-
ing, but could have created few serious difficulties. The mystery is
incapable of complete solution, but a number of possibilities suggest
themselves.

One is that there was something unusual about this particular Tory
Government which led it to disregard the great pressure groups and insist
on its mandate. There is a small amount of evidence to support this view,
but it will not really bear close examination. In its favour is the undoubted
fact that in 1970 the Conservatives were heavily influenced by market
liberalism, and as a result were suspicious of a style of politics involving
deals between government and the great interest groups. The attempted
policy of disengagement from industry and the fact that they were hostile
to NEDC[58] – the epitome of functional representation – are indications of
this sort of thinking. But other than this, the Conservatives showed little
desire to reduce the importance of the functional groups. When, for
instance, Sir Keith Joseph – perhaps the nearest thing to a market liberal
in the Cabinet – came to reorganise the National Health Service in 1971 he

produced a consultative document which, though made available to the interested parties, was never published.[59] Could deference to the system of functional representation go further? The same government in 1972 reversed most of the important policies for which it had received a mandate in 1970, and tried to work out an alternative by detailed negotiation with the TUC and the CBI. Thus the Conservatives' behaviour over the eight pillars can be explained neither in terms of some special attachment to the doctrine of the mandate nor as due to some special dislike of pressure groups.

This only makes the failure to consult seriously with the TUC all the more puzzling, for it means that the Government's behaviour was not only an aberration compared with traditional Tory attitudes; it was also out of character with actions of this particular Conservative administration. A possible explanation for this aberration might rest on three factors: the traditional Conservative view of government; the particular situation in 1970; and the personalities of some of those involved.

Conservative dislike of 'mandate politics' springs from a particular view of the proper functions of government. Tories are elitists: they believe that political leaders should look after the good of the community without pandering too much to the particular views of the electorate; hence they are suspicious of very detailed election manifestos and the populism implied by a stress on the mandate. If there is a consistent thread running through the twists and turns of Mr Heath's time as Prime Minister, it is surely this insistence on strong government independent of sectional interests in the community. By 1970, however, the Tories were convinced that the main threat to the autonomy and strength of government came not from the electorate at large but from the trade unions. They turned to the mandate not because they were populists at heart, but because it promised a source of legitimacy and support in their attempt to restore the independence of political leaders from the unions' power. At the heart of the Conservatives' behaviour, then, lay a quite traditional Tory belief in strong government which, paradoxically, led them to ignore for once their equally traditional suspicion of mandate politics.

The Conservative belief that the unions represented a threat to firm and independent government had been developing gradually over a long period, but it was undoubtedly strengthened by the events in 1969 arising from the publication of *In Place of Strife*. The argument between the unions and the Labour Government concentrated on a number of 'penal' clauses to which the TUC objected, and after prolonged negotiation Mr Wilson and his colleagues retreated, in return for a promise of internal reform from the unions. Although the best guess now is that the Government failed to carry its view because of the behaviour of its back-bench supporters rather than because of the direct exercise of trade-union power, the Conservatives undoubtedly concluded that a weak Government had collapsed in the face of sectional pressure. The Tories made much of this, partly because they believed it was electorally advantageous, but also because it grossly offended their notions of what strong government should be.

In Place of Strife is also important for another reason. Tories believe in the system of pressure-group politics, and are quite prepared to negotiate with functional groups like the CBI and the TUC. But their belief in strong and independent government means that they believe in limits on the power of such groups. The Conservatives believed that in 1969 the TUC had exceeded those limits – had broken the implicit rules of the game – and were likely to do so again given the chance. The Government thus refused to negotiate because it believed – on the evidence of *In Place of Strife* – that the unions were not really interested in the normal process of compromise and negotiation, but wanted only to destroy any measures which would threaten their power. As I shall show in a moment, however, the Government's intelligence was faulty in this respect: the TUC was in fact very ready for negotiation, and compromise could well have bought, if not agreement, at least acquiescence.

The Government seems to have had contradictory attitudes towards the unions: on the one hand, it believed them to be so intransigent that negotiation was pointless; but on the other it also believed that, if it behaved in a determined fashion and put the legislation on the statute book quickly, then the TUC would soon drop all opposition and cooperate. This thinking led to the adoption of what was called the 'big bang' strategy: the Cabinet early on decided that, since the measures were going to be opposed, it was best to put them all in one big Bill, push it through quickly and get the unpleasant business over with as quickly as possible. This underestimation of the amount of opposition which would arise also seems to have sprung from poor intelligence about the unions. In particular, the Government never seems to have realised the strength of attachment by the TUC to the practice of negotiation and consultation in Whitehall. The fact that Carr's insistence that the eight pillars were irremovable unwittingly alienated those very members of the General Council who might have given his case some sort of sympathetic hearing is a striking example of the incomprehension with which the Conservative leadership viewed the TUC.

The Tory belief in strong government combined with the particular circumstances of 1970 go some way to explaining the Conservatives' behaviour, but since what happened was the result of choices made by individuals any satisfactory explanation must take some account of the personalities of those individuals. Of course, 'personality' does not exist in a vacuum: the same Churchill who was the exuberant hammer of the unions in 1926 was by 1951 the instigator of Monckton's policy of conciliation. Nevertheless, certain situations favour the appearance of certain traits in certain people. In this respect Mr Heath's behaviour is important. He has always exhibited to a very high degree the classic Conservative attachment to firm government, an attachment which the events surrounding *In Place of Strife* were calculated to increase. In Cabinet he seems to have been one of the most assertive of Prime Ministers, and in the months after the unexpected election victory of June 1970 his prestige and authority were at their height. If he had chosen to encourage those like Whitelaw who pondered the thought of compromise with the unions, there is little doubt that such a course would have been seriously considered. But in fact he did the reverse: he was one of the main sources of pressure for speedy legislation, which would clear the matter out of the way, and a strong supporter of the Cabinet's 'big bang' strategy. With such a Prime Minister in such a mood, there is little else Carr could have done, even had he wished otherwise. Mr Heath is – to put the matter colloquially – a 'big bang' politician, whose political career has been marked by a series of spectacular conflicts. He made his name as a departmental minister in 1964 with an Act abolishing resale price maintenance, which he pushed through against fierce opposition from interest groups and from his own backbenches; the outstanding achievement of his premiership was the highly contentious legislation taking Britain into the European Economic Community; and his career was ruined – at least for the time being – by the biggest political bang of recent years, the dispute with the miners in 1974.

If, despite Heath, the Government's behaviour remains somewhat puzzling, the TUC's reaction to it is more easily explained. To understand the TUC's reaction it is necessary to recall the position enjoyed by the unions in the political system. For a generation the TUC had been allocated a place near the centre of decison-making, and had almost always been consulted in advance about any public policy which affected the unions. So accustomed had the TUC's leadership become to consultation that when it failed to take place their reaction was very hostile: trade union objections to the 1962 pay pause, for instance, arose as much from the fact that the Government had failed to consult in advance as from any objection to the substance of the policy. The situation was now repeated over the Consultative Document. At the Special Congress in March 1971, the union leaders laid as much stress in their objections on the absence of consultation as on the substance of the measures. According to Lord Cooper, the Chairman of Congress, the failure to consult properly upset the General Council more than any other single action.[60]

There is no doubt at all that the Government's refusal to discuss anything but the details of the Bill was taken as a grave affront by the General Council. What is more, this was a matter which united leaders of very different political opinions: unions which might have had some sympathy with the idea of legislation, such as the General and Municipal Workers, were also those which most valued the practice of consultation and the opportunity it gave the TUC to act as an orthodox pressure group. The Government's behaviour was thus calculated to most offend precisely those members of the General Council who might have been potential allies. This sense that the Conservatives had acted in what amounted to an unconstitutional fashion was well put by Alex Donnet, a leader of the GMWU:

> All British governments know, or should know, that consultation is of special importance and significance to the trade unions because it expresses their members' desire that their representatives should have full and free opportunity of putting forward their views and have them considered before conclusions are reached. This was denied them; and, throughout, the Government have refused to consult the TUC. As a consequence, the TUC has initiated, planned and promoted the most extensive and determined campaign of opposition to the Government's proposals in the history of the Movement.[61]

The fact that union objections to the Industrial Relations Act concerned not only the content of the legislation but also the manner in which it was enacted is important to understanding the unions' later behaviour. Trade-union leaders quite understood the doctrine of the mandate, but only when Carr made the announcement about the eight pillars do they seem fully to have realised that the Tories were entirely in earnest when they invoked it to justify their measures. This is understandable: for a generation the unions had been encouraged to believe that, whatever the outcome of elections, they would have a considerable say over any policies which affected them. Now, this was being denied them over the most important piece of legislation in living memory. In a real sense the unions thought the legislation illegitimate and unconstitutional, not just because of its content but because of the way it had been prepared and passed. As a result appeals to the unions to respect the constitution and the rule of law met less response than might otherwise have been the case, precisely because of this feeling that it was the Government which had first been in breach of the constitution.

With the TUC voluntarily retiring from the scene, arguments over the Consultative Document were now largely conducted between the Government and the employers' spokesmen. In the period allowed for consultation the leaders of a number of employers' organisations met Carr or his officials, while a number of others relayed their views through the CBI. It was the latter which continued to put forward the most comprehensive criticisms. The Confederation's objections continued to be based on the assumption that any workable solution would have to win the support of the union leadership. The CBI also operated on the assumption that such support could be obtained since, as Leonard Neal put it, the unions were 'as interested in getting some order into the situation as we are'.[62] The familiar theme of strengthening national institutions – unions and employers' associations – was repeated, but with even greater emphasis and detail as the CBI looked with increasing concern at the details of the Document. The first meeting with Carr to discuss the Consultative

Document concentrated on the Registrar, the CBI pressing again its desire for a much stronger institution than the Conservatives envisaged.[63]

By the second meeting, the CBI's objections had widened.[64] Most important, as we have already seen, the Confederation had realised that what at first looked like a considerable concession – the possibility of having the NIRC impose legally enforceable procedure agreements – turned out to be potentially very damaging to the whole idea of industry-wide bargaining, since the agreements could only be imposed at company level. At this second meeting, the CBI also began to develop its opposition to the ban on the closed shop. The Confederation objected that any attempt to impose a ban would lead to a confrontation with the unions. And there was a more positive objection: for some time many employers had been aware that the closed shop could be part of a bargain with the unions, whereby union desire for institutional security could be fulfilled, in return for a promise to exercise discipline over the rank and file. In defending the closed shop, the Confederation was reflecting the attitudes of large firms, already highly unionised, especially in engineering. Interest groups catering for small businesses had taken a very different view: the National Association of Manufacturers, in its evidence to Donovan, condemned the closed shop; while the Association of British Chambers of Commerce, in its response to the Consultative Document, complained that even the Conservatives' conditions for granting an agency shop were not stringent enough.[65] The extent to which big business – especially big industrial concerns – defended the closed shop was to be one of the most striking features of arguments over amending the Government's proposals.

The response of the CBI shows clearly the extent to which important parts of the business community, especially the larger industrial undertakings, had responded to the problems of industrial relations by a move in the direction of compulsory collectivism. The pivot of the CBI's proposals was a Registrar who ·could take legal action against individuals and institutions. Added to this was support for the imposition by the state of legally binding procedure agreements throughout whole industries, and support for the closed shop, partly on the grounds that banning it would needlessly antagonise the unions, but also on the grounds that it was a useful disciplinary instrument. Indeed, with the EEF, the CBI argued that the imposed procedure agreements should not be confined to industries where labour unrest existed, but should be extended to peaceful industries as preventive medicine.[66]

This response – particularly in the matter of the closed shop – was echoed by a number of other big-business pressure groups. When the heads of the nationalised industries saw Carr, they endorsed the CBI line, and stressed in particular the problems which would be created by an attempt to ban closed shops.[67] The British Federation of Master Printers similarly funnelled its worries on this issue through the CBI to the Government.[68] An even more significant response came from the motor industry, which had long shown an interest in the disciplinary potential of the closed shop. Through the Motor Industry Joint Council three key features of the proposals were criticised.[69] Doubts were expressed over what was felt to be excessive reliance on an American model of reform. This may be interpreted as another version of the familiar CBI objection about not wanting the law to intrude too much into the detailed workings of industrial relations. Concern was also voiced on two other matters: the closed shop, and the problem of how to prevent unions simply refusing to sign legally binding agreements.

The arguments over the proposals in the Consultative Document opened up the divisions between the Government and the leading employers' pressure groups. The outcome of the consultative process – as reflected in the Bill, which was published in the first week of December 1970 – showed that the Government was unimpressed by the arguments which the employers had put to it. Though Carr stressed that 'even now' consultation was not ended,[70] every one of the key arguments put forward by the employers had been rejected: the Registrar's role remained the same; there was no retreat in the attack on the closed shop; and no attempt was made to meet the employers' desire for the imposition of procedure agreements across whole industries. The liberal provisions in the proposals remained, despite the employers' criticism, and the employers' desires were rejected on liberal grounds. On the matter of procedure agreements, for instance, Carr argued that it would be wrong to allow organisations such as the EEF to secure imposed agreements not only against the wishes of unions, but even against the wishes of some of its own members.[71] There is some temptation to dismiss this argument as public rationalisation: after all, the Conservatives knew perfectly well that to allow employers to impose agreements throughout whole industries would be an extreme provocation towards the unions. But apart from the fact that viewing the party's liberalism as a rationalisation involves discounting numerous statements by its spokesmen, it is the case that over matters such as the closed shop the Conservatives were ready to offend both sides of industry in the pursuit of liberal principles.

The Government's rejection of the employers' arguments meant that the Bill, when published, changed little that was in the Consultative Document. A small number of unfair industrial practices were removed; there was some change in the relationship between the Industrial Relations Court and its lower divisions; and some alteration was made in the conditions governing registration of unions. One of the leaders of the CBI remarked that the employers had got as little out of the Government as had the unions, and the remark is probably accurate. This casts some doubt on the conventional textbook explanations of what makes pressure groups effective. The CBI possessed everything which should have made for success. As a prestigious and established organisation, it had good access to the Department and its ministers; it was undoubtedly voicing the views of some of the most powerful groups and individuals in British industry; in the matter of the closed shop, it had the support of senior officials in the Department of Employment; it had supporters in the ruling party;[72] it had its former Director General in the Cabinet;[73] and it could offer an explicit and reasoned alternative to the Government's proposals in the form of the Neal Report. But it appears that if – as happened here – the politicians make up their minds to pass a particular law there is very little that even a powerful pressure group can do to stop them. Of course, as the final fate of the Act was to show, there is a world of difference between putting legislation on the statute book and actually getting it to operate successfully. Governments can if they wish be relatively autonomous of pressure groups during the making and passing of laws, but the importance of outside groups may rise dramatically when legislation has to be implemented.

The Government's independence of mind was not confined to spurning the interest groups; it also resisted the advice of its civil servants. The Department objected in particular to thrèe provisions: it thought the attempt to outlaw the closed shop incapable of being put into practice; it could see little use for cooling-off periods; and it did not accept the Tory view that secret ballots in certain circumstances could result in moderation on the part of unions.[74] It carried its view on none of these. This is not very surprising. Civil servants exercise a decisive influence on much public policy, but the circumstances of industrial relations in 1970 were not conducive to the exercise of such power: the Tories had come to office with a clear and determined idea of what they wanted to do; they had committed themselves electorally; and the Prime Minister was behind the party's policies. In addition, the Department itself was divided: though support for legislative reform had grown over the years, there were still some civil servants – especially those connected with the conciliation services – who defended voluntarism. In the circumstances, it is not very surprising that the politicians failed to be deflected from their course.

The publication of the Bill marked a new stage in the struggle over the Government's measures. The range of interest groups which were interested in the proposals widened considerably at this stage, and Parliament became a major arena of public debate. It is to Parliament, its role and significance, that the next chapter is devoted.

6 The Parliamentary Battle

In formal terms Parliament lies at the centre of law-making. From the publication of a Bill to its final enactment on receiving the Royal Assent, the familiar stages in both Houses – presentation, Second Reading, Committee, Report and Third Reading – provide a framework for argument and debate. MPs probably spend more time than any other group in public discussion of legislation, and the parliamentary debates constitute a large proportion of the total public argument. This was especially so in the case of the Industrial Relations Bill. Apart from Finance Bills it was the longest piece of legislation to concern Parliament in the post-war years. As its Committee stage was taken on the floor of the Commons, it also occupied more parliamentary time than any piece of non-financial legislation since 1945.[1]

Yet all this effort has a slightly hollow ring. The parliamentary process was largely irrelevant to shaping the initial Bill into the final Act. Each amendment conceded or initiated by the Government required a parliamentary majority, but the Conservative supremacy in both Houses meant that this was always assured. The initiative for amendments generally came from outside Parliament. The irrelevance of the protracted parliamentary stages to the shaping of the legislation is also indicated by the behaviour of the chief pressure groups. The TUC did indeed send an observer to the first meeting of a Parliamentary Labour Party working group preparing opposition to the Bill, but the arrangement quickly lapsed. Indeed the parliamentarians found that such amendments as the TUC proposed tended to arrive after the relevant clauses had been debated. In any case, because of its withdrawal from the whole process of consultation and negotiation, the TUC's attitude was – as it put it to the PLP – that it 'was not in a position to be closely involved in the process of amending the Bill.'[2] Hence the chief trade-union campaign was not at all synchronised with the parliamentary battle. The CBI's campaign similarly neglected Parliament. When all else failed, the Confederation arranged for twenty-five amendments to be put down; only two were ever reached, and both were defeated.[3]

The failure even to discuss most of the CBI's amendments points up another important feature of the debates, especially in the Commons: the quite haphazard discussion of the Bill. Because of the use of the guillotine, the Commons in Committee only discussed selected portions. What is more, while detailed arguments took place over relatively minor amendments, important clauses were not even debated: thus the House spent four hours arguing over the meaning of the word 'responsible',[4] but passed without discussion numerous important clauses, including some concerning the operation of the agency shop and the activities of the Court. Even the debates which did take place were – viewed from the point of view of a detailed argument about the problems of industrial relations – a shambles. Back-bench contributions in the Commons, in particular, were largely a rambling farrago of political abuse, anecdote and misused statistics. The Lords' debates, though more ordered and better informed, were mainly used by the Government as occasions for inserting amendments agreed with the relevant interest groups.

None of this is very surprising. The formal institutions of Parliament are in most cases peripheral to the shaping of legislation, and this is especially the case when a party is as committed as were the Conservatives to a particular line of action.[5] MPs can and do influence Bills, but they do not often do so by speaking on the floor of the House of Commons.

If Parliament was so irrelevant to the whole business of shaping the Industrial Relations Bill into an Act, what was the whole furore about? For it must be emphasised that there was a furore: there was a long, bitterly argued Committee stage on the floor of the Commons, and the Opposition forced numerous all-night sittings and long voting sessions in an effort to make the Bill's passage as difficult as possible and generally to obstruct the Government's parliamentary timetable. Just how acrimonious the arguments were is best indicated by the fact that at two important points the normal rules governing procedure broke down. One episode involved a group of mainly Tribunite Labour MPs – including Eric Heffer, a front-bench spokesman on the Bill – who crowded round the Speaker's chair, obstructed the business of the House and caused the proceedings to be suspended. The second episode is perhaps more significant. In the face of the Opposition's attempts to delay the Bill for as long as possible by debating every line in detail, the Government imposed a guillotine. But this was done without consultation through the usual channels – the whips' offices – and led to the suspension by Labour of the normal arrangements – such as pairing – which make parliamentary life bearable. All Oppositions foam at the mouth at the sight of a guillotine motion, but Labour's suspension of the usual arrangements reveals something more than synthetic anger. The bitterness of Labour's opposition to the Bill can be explained in terms of two considerations: one had to do with the Bill itself, the other with the place of Parliament in the political system.

One of the chief reasons why so many Labour MPs sounded angry and bitter during the passage of the legislation was that they *were* genuinely angry and bitter. Most of the parliamentary fireworks – such as the action which led to the suspension of the House – came from a relatively small group of MPs on the Labour benches associated with the Tribune group. The debates were dominated by MPs such as John Mendelson, Norman Atkinson, Joe Ashton and – from the front-bench – Eric Heffer, who had opposed their own Government's attempts to reform industrial relations in 1969, and who were quite sincerely convinced that attempts to change the law were an attack on working people. In their eyes the Tory Bill was class legislation designed to strengthen employers and weaken unions. Given this anger their behaviour is quite explicable: if the Bill really was a vicious attack on working people, there was little point in treating it as an ordinary piece of legislation subject to the usual gaze of parliamentary scrutiny; ridicule, obstruction and blanket denunciation were far more appropriate.

Apart from this group of MPs, who really were angered by the Bill, there was another section of the PLP – typified by Barbara Castle, who led for the opposition – who had more tactical reasons for denouncing the proposed legislation. Mrs Castle's fiery denunciations of the measure were undoubtedly inspired in part by a desire to mend her fences with the trade union leadership and with her own back benches. As Conservatives delighted to point out, there were some remarkable resemblances between their own proposals and those which Mrs Castle had sponsored in *In Place of Strife*; the sharpness of much of her language arose from an attempt to convince the unions that she and the party leadership generally were now opposed to legal intervention. This is not to say that the denunciations of the Tory measures were insincere; on the contrary, the behaviour of the Labour Party's leaders since 1970 shows their complete conversion to the view that no attempt must be made to alter the laws on industrial relations without the support of the trade unions. In 1970, however, this conversion was so recent that the party's leaders generally, and Mrs Castle in particular, had to go out of their way to convince the unions of the sincerity of this change of heart.

This tactical consideration is linked to the second general reason for the behaviour of parliamentarians during the passage of the Bill: the place of Parliament in British politics. The experience of this particular legislation suggests the not very surprising conclusion that the main function of the House of Commons, in particular, is not to scrutinise legislation but to publicise the views of the main antagonists in a debate. Thus arguments about the proposals were really extensions of the general battle between the parties. The debates performed a publicising function, signalling to observers within and outside Parliament the differences between groups and individuals. The hours spent in apparently futile argument over the meaning of 'responsibility' in the conduct of industrial relations allowed front benchers and backbenchers of both main parties to state their views about industrial relations and about the conduct of economic policy generally.

This explanation also makes sense of much else about the behaviour of parliamentarians. The Government's decision to take the Committee stage of the Bill on the floor of the House of Commons, for instance, which surprised the Opposition, looks like an irrational act: it tied up a large amount of parliamentary time unnecessarily and exposed the Conservative benches to a long series of exhausting sittings. It was adopted, however, in the belief that it would expose divisions within the Labour Party, and publicise further what the Tories believed were their own more attractive policies.[6] Similarly, the behaviour of the PLP is explicable in terms of the desire for publicity. Labour's essential problem was to demonstrate clearly to the unions its goodwill after the differences over *In Place of Strife*. As one backbencher remarked: 'We will not convince hon. Members opposite by our arguments, but I hope that we can convince . . . the trade union movement . . . that there is more discussion on trade unionism at the moment . . . than has taken place since 1927.'[7] Viewed in this light Labour's tactics are not at all puzzling: select a few issues, such as the closed shop, on which the party is united, and which bear closely on the institutional interests of the unions; concentrate on these in debate; and make life as uncomfortable as possible for the Government by forcing all-night sittings and long voting sessions. Labour's behaviour may be seen as an attempt to expiate the 'sins' of the previous Labour Administration. Most of this remained on the level of speeches, but the attempt by a group of backbenchers to disrupt the proceedings by crowding round the Speaker's chair had a similar symbolic purpose.[8] As Eric Heffer, one leader of the group, put it later: 'Many thousands of workers had lost pay in taking leave from work to demonstrate against the Bill. In some way or other we had to show these workers that we were just as serious in our attacks on the Bill.'[9]

The fact that the main function of the parliamentary battle was publicity thus explains much about the character of the debates. The apparent irrelevance of many speeches to the matter ostensibly under discussion – that a speech on registration, for instance, could turn into a defence of the closed shop or an attack on the Government's economic policies – is accounted for by the fact that the point of the whole exercise was to deliver such general attacks. Thus Mrs Castle remarked of the Committee stage, whose formal purpose is to consider the details of a Bill, that during it 'we concentrated on the points of profound principle and disagreement.'[10]

This interpretation also makes sense of the differences between the debates in the Lords and the Commons. Debates in the former, though they largely repeated arguments already voiced in the lower House, were more decorous, addressed more directly to the topic in question and less likely to be littered with abuse than was the case with the Commons. This may reflect the superior calibre of speakers in the Lords, but it also springs from the fact that the publicity function was not so important, nor the party battle so intense. This does not mean, however, that the Lords played a more positive role than the Commons in shaping the final Act. One common argument for a second chamber is that it can do a great deal of good work in tidying up the details of legislation. The Lords' stages were certainly used for this purpose, because the Bill was so large and complex that large numbers of amendments were necessary simply to remove unintended consequences arising out of faults in drafting. In addition, the Lords' stages were used to introduce many of the really significant amendments to the Bill. But hardly any of this was done at the initiative of the Peers, but was introduced by the Government itself. What the passage of the legislation through the upper House did was to give the Government more time to hear the views of the interest groups, to ponder the implications, large and small, of what was in the proposals, and then to introduce changes as it saw fit.

The peripheral position of Parliament in shaping the legislation poses problems in describing the passage of the Bill. On the one hand, to follow the chronology of the parliamentary stages would be to relegate to a secondary place what went on outside Parliament, where the really important events were taking place. Yet to ignore the speeches in both Houses would be to omit what concerned the key actors – and engaged the attention of the mass media – during the passage of the legislation. The best solution seems to be to treat the parliamentary debates as what they were intended to be: attempts to express publicly the grounds for opposing and supporting certain policies on industrial relations. As far as substantively amending the Bill is concerned, MPs were largely adjuncts to the pressure groups, and their role in this respect is best described when we come to look at the place of such groups in changing the Bill.

It may be objected that an examination of the public statements of MPs amounts to little more than a study of public rhetoric, bearing little relationship to either 'real' beliefs or behaviour. It is of course necessary to take care in interpreting public statements, but the view that they are in some way 'unreal' is surely misplaced. When we describe a speech by a politician we are describing behaviour, albeit rather different behaviour from a decision to implement a particular policy. Even if politicians say one thing, and do something completely different, what they have said is still significant: the public justifications for actions are as important as the actions themselves.

But, even apart from this consideration, it is not in fact the case that over industrial relations there was a wide gap between what the politicians said and what they did. In the case of the Conservatives, for instance, the frequently expressed concern with the closed shop reflected an enduring and widespread worry in the party, and was in turn reflected in the policies which were adopted. Similarly, one of the constant themes of Barbara Castle's speeches – that the law was an inappropriate instrument of reform – while contradicting the policies of 1969 yet arose from a real shift in Labour thinking back to voluntarism. In the same way Harold Wilson's constant claim that the Bill was likely to undermine the official institutions of trade unionism reflected a concern with institutional stability which marked his attitude to industrial relations while he was in office.[11] The speeches during the parliamentary stages offer the most sustained exposition we have of how British politicians view industrial relations, what they believe to be the purpose – if any – of legislation, how they account for industrial conflict, and how they would set about securing industrial peace.

THE POLITICIAN AND INDUSTRIAL RELATIONS

The first task the politicians faced was that of accounting for the existence of the Conservative proposals. The Tory justification for introducing the legislation was, not surprisingly, an echo of what had gone before. Carr's most important image was 'disease', the chief symptom of which was an accelerating level of unofficial disputes.[12] This underlying disease consisted of the destruction of an institutional order: 'the breakdown of stable and constructive collective bargaining, particularly at company and plant level.'[13] This theme was developed by the Prime Minister during the Second Reading, in his longest contribution to the debate over reform. A new set of rules, he argued, would bring order into a situation where 'the competitive pressures inherent in the existing system of collective bargaining and the consequences of industrial disputes . . . have pushed up money wages beyond what both sides in the House recognise to be possible.'[14] General economic measures would increase productivity; the elimination of 'unnecessary' restrictive practices would allow unions and management to improve efficiency; and a tougher bargaining environment would produce more professional trade unions.[15] The Conservative back benches echoed this stress on the breakdown of order and stability.[16]

If there was agreement among the Conservatives about the underlying justification for the proposals, the same could not be said about Labour's explanation for their existence. Two separate accounts were offered.[17] On the one hand, it was argued that the Bill was a product of Conservative legalism, a lawyer's paradise introduced, according to Mrs Castle, by 'legal maniacs' striking a 'theoretical pose'.[18] An even simpler version asserted that it was the 'Bill of the Solicitor General.'[19] This view of the proposals as a product of ill-informed legalism was strongly echoed by Wilson,[20] and was also a theme of back-bench contributions.[21] But a rather different account, based on a 'class' interpretation of the legislation, was also put forward, chiefly by members of the Tribune group of MPs. On the front bench, this view was expressed by Eric Heffer, a Tribune MP coopted onto the front bench to fight the Bill. He argued that it was 'class legislation' whose rules were employers' rules designed to 'cripple the trade union movement'.[22] An even more explicit statement of the class interpretation came from the back benches: 'this Bill is about wages. . . . It is (the government's) method of intervening in the question of wage bargaining, in the hope that they will strengthen the employer.'[23]

These two views were sometimes used together: Heffer tended to express both,[24] while remnants of the class interpretation appeared occasionally in Mrs Castle's remarks.[25] But they tended to lead in different directions. The 'excessive legalism' argument produced a condemnation of the Bill on the grounds that it was irrelevant to the realities of the industrial situation.[26] It was also associated with a 'human relations' explanation of industrial conflict, an almost Burkean defence of piecemeal reform in industrial relations and a stress on the limits of law. The class interpretation, on the other hand, was less prone to see the Bill as a reflection of ignorance[27] since it saw it as a response to the demands of employers, while it explained industrial conflict not in terms of 'human' problems but as an expression of class antagonism between workers and employers.

Since there was general agreement that the causes and consequences of strikes were at the heart of the whole argument over legislation, the most important divisions tended to appear in the accounts offered of industrial conflict. On the Conservative side two distinct, though occasionally overlapping, explanations appeared. The first, based essentially on a human relations interpretation, reflected long established Tory views about the causes of strife.[28] The size and complexity of modern industries, it was argued, created problems: 'fear and bad communications can poison relations within a company.'[29] In such a situation, 'bad working conditions and dull, frustrating and repetitive work can lead people to take actions which are not always as wise as they should be.'[30] On this interpretation strikes were an irrational but understandable outburst by workers subject to deep-seated frustrations. But an alternative account stressed the importance of disruptive groups and individuals. 'The British working man,' remarked William Clark, 'is a decent chap. . . . But he is lethargic and one of the problems of the trade union movement is that his lethargy permits others to take control.'[31]

The Labour benches offered a wider set of explanations for conflict, but again the human relations motif dominated. From the front bench Mrs Castle offered the most graphic account in these terms. Strikes, she remarked, are 'a reflection of the deep malaise of modern industrial society, with its bewildering technological change, its ever present threat of redundancy, its job insecurity . . . the failure to involve the worker constructively or excitingly in the decisions which govern his whole working life'.[32] This was widely echoed. The Chairman of the PLP observed that the problem arose because workers feel 'propelled helplessly along by hidden forces',[33] and it was similarly argued that good industrial relations depended on making 'the worker feel that he has some part to play in the operation of the company of which he is a member.'[34]

This explanation for conflict, though it dominated Labour contributions, was, however, supplemented by two others. First, there was some reference to the 'agitationist' account which had been voiced on the Tory side. Mr Wilson, for instance, though he clearly accepted the human relations approach,[35] also invoked more sinister forces. The growth of shop-floor power, he explained, was partly 'spontaneous', but part was 'capable of being created by unscrupulous unofficial leaders.'[36] The view that conflict can be fomented by small groups of agitators was also implicit in the frequent condemnations of the Bill by Labour on the grounds that it would make the job of militants easier.[37]

These two accounts of the sources of industrial conflict were joined by a third, based on a class interpretation of industrial relations: according to this view, strikes were a reflection of a fundamental conflict between workers and employers. This classically socialist explanation was only weakly represented in Labour speeches, and was confined largely to Tribunites.[38] The argument was by no means as clearly developed as the human relations view, and it emerged less in explicit statements than in detailed criticisms of the Bill.

Labour interpretations of the origins of industrial conflict implied a wider view of the nature of industrial relations generally, and this in turn shaped the objections which were raised to the Tory proposals. The first line of attack concerned the very use of law. Here, the human relations approach could be used to support a condemnation of legal reform, for if good industrial relations depended on 'the atmosphere . . . the ambience of industry',[39] then the law was largely irrelevant. If the industrial relations system was a delicate, organic mechanism, then 'the rigidity of law enforcement' was quite inappropriate.[40] The core of Labour's objections rested, however, not on general points about the role of law but, not surprisingly, on criticisms of the content of the Tory proposals. The most common objection was that the Bill weakened the unions. But it turned out that different sections of the Party were referring to different kinds of weakness. Most Labour objectors feared that the effect of legislation would be to weaken the power that the official union leadership could exercise over the rank and file,[40] while a minority were afraid that the Bill would weaken unions and workers in their struggles with employers.[41] The two objections were, of course, very different, but they allowed Labour to unite against the Bill, and also facilitated agreement on what were the most objectionable proposals. They resulted in particular in a concentration on the question of the closed shop, which was obviously a key institution both for those who wanted a disciplined movement in the control of officials and for those who wanted to strengthen worker resistance to employers. Labour MPs spent more time attacking Clause 5 of the Bill — which dealt with the closed shop — than any other, and also turned many of the other debates into attacks on the closed-shop provisions.

The accusation that the Bill would weaken the capacity of trade-union leaders to control their members was linked to the human-relations interpretation of industrial relations. As Mrs Castle remarked: 'If we want to reduce strikes, we do not need more legal restrictions: we need better psychology.'[42] Part of this improved psychology consisted in ensuring that union leaders were insulated from the pressure of militants in the rank and file. The pith of the Labour case was that key provisions in the Bill – especially those allowing individual workers some say through strike ballots and ballots on union recognition – would undermine the official leadership. The various ballot procedures, Mrs Castle argued, constituted a 'charter for militants'.[43] The trade-union leadership, she contended, was fighting 'a rearguard action against their own militants' on such matters as wage demands.[44] She was echoed by Wilson, who observed that the Bill was a 'Trots' charter', because 'it is the militants who will be encouraged.'[45]

This concern with institutional stability and discipline emerged most clearly in the attacks on the agency shop provisions. 'Sensible' employers, urged Mrs Castle, did not want agency shops, since the proposal would undermine the authority of official trade unionism.[46] Wilson was even more explicit. Citing the Pilkington affair[47] – when workers employed by the well-known glass firm had unsuccessfully rebelled against the official leadership of the GMWU – he argued that the agency shop proposals would undermine disciplined trade unionism. The problem at Pilkingtons, he suggested, was the existence of a 'militant' breakaway union: 'the breakaways were in the end . . . repudiated by firm leadership by moderate trade unionists.' The agency shop provisions could, had they existed, have been used 'in the last ditch fight to prevent the return to work and the end of the strike.'[48]

That this line of attack reflected widespread fears in the PLP is indicated by the extent to which it was repeated in back-bench contributions. The chief back-bench accusation was that the Bill would increase militancy by weakening the official leadership, and that the most blatant cases of this process occurred in the ballot procedures, especially as they concerned union recognition and the agency shop.[49] The criticisms tended to start from the assumption that – as Tom Williams put it – there was no quarrel between the parties on the need to improve industrial relations: 'we can concede immediately that there may be a need for a more disciplined society.'[50] The criticisms were based on a collectivist view of industrial relations in which the unions were the most important collectivity. Unless there existed unions where a strong hierarchy, preferably backed by a closed shop, could exercise firm discipline, then there would be a sharp increase in industrial strife.[51] As a result of this view, the attacks concentrated on the disruptive effects of the 'liberal' measures. Thus a former chairman of the back-bench group of union MPs argued that the legislation would destroy the stability secured by the operation of the Bridlington rules.[52] Reopening the whole question of agency shops and recognition for members 'could well provide for the escalation of militancy between unions.'[53] The essential problem was that workers, if freed from the disciplinary constraints of official unionism, would 'clearly always be tempted to join the most militant of the unions.'[54]

The alternative criticism of the Bill – that it would weaken unions not against their own members but against employers – reflected a class view of industrial relations, and was stated in the main by MPs associated with the Tribune group. On the front bench it was Heffer, not surprisingly, who took this alternative line. His attacks on the banning of the closed shop ignored the argument that it was a useful device for suppressing militancy. Instead, he suggested that a ban would tilt the balance of power in favour of employers.[55] Similarly, from the back benches Stanley Orme argued that the closed shop was necessary if workers were to match the power of employers,[56] while Norman Atkinson, who developed the most comprehensive version of the class interpretation during the debates, argued an essentially similar case.[57]

The two separate critiques of the Bill which emerged from the Labour benches implied two very different views of the nature of industrial relations. The most common line of argument sprang from a human relations approach which stressed the organic character of institutions, the desirability of limited change and the importance of official trade unionism as a disciplinary influence on the work force. The class interpretation stressed the conflicting interests of, on the one hand, workers and unions – whom it tended to treat as synonomous – and, on the other, employers, and saw the Bill as designed to strengthen the latter at the expense of the former. Labour was thus united by its attachment to collectivism. But the predominant view saw unions as managers and mediators of conflict, seeking to achieve common aims with other interested parties, such as governments and employers. Rank-and-file workers were viewed with caution, if not suspicion. Either through failings in human relations, or because of the activities of agitators, or both, pressures for militant action were likely to develop if the power and authority of unions over workers were relaxed. Hence the opposition both to the ban on the closed shop and to the prospect of workers having a direct say through ballots.

One of the most striking features of this view, and one of the main reasons for taking it seriously, is that it closely reflects the stance on industrial relations of the Labour Government before 1970. Labour's change of policy after the defeat over *In Place of Strife* and the loss of the 1970 election did not therefore represent any significant change in outlook, but rather a tactical shift. Having spent much of the period between 1966 and 1970 using the power of the state to buttress official unionism, Labour after 1970 retreated from state compulsion on the unions. But the aims of policy, and the fundamental assumptions about the nature of industrial relations, remained the same. The class interpretation remained a minority view. Though the differences between the views could be obscured by a concentration on a few issues, such as the ban on closed shop, which deeply offended both groups, the implications were very different. The most common view implied moderation on the part of unions over such matters as strikes and wage claims, whereas the minority view implied that, since unions existed to advance the interests of workers in a hostile society, 'the first function of a trade union is to protect its members and do what it can for them – not to look to the national interest.'[58]

Labour's approach to industrial relations was, as we have seen, marked by two very different forms of support for collectivism. Dualism also marked the Conservative contribution to the debates, but in this case it consisted of the familiar tension between liberalism and collectivism. It emerged most clearly in the Tory response to the Labour attack on the proposals to outlaw the closed shop. The front bench retort to the accusation that the result would be to increase militancy was twofold: to deny that undesirable consequences were likely to occur;[59] and to argue, in contradictory fashion, that if there were costs these were worth paying. Thus Carr admitted that there was a danger of dissatisfied members deserting their unions, but asserted: 'I do not believe that [closed shops] are the sort of means that we in this country . . . ought to seek to retain.'[60] This argument, which was derived from the moral rather than the market aspect of liberalism, set the tone of Conservative contributions. Justification was primarily expressed in terms of lessening the coercive power of unions over members, rather than freeing the market of the distorting effects of labour monopolies. This moral objection arose from a belief that, whatever the virtues of unions, they were guilty in many cases of intimidating workers. As Dudley Smith, one of Carr's junior ministers and a member of the policy groups before 1970, remarked in justifying the ban on closed shops: 'there has been a crying need in this country . . . for the introduction of some sort of justice for many people who have been exploited by unions'.[61]

Suspicion of the closed shop thus reflects a wider belief in the intimidatory potential of working-class organisation.[62] The links between this and the sentiments of moral liberalism are nicely seen in the defence of a clause making it illegal to picket a private home in a strike. The clause – which reenacted a similar one in the 1927 Trade Disputes Act[63] – was admitted to have no bearing on a significant problem of industrial relations,[64] while it was of course insulting to the trade unions. Not even its defenders argued that such picketing was a common occurrence. It was rather, argued Geoffrey Howe, that the non-conformist who wants to opt out of a strike 'is entitled to cherish his little shred of courage in his own home.'[65]

Remarks such as these make the Conservative front bench sound like extreme supporters of moral liberalism, but as their advocacy of the agency shop indicated they were prepared to go a long way to meet collectivism.

The agency shop, it was suggested,[66] solved the moral problem of the 'free rider' by requiring dues not paid to a union to be given to charity and it relied on the force of inertia and habit to ensure that most workers did actually join, thus ensuring institutional stability. At the same time, the use of arguments about the need to strike a balance between the freedom of the individual and the collective requirements of industry[67] were sufficiently vague to allow amendments to the legislation during its passage.

Front bench speakers on the Conservative side tended to present themselves as balanced between the pressures of liberalism and collectivism. Tory backbenchers, on the other hand, were much more explicitly divided into those who expressed libertarian, and those who expressed collectivist, sentiments. It is unclear how far this represented a deep division in the party and how far it reflected the somewhat fragmented character of back bench contributions, which tended to alight on particular points rather than – as in the case of front benchers – consisting of set speeches on a wide range of questions. What is clear is that there were divisions, especially over the concessions on the closed shop made during the Bill's passage.

Libertarian objections to the closed shop came in a wide variety of forms. Some consisted of blanket denunciations. Geoffrey Stewart-Smith attacked not only the pre-entry closed shop, but even the Government's own agency shop proposals. The closed shop was, he argued, a tyranny in itself, and gave rise to further abuses such as 'kangaroo courts'.[68] This revealed yet again the Tory belief in the intimidatory potential of unions; and more measured Tory statements also tended to dwell on examples of compulsion against individuals by particular unions.[69] In a number of cases, however, abstract principle was clearly reinforced by other considerations. For instance, the most common example cited of the alleged abuse of union power referred to the campaign by unions such as the Draughtsmen (DATA)[70] to exclude from negotiating rights 'professional' unions such as the United Kingdom Association of Professional Engineers (UKAPE). In other words, opposition to the closed shop on libertarian grounds was reinforced by a desire to defend professional and 'moderate' unions against militant organisations.[71]

During the course of the parliamentary debates, several Labour MPs – most notably the ebullient Brian Walden in a justly praised contribution[72] – argued that there was a deep cultural division between the two sides of the House: on the Labour side a collectivist outlook springing from the traditions of united working-class action; on the Tory side an individualist, middle-class set of attitudes. Labour was certainly collectivist, though as we saw earlier this was only partly explicable as an expression of working-class communality; much of the party's collectivism sprang from a distrust, even a fear, of the explosive potential of workers' power and a determination to use hierarchical institutions to secure peace and discipline. Conversely, though moral liberalism was certainly very well represented on the Tory benches, the preoccupations of so many Labour MPs – institutional stability and industrial discipline – were also in evidence on the Conservative side.

These concerns found expression in a number of ways. First, an unsuccessful attempt was made to amend the Bill so as to meet the demands of employers' federations that the imposition of legally binding procedure agreements be allowed throughout an industry.[73] Second, a number of attempts were made to mitigate the institutional instability which some thought might follow from banning the closed shop. The weakest suggestion, which was accepted by the Government, was that a positive recognition of the virtues of belonging to a union, and of employers' recognising unions, be written into the Act and the Code of Conduct.[74] A more significant demand came from a number of Conservative back-benchers who supported the argument that in a number of occupations – especially acting and shipping – special circumstances made it necessary to offer something more than an agency shop.[75] These arguments were finally accepted by the Government though, as we shall see, almost certainly not because of back bench pressure. The final expression of a concern with institutional stability came in response to the Government's decision to meet the special problem of a few occupations by amending the Bill so as to allow in certain circumstances the setting up of approved closed shops.

This concession indeed provided the spectacle of a public argument on the Tory back benches between supporters of moral liberalism and defenders of the stability of institutions.[76] The Government's insistence on setting up a general procedure by which approved closed shops could be obtained produced an extended restatement of the liberal case against closed shops from John Boyd-Carpenter, a senior backbencher, who argued that using the law to compel workers to join unions involved the danger of a corporate state: 'the party to which . . . I belong has for a long time believed in the right of the citizen to join or not to join a union, and the closed shop is a serious interference with that right.' Boyd-Carpenter argued that there were valid grounds beyond those of conscience for refusing to join a union, and that simply disliking the leadership, for instance, ought to constitute one such ground.[77] But Peter Emery, another prominent backbencher, not only welcomed the approved closed shop, but argued that obtaining it should be made easier, that it could contribute 'towards obtaining industrial discipline', and that it was relevant not just to seamen and actors but could be used by unions such as the TGWU to discipline militants.[78]

The discussions over union membership, and in particular over the closed shop, illuminate the conflict in Tory attitudes towards the unions. On the one hand, Conservatives wanted to strengthen order, authority and discipline in industrial relations, all of which implied a strong official trade unionism which could control its rank and file. On the other hand, they wanted to maximise the freedom of individual workers to decide whether or not they would join a union. Sometimes the conflict expressed itself in an argument between individuals, as when a collectivist Emery met a liberal Boyd-Carpenter, but the contradictions were endemic to Tory thinking and Tory policy. The initial Bill, though frequently justified in terms of strengthening official trade unionism, was essentially a liberal measure: in other words, as its critics often remarked, it demanded that the unions act in a disciplined, hierarchical fashion, but declined to offer them the means of controlling their members.

During the passage of the legislation, the liberal features of the proposal were considerably modified, though not sufficiently to please the collectivists – either employers or trade unionists – in industrial relations. While amendments to the legislation coincided with the parliamentary stages, little was owed directly to the intervention of MPs. All of the noise and fury of the battle contributed only a small portion to the final shape of the Act. To discover who the authors of change were we must look to the campaign outside of the parliamentary arena. This is the purpose of the next chapter.

7 The Campaigns Against the Bill

The passage of the Bill was marked by two distinct campaigns: the first, one of mass agitation and action, was initiated in the main by the unions, and by the TUC in particular; the second, a much more conventional campaign focussed on Whitehall, involved a wider range of pressure groups. Though the two overlapped at certain points, they ought to be discussed separately since they differed not only in the methods they used but in their aims. The mass campaign was a root-and-branch attack on the legislation, whereas the groups that concentrated their activities on Whitehall and Parliament – mainly on the former – coupled their more orthodox tactics with a more limited set of demands for particular amendments to the Government's proposals.

THE TRADE UNIONS AND MASS ACTION

Pressure groups typically try to exercise influence at three distinct levels in British politics: in the Whitehall executive; in Parliament; and among the public at large. In boycotting any consultations with the Government after 15 October 1970 the TUC was rejecting the first. Its interest in the parliamentary process was, as we have seen, perfunctory. This left a campaign of mass agitation and propaganda as the only remaining alternative.

The General Council meeting which rejected further consultations also took a series of decisions which set this campaign on its way.[1] On 12 November 1970 a meeting of principal officers of affiliated unions was held at Transport House to discuss strategy; a series of weekend conferences of full-time officers was held during the first half of 1971 to inform them of the implications of the legislation, and to enable them in turn to explain the unions' position to the rank and file; in the first two months of 1971 nine regional conferences were held, and the TUC provided speakers for numerous other public meetings; on 12 January 1971 the TUC sponsored work-place meetings against the legislation in which it claimed that 'several million' workers took part; it also held a national rally at which Feather, Wilson and others spoke; and on February 21 – a Sunday – it organised a march in London attended by an estimated 140,000 people. In addition, the unions poured out a deluge of paper: advertisements in national newspapers were placed after consultation with an advertising agency; the distribution was arranged of half a million copies of *Reason*, a detailed critique of the Bill; three thousand 'campaign kits' were distributed to union officers; and several million copies of leaflets and broadsheets were distributed to the public at large.[2] The sheer volume of all this activity is impressive: the 21 February demonstration, for instance, was probably the largest peacetime political gathering since the days of the Chartists, and indicates what a pressure group with a mass membership can achieve even when many of its own members are doubtful of its policies.

The purposes of this campaign were twofold. The first was, as the TUC put it, 'to explain clearly to all active trade unionists the dangers to the trade union movement contained in the Government's legislation, to inform them of the reasons for the TUC's opposition to it, and to enlist their active participation in opposing it.' Secondly, the campaign was aimed at influencing public opinion generally against the proposals, in an attempt to persuade the Government to 'reconsider its intentions.'[3] The problem the unions faced in turning to the public at large was that, according to opinion polls, not only did an overwhelming majority of electors support the Conservative proposals, but a majority of trade unionists felt the same.[4] The campaign is best seen as an attempt to remedy this situation, and in this it seems to have achieved some limited success: though overall public support for the Government did not significantly waver during the passage of the Bill, there is some evidence from the polls that rank-and-file union opposition to the measures did increase, though not by any enormous amount.[5]

The failure to undermine popular support for the Government was not, however, particularly serious, because despite the formal claim that the TUC hoped to persuade the Government to drop the legislation, the campaign was aimed not so much at the Bill as at the Act which would follow it. Indeed as early as October the General Council had virtually accepted the inevitability of legislation in deciding to reserve its main effort – the calling of a Special Congress – until the Bill was well on its way to the statute book. Similarly, the campaign to inform union officials of the implications of the legislation was simply a prelude to the educational campaign designed to enable them to frustrate the workings of the Bill when it was finally enacted.[6]

The Bill could only have been defeated under three circumstances: if the Government could be convinced that its case was unfounded, clearly a most unlikely possibility; if the Bill were defeated in Parliament, which was almost as unlikely; or if the Government were forced to abandon legislation by industrial action. Although a small minority of union leaders flirted briefly with this third possibility,[7] it was never likely that it would be considered seriously. In this rejection of any attempt to force the Government to drop the Bill lay the key to the TUC campaign; and at the root of this decision in turn lay a deep attachment to constitutionalism.

This constitutionalism manifested itself in two ways. In the first place, one of the chief union arguments against the Government was that the Conservatives were themselves acting unconstitutionally in not observing the normal rules of consultation. Secondly, almost as soon as the unions realised that the Bill would become law they concentrated on destroying it by constitutional means. In December 1970, when the Bill was only just beginning its passage through the Commons, the TUC set up a Liaison Committee – composed of prominent members of the General Council – to negotiate with leading members of the Labour Party a replacement for it.[8] It was this Committee which finally produced the package of measures embodied in the social contract which Labour implemented after 1974. The twin aims of trying to undermine popular belief in the usefulness of legislation, and ensuring the return of a Labour Government which would repeal any Conservative legislation, both made it imperative that the unions court public opinion and in turn ruled out any attempt to force the Government's hand by industrial action. The bulk of the TUC leadership was conditioned by the fear – stretching back at least to the General Strike of 1926 – that any attempt to use industrial action would be seized on by the Tories as an excuse for a 'who governs Britain' election at which Labour would be routed and the unions would suffer an overwhelming moral defeat. As Len Murray – at that time Vic Feather's deputy – put it: 'The Tory Government have only to get one sniff of a strike – and they will go to the country again. And what is more, they will win.'[9]

This commitment to constitutionalism makes sense of much that would otherwise seem pointless about the TUC's campaign during the passage of the Bill. Holding work-place meetings outside work hours and a mass demonstration on a Sunday so as not to disrupt production was very unlikely to make any impact on the Government. On the other hand, it helped increase the union solidarity which would be necessary if a policy of noncooperation were to work, and demonstrated the extent of union opposition to the public while avoiding any suggestion that the unions were trying to impose their will on the rest of the community. It is no exaggeration to say that much of the point of the TUC campaign was not to prevent the legislation reaching the statute book but to ensure that the Government would have no excuse for arguing that its legal authority was being frustrated by the unions.

The extent to which the majority of union leaders were committed to an appearance of moderation and responsibility as a means of courting public opinion emerged most clearly in their response to challenges to their strategy which came from a minority in the trade union movement. It had two sources: within the General Council there was a challenge from a group amongst whom Hugh Scanlon was prominent;[10] and a more fundamental threat was presented by a body known as the Liaison Committee for the Defence of Trade Unions. Though the strategy of the majority survived the challenges both from within the General Council and from below, for a time they were a serious embarrassment.

Though Scanlon's position tended to be popularly represented as one of extreme militancy, his behaviour was actually more ambiguous than such a description implies. As was to emerge later he was quite deeply attached to constitutionalism, albeit in a modified form. But his political position was made difficult for a number of reasons, all of which illuminate the problems facing the General Council in trying to hold the constitutionalist line. The engineering industry, which Scanlon's union dominates, was likely to be influenced more than any other by the proposed legislation, for it was in engineering that all the symptoms of what Conservatives considered the diseased state of industrial relations – the closed shop, wage drift, unofficial strikes and worker militancy – were most highly developed. The militants in the industry had most to lose under the Bill, and it is thus not surprising that resistance in the form of industrial action came most often from engineering and that Scanlon reflected the pressures from below. His particular political position made this the more likely, for not only is the structure of Scanlon's union such as to give a large say to the active militant minority rather than to full-time officers or the largely apathetic mass of members, but his own power rested on an alliance of Labour Party left-wingers and Communist Party supporters who after 1970 believed the General Council's line to be too timid.

The Liaison Committee, which presented the challenge from below, was originally formed in 1966 to fight wages legislation, at a time when the majority of the official leadership had acquiesced in the Labour Government's statutory incomes policy.[11] The fact that it represented a challenge to the official leadership provided an important undercurrent in its relations with the TUC. The Committee was usually described as a Communist front[12] but the truth seems to have been more complicated. It was undoubtedly under Communist influence, which is hardly surprising since the Communists are the most numerous and best organised dissident leftist group in the unions, but during the campaign against the Bill the Committee gathered under its wing all sorts of people – from old-fashioned Labour Party left-wingers to Trotskyists – who were unhappy with the official TUC strategy. At its first meeting to coordinate opposition to the legislation, the principal speakers were Norman Atkinson, a left-wing Labour MP sponsored by the AUEW, and Eddie Marsden, the Communist president of the construction section of that union. Opinion among the 1800 people present ranged from those who wanted an immediate general strike to those who supported a limited series of one-day stoppages.[13] This meeting rejected the call for a general strike, condemned the TUC for its delay in calling a special Congress, and called for a one-day stoppage on 8 December, the TUC day of protest against the legislation.[14]

The response to this and subsequent strike calls illuminates the complex relationship between the unofficial groups and the national leadership.

The possibility of extensive unofficial stoppages threatened the official strategy in two ways: it could undermine the desire to appear moderate and responsible, and it could also give the appearance that the official leadership was unable to control its members and thus further strengthen the case for legislation. Defenders of the General Council thus made strenuous efforts to dissuade workers from striking, and to minimise the significance of the stoppages that did occur.[15] Among a minority on the General Council, however, the response was more ambiguous. Scanlon, for instance, had originally argued that TUC protest meetings should be held in working hours,[16] and was to maintain demands for a more militant campaign throughout the Bill's passage. Unions in engineering were at this time coming under pressure from various unofficial 'ginger' groups to support industrial action on 8 December.[17] On the other hand, to give any sort of official backing to strikes would be to defy both the letter and the spirit of the General Council's policy. As a result, even those unions who wanted a more militant TUC line adopted a cool attitude to the call for industrial action. Only one – in the printing industry – made the stoppage official; an attempt to commit the Confederation of Shipbuilding and Engineering Unions to support failed, though the London region of the CSEU did give its backing; and, perhaps most significant of all, the executive of the engineering section of the AUEW refused to commit itself either way.[18]

Despite the coolness of the official leadership, even on Government estimates 350,000 workers were involved in stoppages on 8 December 1970.[19] More important perhaps, the disruptive effects were highly publicised since newspaper publication was interrupted. Despite Feather's remark that nine and a half million workers went to work 'in the face of attempts by a front organisation to mislead them',[20] there is no doubt that the unofficial campaign posed problems for the TUC, caught as it was in the familiar dilemma of trade union leadership: trying to balance a policy of caution and constitutional opposition against the fear of losing control to unofficial leaders. On 16 December 1970 the problem was ventilated at a General Council meeting where the original supporters of some strike action – including Jack Jones and Dan McGarvey, the Boilermakers' leader – argued that there was a danger of losing the initiative to unofficial elements.[21]

Though this produced no change in TUC policy, it did signal a more determined campaign to convert the General Council to a more militant line. In February 1971 the TGWU and the AUEW combined to try to commit first the 'cabinet' of the General Council, and then the Council itself, to support for one-day stoppages, but remained in a small minority in both bodies.[22] But the strikes campaign received a considerable fillip from the decision of the AUEW on 11 February to break with TUC policy in advance of the Special Congress called for 18 March, by giving official support to one day stoppages on 1 March and 18 March.[23] Attempts by the Liaison Committee to organise stoppages in January had met only limited success,[24] but the two March strikes told a very different story: on both occasions the engineering industry was virtually paralysed, and no newspapers appeared.[25] The opinion polls might suggest that a majority of rank-and-file trade unionists actually approved of the Bill, but this still left a considerable minority in opposition, and this minority tended to be concentrated in key occupations where stoppages could result in spectacular and economically damaging effects.

As might have been forecast from the disposition of forces on the General Council, however, the attempt at the March Congress by the AUEW and the TGWU to commit the TUC to a series of strikes ended in failure.[26] It also ended the challenge to the strategy of courting public opinion and resisting the Bill by constitutional means, since both unions abandoned any further attempts to challenge TUC policy, in respect of the Bill at least.[27] This removed the spine from the strike campaign, and exposed the very disparate nature of the groups which the Liaison Committee was trying to organise: the final meeting concerned with opposing the Bill – held at the end of April 1971 – ended in fighting and a rather desultory call for a TUC-sponsored day of industrial action.[28] By then the national leadership of the unions had turned to the task of facing the problems raised by the Act, which would shortly come onto the statute book.

Viewed as an attempt to stop the passage of the Industrial Relations Bill the TUC campaign was a failure. There never was any likelihood that argument, publicity and the avoidance of disruptive action would alter the Government's determination to place an Act on the statute book. But this was not the essential point of the campaign and, viewed in terms of its other aims, it was strikingly successful. The meetings, marches and demonstrations kept the rank and file occupied; events such as the mass march in London publicised the union case without causing any serious inconvenience to the public; and the process of securing an agreement from the Labour Party to repeal the legislation was begun. Above all, the challenge from the supporters of strikes was rebuffed. In this, the behaviour of the national leadership was crucial. The Liaison Committee, though it embarrassed the TUC, was never the tightly-organised effective body which its opponents – and perhaps some of its supporters – pretended, and there is a marked contrast between the rather modest response to the strike call in January 1971 and the overwhelming support which the AUEW received in March. Either because they supported the policies of their leadership, or because of the desire for a quiet life, the mass of AUEW members were quite clearly prepared to respond positively to a strike call. This potentially serious challenge was resisted because of the determination of the overwhelming majority of the General Council not to countenance industrial action, and the reluctance of the minority, faced with this position, to break with established policy. The final rejection of militancy in the campaign against the Bill was signified by the result of the voting at the March 1971 Special Congress. But by then the TUC had ceased even formally to contest the Bill, and was turning its undivided attention to the implications of the Act. By then, also, the more orthodox campaign by a wide range of pressure groups – including some unions – to amend the proposals in piecemeal fashion was entering its final stages. It is to this campaign that we now turn.

PRESSURE GROUPS AND THE AMENDMENT OF LEGISLATION

The shaping of Government-sponsored legislation in Britain normally follows a regular pattern: serious bargaining between the Government and interest groups takes place before Governments commit themselves in the form of a Bill. As a result, the most important concessions and adjustments have often occurred prior to the parliamentary stages.[29] As in so many other ways, the Industrial Relations Bill did not conform to this pattern. One of the most striking features of the evolution of Conservative policy both before and after the June 1970 election was the very limited influence exercised by normally powerful interest groups. During the parliamentary stages – though not primarily as a result of parliamentary intervention – the pressure groups did, however, succeed in securing significant amendments. Two sets of calculations influenced the changes made by the Government: one concerned the likely effect of the proposed measures on the stability of existing institutions in industrial relations; the other involved the problem of securing the unions' compliance with the legislation.

The chief threats to institutional stability came from three sets of measures: those concerning union representation in collective bargaining, affecting in particular the closed shop but also concerning the matter of recognition of unions by employers; those relating to registration; and those involving the legal enforceability of agreements. Of all these matters, none aroused as much argument as the clauses affecting the closed shop.

During discussions on the Consultative Document the main employers' organisations had expressed their scepticism about the proposals to ban the pre-entry closed shop and to replace it with an agency shop which could only be obtained with the consent of a substantial number of affected workers and which would contain significant safeguards for conscientious objectors to unionism. With the publication of the Bill, these objections were repeated: thus the EEF, in a circular to members in January 1971, singled out these same clauses as a likely source of future disruption.[30] But the main objections during the Bill's passage came from particular industries where closed shops were felt to perform key functions in retaining stability and discipline. Of these, the most important have already been mentioned: shipping and acting.

The problems of these two occupations were similar: a shifting and geographically dispersed labour force; small work units; and a multiplicity of often small employers. Both had developed a highly effective pre-entry closed shop. This was advantageous to the unions in a number of ways. The arrangements between the National Union of Seamen and the Shipping Federation allowed the union to cut out rivals, increased NUS control over its members, and solved the otherwise almost intractable problem of recruiting and retaining members scattered in small groups throughout the globe. For Equity, the actors' union, the usual attractions of the closed shop were reinforced by the market position of members. The supply of potential actors and actresses far outran demand for their services, and Equity was able to use control at point of entry to restrict the numbers in the profession, thus easing the problem of unemployment among members and using its monopoly of the labour supply to deter anyone who might be tempted to work at below union rates. The problems presented by the agency shop to these two unions – and a few smaller organisations[31] – were twofold: banning the pre-entry closed shop removed the critical weapon of control at point of entry; and the safeguards in respect of individual conscience made them nervous that an agency shop would be insufficient to retain members.

The chief employers' organisation in the shipping industry – the Shipping Federation – had just as much interest as the NUS in defending the stability which the closed shop was believed to produce, but it also had more immediate reasons for wanting the proposals changed. In the original Bill even agency shops could apparently only be obtained by an agreement between a union and an individual employer. Such a system, if implemented, would considerably diminish the Federation's importance.[32] The consequence was that both the NUS and the Federation argued, directly to the Department and to the minister in Parliament, that the industry should be explicitly excluded from the provisions banning the closed shop, an argument similarly advanced by Equity for the acting profession.[33]

The arguments of particular industries were reinforced by more general defences of the closed shop. Not surprisingly, the trade-union leadership strongly defended its contribution to institutional stability in industrial relations;[34] but industrialists – especially those representing big business – were just as anxious for its retention. The big employers' organisations, the leaders of the nationalised industries and spokesmen for the motor industry all weighed in at various times with criticism of the proposal to ban closed shops,[35] while during the Second Reading debate in the Lords an impressive array of leading businessmen voiced similar views.[36] The Government was thus faced with a number of separate demands: the unions as a whole were opposed to any attack on the closed shop; a small number of unions were concentrating on getting their own industry exempted from the provisions of the legislation; federations of employers such as that in shipping not only wanted their industry exempted but also wanted to ensure that nothing in the final Act undermined their own importance; while industrialists generally were attempting at least to mitigate the effect of any ban by, for instance, narrowing the grounds on which workers could refuse to join a union.[37] These last efforts spilled over into attempts to make it easier for a union to gain recognition and more difficult for it to be displaced once it was established.

The second feature of the Bill which came under attack on the grounds that it would undermine institutional stability in industrial relations concerned the matter of registration. Registration had of course been a bone of contention between the chief employers' organisations and the Government ever since the former realised that the Conservatives had no intention of turning the Registrar into the main instrument for implementing the Act. But during the Bill's progress onto the statute book the chief argument concerned the effect registration would have on a number of organisations which combined the bargaining functions of a trade union with other roles, such as that of professional association. The decision taken some years previously – and now reflected in the Bill – to make registration virtually the defining characteristic of a trade union posed important problems for these bodies. Put briefly, if they registered as unions they lost their entitlement to substantial tax concessions available to them as registered charities; but if they failed to register, it was possible that they would be unable to fulfil their functions as collective bargaining agencies.[38] Registration thus threatened the interests of powerful pressure groups such as the British Medical Association. This in turn raised a responsive chord in the Conservative Party. If the BMA were forced to withdraw from collective bargaining, or if its position were weakened, the likely replacements included aggressive organisations such as the Association of Scientific, Technical and Managerial Staffs (ASTMS).[39] It was clear from the debates in Parliament that there existed a considerable reservoir of sympathy within the Conservative Party for professional middle-class associations, such as the BMA, especially when they were under challenge from militant unions.[40]

The final matter which concerned institutional stability bore on the position of the various federations of employers' associations. One of the main features to emerge from an examination of the various debates on industrial relations is the extent to which the federations have interests additional to – and sometimes even in conflict with – those of individual employers. During discussions on the Consultative Document, one of the chief aims of the most important bodies – the CBI and the EEF – had been to defend industry-wide bargaining and the central role of the Federations in the system. Arguments about the Bill saw the pattern repeated, as in the claim by the Shipping Federation that it, not individual employers, should operate any closed shop or agency shop agreements. Attempts were also made to reverse the defeat which the Federations had suffered during consultation over the matter of the imposition of legally binding procedure agreements, when the Government had allowed the possibility of such imposition but only in the case of individual undertakings, thus opening up the prospect that even the non-imposed agreements negotiated by the federations would be deserted.[41]

Moreover, the Bill seemed to restrict the federations' role even further. If there was one matter on which all the contestants in the argument about reform agreed, it was that that the provisions in the 1871 Trade Union Act which forbade unions and employers' associations to sign legally enforceable agreements should be repealed. But the Bill not only excluded the federations from applying for imposed agreements, it did not even make it clear that they could voluntarily enter into legally binding agreements with unions.[42] It thus raised the spectre of a wholesale devolution of bargaining away from the national level to the level of company agreements sanctified by law.

The extent to which the Government compromised on the three main areas of controversy – closed shops, registration and the role of employers' associations in the negotiation of agreements – is to be explained by two sets of considerations: the fact that some of the ways in which the Bill threatened institutional stability were unintended; and the fact, already mentioned as a major influence on the Government's behaviour, that it was beginning to worry about how to mobilise consent for the Act. It is not surprising that the amendments which the Conservatives found it easiest to concede concerned the unintended consequences of their proposals. Thus it was never in any serious doubt that some way would be found to accommodate the problems faced by associations such as the BMA over the registration requirements: the unintended nature of the problems, the powerful position of the BMA in the interest-group universe and the sympathy within the Conservative Party for professional associations challenged by militant unions all meant that it was only a matter of finding a suitable solution. In the event, the problem was dealt with by treating the professional associations as a special case: a separate professional register was created, which allowed them to register in such a way as to combine their collective bargaining functions with their other roles; and their interests were further safeguarded by guaranteeing them a statutory member of the Commission on Industrial Relations.

The question of allowing employers' associations to enter voluntarily into legally binding agreements with unions similarly posed few problems. Though the failure of the Government to make it clear in the Bill that this was permissible may reflect Conservative ambiguity about the role of industry-wide bargaining, it is certain that it was never intended to exclude employers' associations from such agreements, and an amendment introduced during the Lords' stages made this clear.[43]

The other contentious matters were not settled so easily. The Government proved adamant in its refusal – first expressed in discussions on the Consultative Document – to allow employers' associations to secure the imposition of legally binding procedure agreements on trade unions. Thus the hesitations induced by Conservative liberalism were yet again bringing the Government into conflict with the more full-blooded collectivism of employers' associations. The Government did, however, give some ground on the matter of ensuring the stability of trade-union membership. It accepted a Commons' back-bench amendment writing into the legislation the virtues of union membership and recognition;[44] it similarly eased the ballot requirements for obtaining an agency shop;[45] and most important of all it dropped its attempt to impose a total ban on pre-entry closed shops. The decision to supplement agency shops by the device of what the Act was to call the 'approved closed shop' was the most significant concession made by the Government to the defenders of institutional stability. An approved closed shop differed from an agency shop in a number of important ways: it was more difficult to obtain, requiring the consent of more of the involved parties; it was much more difficult – indeed almost impossible – for a worker to opt out of the payment of union dues; and above all it gave the approved union control at point of entry to an occupation, since the holding of a union card was effectively a condition of employment.[46] It was this final consideration which was crucial as far as the most vocal groups – Equity and the National Union of Seamen – were concerned.

The concession of an approved closed shop was explained by Government spokesmen in terms of the special problems faced by acting and shipping,[47] and there is no doubt that this partially accounts for the Government's change of mind. In other words, the threat to the stability of industrial relations was absolutely unintended, and when this was spelt out both in Parliament and in direct representations to Whitehall then some way was sought to rectify the error. But this cannot explain the particular device used. What Equity and the NUS wanted was simple exclusion from the provisions in the Bill which banned pre-entry closed shops:[48] such a device would be simple; it would not disturb the status quo, which was already highly advantageous to the established institutions; and it would mean that the unions in question need have nothing to do with the Act, an important consideration as it became increasingly clear that the TUC was going to try to boycott it. The Government gave something very different. A highly cumbersome process had to be gone through before an approved closed shop could be gained; there was no guarantee that any particular union would be able to fulfil the necessary conditions; and, most important, a union had to be registered before it could even apply for such an arrangement.

The Government rejected the argument for a simple exclusion clause on the ground of impracticality; but this was not in fact its main concern. The principle of excluding seamen from the provisions of labour law has, for instance, long been practised on the grounds that the special problems of maintaining discipline aboard ship require more restrictive legislation than that applied to workers generally. The clue to the Government's real attitude lies in its concern with securing trade union compliance with the Act, and its dawning realisation that the TUC was really serious in its determination to oppose registration. We have it on the authority of both Sir Denis Barnes and the leading politicians involved that the Government believed that after initial opposition the union movement would quietly register and cooperate. Neither the Conservatives nor the civil servants foresaw that non-registration would be so widespread or so long-lasting. The way the approved closed shops were to be granted represented the opening shot in what the Government had now come to realise would be a serious battle to secure union cooperation.[49]

Long before the 18 March Special Congress which made non-registration the key to the TUC's campaign against the Government's legislation, it was clear that this tactic was going to be the key to TUC opposition. In the winter and early spring of 1971 the arguments within the General Council were not about whether to register or not, but about whether Congress should 'require' or 'advise' non-registration. Since registration was the key to the operation of the whole legislation, the Government was anxious to ensure that the legislation could not be boycotted in this fashion, and the device of offering an approved closed shop was useful in a number of ways. First, since unions such as Equity and the NUS would now have to register to retain the closed shop arrangement on which their survival depended, this promised to breach the unity of the TUC, and to encourage other unions to register. Second, since approved closed shops were not to be confined to shipping and acting, they offered an inducement – though because of the rigorous process which had to be gone through not a very enticing one – to other unions to register in the hope of securing such arrangements. As it turned out, both these calculations proved correct, and as a result the TUC's campaign of opposition was very nearly wrecked.

The Government's chief efforts to secure TUC compliance were, however, centred on two other potential amendments to the legislation. One of these the Government refused to concede, even though there is evidence that it would have rectified an unintended effect of the legislation, while the other it originated itself. One of the chief benefits of registration under the laws in force before 1971 arose from tax relief on the provident funds of registered bodies. Unions which declined to register under the new Act lost this relief, a particularly heavy blow to the rich, well established unions like the GMWU and the TGWU which have large funds.[50] This severe financial penalty was, initially at least, quite unintentional. Carr argued at first that the problem could be overcome with existing legislation on friendly societies, but it turned out that this was not the case.[51] Having stumbled unawares on a weapon in the fight to secure TUC compliance, the Conservatives decided to use it. Though the loss of tax relief strengthened union resentment against the Act in the long run – particularly as it seemed to be aimed at their welfare activities rather than at industrial militancy – its short-term effect was, as we shall see, to push some unions nearer registration.

But the most important tactic adopted by the Government in its attempt to secure union compliance concerned what was known as the 'provisional register'. Under the original Bill, all unions registered under the old laws – which included most TUC affiliates – were to be transferred to a provisional register, which would remain in force for six months. At the end of this period any union which had not been transferred to a permanent register – either because it had not applied, or because its application had been rejected – would simply have the status of an unregistered organisation of workers. As such, it would be excluded from most of the rights, but not many of the limitations, contained in the Act. The procedure accurately reflected the expectation that once the legislation got under way the unions would be supplicants queuing up to register. The TUC's determination to ensure total non-registration changed this expectation, and the Government responded – apparently at Howe's suggestion – with a very simple amendment: unions on the provisional register would now be deemed to have automatically transferred onto the permanent register unless they took steps to have themselves removed.[52] By placing the onus on unions to de-register, the Government created enormous problems for the TUC. This single amendment came close to destroying the campaign of opposition to the Act.

The Act which finally received the Royal Assent in August 1971 was more collectivist both in its spirit and in its provisions than the Bill which had been published eight months previously. It now in effect exhorted the parties to industrial relations to be good collectivists: it encouraged workers to join unions, and employers to recognise them; it made it easier for an established union to secure a stable bargaining position with an employer, and to have that position reinforced by law; and in the easing of the agency shop requirements and the introduction of approved closed shops it promised more of the stability which the key institutions in industrial relations desired so strongly. The Government had made these concessions partly at the behest of the various pressure groups; but in a real sense the pressure group which most influenced the Government's behaviour ostentatiously took no part in the negotiations. The TUC's boycott of the discussions about the Bill, and its increasingly obvious determination to fight the Act by a policy of non-cooperation, was a key influence on the decisions taken by the Government about amendments. The effect of the Government's tactical and substantive amendments on the unions' capacity to organise a successful campaign of resistance to the Act will become clear in the next chapter.

8 The Politics of Defiance

Studies in the politics of public policy – especially studies of legislation – tend to follow a familiar pattern. They move from an examination of the origins of a measure through an analysis of its development until the point where it reaches fruition either as a law or as some other decision of government.[1] The implicit assumption is that what happens afterwards is the concern of others, such as specialists in the particular field with which the policy is concerned. As a rough and ready division of academic labour this probably makes sense; yet clearly any discussion of the politics of the Industrial Relations Act which stopped at the point where it reached the statute book would be quite incomplete. The most interesting feature of the Act was that the attempt to make it work failed, and did so largely because of the behaviour of key interest groups. This chapter tells the story of resistance to the legislation, in particular the campaign waged against it by the unions. But the account given here is highly selective, effectively ending in the summer of 1972. This means that some of the most spectacular cases of resistance – in particular those involving the AUEW – are only dealt with briefly. This is because the argument here is that by the autumn of 1972 the unions had won the key battle with the Government: the jailing of the London dockers and the success of the TUC's non-registration campaign combined to ensure that the Act would no longer be an important part of the Government's strategy. By then the Government – spurred on by the miners' victory in their 1972 strike – had turned to tri-partite talks with the CBI and the TUC in an effort to secure acceptable economic policies; the confrontation associated with the Act was now simply an embarrassment. The spectacular cases involving the AUEW served not to cause the Act's failure – that was already assured – but to remind the Government of the legislative millstone which hung round its neck.

'Failure' in this context has a particular meaning. In some limited ways the Act was a success. Particular clauses, such as those concerning unfair dismissal, were widely used and a substantial case law was built up.[2] Even those parts of the legislation which the unions tried hardest to destroy were often implemented. Thus the attempt to operate a complete boycott of institutions such as the NIRC and the CIR quickly collapsed when it threatened the interests of unions. When it became clear that failure to answer a charge before the Court would result in contempt proceedings and sequestration of assets, the General Council quickly gave its assent to 'defensive' appearances.[3] The experience of the CIR is even more illuminating, since in its concern with such matters as recognition the Commission was trespassing in areas very important to the TUC. When unions found their institutional interests threatened by the CIR's enquiries, they hastened to try to influence them, by direct submissions to the CIR and by using the Department of Employment as a 'postbox'.[4] Some unions, while publicly supporting the policy of complete boycott, developed substantial covert contact with the Commission. The TGWU, for instance, while publicly repudiating all cooperation, was in frequent communication with the Commission, on occasion even initiating the approach itself. But, viewed in the terms in which both the unions and the Government defined victory or defeat over the legislation, these were small matters. The key struggle from the point of view of both unions and Government concerned registration. To understand how this came about, it is necessary to begin with an examination of how the TUC prepared to fight the Act.

'CONSTITUTIONALISM', THE UNIONS AND THE ACT

The key to the TUC campaign against the Bill had been its adherence to a strategy of constitutionalism: try to convert the public to the unions' point of view by mass propaganda; create a popular climate unfavourable to legislative intervention in industrial relations; avoid any strikes which might antagonise public opinion; secure a commitment to repeal from the Labour Party; and hope that the resulting political climate would shortly return a Labour Government. Since the campaign against the Bill merged imperceptibly into resistance to the Act, it is not surprising that the concern with constitutionalism was to reappear, but the divisions within the union movement at this stage were more marked than those which appeared over the Bill. The vast majority of the General Council believed in constitutional resistance, but there were three distinctive shades of opinion.

First, there were what can be designated 'extreme' constitutionalists, the representatives of the 'government must govern' school. At the March 1971 Congress Frank Chapple and Jack Peel, though casting their unions' votes in favour of the General Council's recommendations to boycott the Act, made speeches which in effect supported cooperation. The elected government, they argued, had a right to have its laws obeyed, and the appropriate place to get rid of a bad law was in the ballot box.[5] This was the sort of response which might have had more influence on the TUC's reception of the initial Bill if the Government had not so offended the constitutionalists by its attitude to consultation.

The extreme constitutionalists were a small group on the General

Council but the second group, the 'moderate' constitutionalists were in an overwhelming majority. They had shaped the TUC's response to the Bill, and now they did the same with regard to the Act. The seven recommendations from the General Council which the March Congress discussed and accepted essentially represented their point of view, which could be summed up as attachment to constitutionalism modified by passive resistance to the Act; but this opposition was carefully restrained so as not to result in any breaches of the law. Four of the recommendations concerned a boycott of the detailed provisions of the legislation: unions were to ensure that they signed no legally binding agreements, by insisting that managements insert an exclusion clause into all relevant documents; they were to refrain from initiating the procedures for securing binding agreements; they were not to use the Act's provisions to undermine the Bridlington or the 'Croydon' procedures;[6] and all trade unionists were to be strongly advised not to serve on any bodies which implemented the legislation. A fifth recommendation would give the General Council discretion to pay the costs of a union which became entangled with the courts, and in very exceptional circumstances would give it power to indemnify a union against damages.[7]

But it was two other recommendations which were crucial. The first instructed the General Council to seek an 'explicit and unconditional' assurance from the Parliamentary Labour Party that it would repeal the Act; the second 'strongly advised' affiliated unions not to register under the legislation.[8] The two recommendations crystallised the views of the moderate constitutionalists: they confirmed the strategy of trying to get rid of the legislation through the ballot box, but tried also to minimise its effect on the existing system of industrial relations. The two aims were closely linked, since there was general agreement that, if unions were to register, and the Act were to weave its way into the fabric of industrial life, then the problem of repeal would be enormously complicated.

The third shade of opinion on the General Council might be called 'qualified' constitutionalism. What this meant was a general acceptance that the law should be obeyed and the authority of government respected, but not in the specific case of the Industrial Relations Act. Hugh Scanlon, the main spokesman for this view, put it thus:

> Let us . . . make it perfectly clear that generally speaking the trade union Movement accepts, operates and conforms with the law of the land. Our opposition and determination is quite specific. It is to this law, to this Act and to the courts set up thereunder. The courts which are active under the Act, particularly the NIRC, are brazenly political and do not appear to operate under the ordinary rules applying to other courts.[9]

The usefulness of this line was that, while allowing union leaders to stay within the fold of constitutionalism, it allowed them also to advocate policies supported by militant opinion in their own unions, much of which was not constitutionalist.

These three types of constitutionalism produced three different responses to the Act. Extreme constitutionalism, though it had the sympathy of leaders such as Chapple and Peel, was actually only embraced by a small section of middle-class trade unionism.[10] It involved, of course, accepting and working the Act, albeit reluctantly. Moderate constitutionalism involved in effect passive resistance by the TUC: unions were to boycott the legislation, but Congress was to do little more than exert its moral authority to ensure that the boycott worked. Thus non-registration was advised, not requested, and the contingency preparations for a battle with the courts amounted only to the very weak suggestion that in exceptional cases the TUC might assist with court costs and fines.[11] In the past, Feather argued, in putting the moderates' position, unpalatable laws had always been got rid of by political, not industrial, action,[12] and this was going to be the case with the Industrial Relations Act. The qualified constitutionalists supported the idea of extracting an explicit promise of repeal from the Labour Party,[13] but in the meantime they wanted an active campaign on the industrial front. During the campaign against the Bill the TGWU and the AUEW had both come round to supporting one-day stoppages, and the latter had even defied General Council policy in calling out its members on the day of the March Congress.[14] At Congress, the main attack on the moderate line focussed in part on the feebleness of its policy on the industrial front and there were calls – to be repeated at later Congresses – for strikes and for the setting up of a common defence fund.[15] The moderate constitutionalists were in a large majority on the General Council and on its important committees, but because of the voting power of the AUEW and the TGWU the challenge to the majority was defeated by only a relatively narrow margin.[16]

But the deepest division at the March Congress concerned not strikes but the question of registration, since in registration lay the key to resistance to the Act. Non-registration became the centrepiece of the TUC's campaign against the legislation for a number of reasons. It made a sort of tactical sense since it was simple, visible and symbolically a clear form of resistance. But there were two deeper reasons: one arose from the nature of the Act itself, the other sprang from the respect for constitutionalism which so characterised the outlook of the union leadership throughout the dispute.

Registration was the coping stone of the Tory proposals. All the significant rights that the Act gave – legal protection in trade disputes, recognition and bargaining rights and the approved closed shop – were only extended to registered organisations. Unregistered bodies were doubly penalised: excluded from the benefits of the legislation, they were nevertheless subject to many of the restrictions it imposed on registered bodies. This double discrimination – which had been made more severe by amendments passed when the Tories realised how the unions were going to oppose the Act – reflected the Conservative belief that every possible pressure must be put on the unions to register, for since registration was the coping stone, it followed that mass non-registration could lead to the collapse of the whole structure. Any Act which tried to reform industrial relations while being ignored by the majority of the big trade unions had a bleak future.

The character of the Act also gave the unions an additional reason for concentrating their efforts on non-registration, for while they had a great deal to gain from the success of such a campaign they had an equal amount to lose from its failure. If wholesale registration occurred, then the other measures of boycott would collapse: why refuse to cooperate with the Court or the CIR if they were making judgements about your union? The Act was – to change the metaphor – like a spider: once it caught a union in the thread of registration complete entanglement was unavoidable. 'If anyone believes,' remarked the leader of the Draughtsmen, 'he can register and then continue opposition to the Act through non-compliance . . . he is grossly deceiving himself.'[17] If unions registered in large numbers and obtained benefits such as agency shops under the Act, this would make repeal nightmarishly difficult, thus undermining the whole constitutionalist strategy.[18]

But non-registration had an added attraction for the constitutionalists: it was perfectly legal. Since registration was voluntary, opposition to it was consistent with the claim that the unions were not challenging the legal authority of either courts or governments. Of course this still raised the danger of confrontation with the Act since an unregistered body was in a very exposed legal position; but that the vast majority of the General Council hoped to avoid such a clash is shown by their refusal to make any serious provision – such as setting up a defence fund – for any battle with the courts.

In view of all these considerations it is not surprising that registration was the chief preoccupation of the union leadership. The great argument between them concerned the degree to which the TUC should insist on non-registration, and in turn what should be done with any union which broke ranks.

THE POLITICS OF NON-REGISTRATION

The opposition of the TUC to registration was complicated by three matters: differences between the varying shades of constitutionalism; fear of the extension of TUC authority, especially among the smaller unions; and, above all, the threats posed by non-registration to the institutional interests of unions. Despite strong attempts by both the TGWU and the AUEW to commit the General Council to a policy of 'requesting' unions not to register,[19] the March Congress was presented with a much more permissive formula: affiliates were to be 'strongly advised' not to register, and if they felt compelled to do so they were to consult the General Council who would make 'observations' on each case.[20] Alan Sapper later remarked on the obvious problem with this tactic:

> What is going to happen if a union before it decides to remain on the register goes to the General Council and says, "Yes, we have terrible problems. We are going to register." The General Council then raises its finger and says, "No, no. Naughty, naughty!" and the union goes and registers. What would happen then?[21]

There were three reasons why the majority at the March Congress supported a permissive line in spite of this sort of objection. First, there were a number of unions who were seriously contemplating registration — the Seamen are an obvious example — and thus favoured permissiveness. Second, a number of others, though committed to non-registration, were concerned about the implications of giving the TUC power to instruct affiliates to de-register.[22] To some extent this may have been a public rationalisation on the part of unions anxious not to close off the option of registration, but there is undoubtedly a strong impulse towards autonomy in many unions, and the idea of a mandatory policy offended this. Finally, extreme constitutionalist opinion was concerned over the mandatory line. Indeed, it even had doubts about a permissive TUC policy. Though non-registration was perfectly legal, Chapple warned that it contained 'the final seeds of a confrontation with the Government.'[23]

The TUC thus embarked on its permissive policy with its ranks divided. This division occurred not just between, but also within, the affiliates: Lawrence Daly, the left-wing general secretary of the National Union of Mineworkers, was tied by his executive to arguing against making de-registration mandatory;[24] while Sidney Greene, the sedate and cautious leader of the Railwaymen, was obliged by his executive to oppose the General Council's recommendation.[25] It is hardly surprising in view of all these divisions that the permissive line which was adopted by the March Congress soon began to crumble.

In the end, a union decided whether or not to register by balancing the advantages and disadvantages of non-registration. By joining the permanent register a TUC affiliate stood to suffer in several ways. First, there was the moral opprobrium associated with breaking the solidarity of the unions' opposition. It was on this that the General Council was clearly relying for the success of its approach to the problem. The importance of moral and social pressure in the rather enclosed world of trade unionism should not be discounted; but for a large number of unions it was not, as we shall see, an overriding factor. What is more, this sort of sanction could only work where the line was held and a small number of unions could be singled out as collaborators. But in the sort of situation existing after 18

March, where a large number of unions were considering registration, this condition was not fulfilled.

It was this problem which the AUEW and the TGWU sought to solve with their proposal that unions be instructed to de-register. But it was far from clear at the time how far this changed the situation. Superficially, it implied that a second set of sanctions beyond moral and social ones would be invoked. The most obvious was expulsion. But in arguing the case for a mandatory policy at both the March and the September Congresses in 1971 the speakers were careful to avoid such an explicit commitment;[26] indeed, an attempt by one of the printing unions to spell out this sanction failed to receive the support of a single large union.[27] This was partly because the supporters of a mandatory policy were divided among themselves about just how far they were prepared to go to enforce TUC instructions. If only a small number of affiliates had to be expelled, then this was a feasible course, but it would clearly be self-defeating if Congress ended up expelling a large proportion of its membership. This hesitation was reinforced by the knowledge that in voting for expulsion a union would actually be voting only for the possible expulsion of smaller unions since, as the leader of NALGO remarked tartly, 'We all know . . . that if circumstances should arise to force the AUEW or the TGWU to register there will be no question of their expulsion'.[28]

But aside from such problems expulsion was a doubtfully effective sanction even when used against a small union. The most important potential losses came in two forms: influence on government and membership stability. Since the early 1960s governments have shown an increasing predilection for dealing with the TUC rather than with individual unions. This fact had been one of the chief considerations in the original affiliation of white-collar unions such as NALGO and the National Union of Teachers,[29] who were now wavering over registration. In addition, since the TUC largely controlled union membership of government advisory bodies and committees, individual leaders faced the possibility of exclusion from the prestigious and satisfying activity of serving on them. But to balance against this was the fact that exclusion could hardly have a dramatic immediate effect, while any union which helped break TUC resistance to the Act would not lack friends in Whitehall.

Membership stability was potentially a more serious consideration. Though there is continuing and fierce competition in this area, TUC members have long sought to stabilise matters through the operation of the Bridlington rules. It is unclear how effective these are, but they certainly express a deep-seated preference for stability on the part of the official leadership. Any union expelled from the TUC faced the possibility of having its members poached. But the reverse was also the case: the expelled organisation could poach in turn, and the Act gave it some effective weapons if it wanted to use them. Add to this the fact that one union seriously considering registration was ASTMS, an aggressive recruiter in a wide range of occupations, and the option of expulsion appeared as even less attractive. Indeed, even when it turned out that the number of affiliates to be expelled was relatively small, the TUC did its best to ensure peace on the recruitment front by trying to maintain the Bridlington arrangements.[30]

The TUC's capacity to enforce non-registration on its affiliates was, therefore, limited. To complicate its task even more, there were a number of factors – present in varying combinations in different unions – favouring registration. There was, for instance, the influence of what was earlier called 'extreme constitutionalism'. In May 1971 the annual conference of the National Union of Bank Employees revolted against the majority of its Executive Committee and voted not only to register but to demand that the TUC drop all of its opposition to the legislation.[31] Shading into this attitude was that displayed by a number of leaders of unions of manual workers – such as Lord Cooper and Frank Chapple – who still reflected the concerns of national leaders about the loss of authority to unofficial groups. Both made it clear shortly after the March Congress that they would advise their own unions to stay registered.[32]

More important than beliefs about the constitution, or about the desirability of legislation, were a whole complex of factors affecting the institutional situations of different unions. At the most extreme were a number of unions – most notably Equity and the NUS – who believed that they might cease to exist unless they registered and obtained an approved closed shop. Both had tried to solve their problems by having their occupations excluded from the Act's provisions, which would of course have reduced the importance of registering. The Government, by making an approved closed shop dependent on a joint application to the NIRC by union and employer, and insisting that only a registered union could make such an application, made registration imperative. The General Council's suggestion to the NUS – that it solve its problem by arranging a collusive closed shop with the Shipping Federation – was, not surprisingly, rejected by the Federation.[33] Similar problems, though of a less acute nature, faced the Union of Shop, Distributive and Allied Workers, and one of the bakers' unions.[34]

These institutional problems had been considerably complicated by the amendment introduced by the Government placing the onus on unions to remove themselves from the register. Not only did this leave the decision about de-registration in the hands of the unions themselves, it created severe legal problems. The National Graphical Association, for instance, announced that it would be forced to register, since to do otherwise would involve first winding itself up.[35] Many unions found it necessary to call special rules revision conferences, while the Iron and Steel Trades Confederation was obliged to ballot its members and failed to get the majority required for de-registration.[36] Perhaps most important of all, the requirement to call rules revision conferences allowed a number of unions to prevaricate over de-registration while waiting to see how others behaved.

Financial problems also lay at the root of another difficulty faced by the unions. De-registration was expensive in a number of ways. Because of the Government's refusal to amend the legislation, unregistered unions lost tax relief on their provident funds; in the TGWU the annual loss was estimated to be as high as £750,000.[37] But de-registration could be expensive in other ways: there were no limits to the damages which could be awarded against an unregistered organisation, and there was the possibility of loss of funds through loss of membership. These losses were potential not actual, but some unions were in such straits than one expensive court case could bankrupt them. The National Union of Agricultural Workers gave finance as its main reason for staying on the register,[38] while financial problems were also an additional cause of the registration of the NUS.[39]

The final institutional factor pushing unions towards registration was perhaps the most important of all. It concerned membership recruitment. In this respect the Act offered several opportunities, particularly to unions operating among non-manual workers. It offered any union which had developed a formal or informal closed shop the chance of at least mitigating the effect of banning the pre-entry closed shop by applying for an agency shop, or even an approved closed shop. USDAW, for instance, found that the Cooperative Union threatened to withdraw its closed shop agreement, and at its conference in 1971 decided to stay on the register.[40] A second membership opportunity offered by the Act was much more important: it opened up to aggressive recruiters such as the National Union of Bank Employees (NUBE) and ASTMS the chance of rich pickings in the commercial sector, such as in banks and insurance companies. White-collar employment has for some years been the great growth area as far as recruitment is concerned, and the historically little-organised commercial sector is most attractive of all, as employees have increasingly turned to unions because of the impact of incomes policies and the threats to jobs posed by mergers and rationalisation.

But the unions faced severe problems: hostile employers; persecution of active unionists; and the presence of house unions, often encouraged by employers as a rival to outside organisations. The Act offered several remedies. It not only gave a legal right to join a union, but actually encouraged union membership and recognition. More important, the provisions governing recognition of unions and the granting of sole bargaining rights were, under the final Act, not especially difficult to fulfil. Indeed, since the CIR could make recommendations without strict reference to the numerical strength of a union there was every reason to think that if a registered organisation could get a foothold in a firm then the use of – or even the threat to use – the Act's provisions would quickly secure bargaining rights.

Registration was thus a key to success in the commercial sector. It was made all the more imperative because the occupations were non-unionised: a union which lost out in the initial scramble would find it difficult to dislodge those established under the Act. The TUC unions were also faced with the problem that the house unions were certain to try to register and some at least would be successful. If the TUC line held, there was thus the chance that the rich recruitment possibilities would be available to unions outside the TUC with whom NUBE and ASTMS had a long-standing rivalry.

There was one additional reason which made membership crucial: money. The large unions of manual workers which dominate the TUC also tend to be rich unions: they have large capital funds which are both a source of additional income and a reserve in case of a financial mishap such as a court fine. They are also enabled to weather without too much difficulty a decline in members. By contrast, white-collar unions, especially those which have grown fast recently, tend to be relatively poor. In 1972, for instance, the TGWU had more than twenty-two million pounds in its general fund, compared with reserves of less than a million pounds in the case of ASTMS. All but a tiny proportion of the latter's income came from membership fees.[41] Many white-collar unions resemble firms which have expanded rapidly on a narrow capital base: they require a high rate of cash flow – in the form of subscriptions – to fund current and future expenditure. Because of this, the recruitment possibilities opened up by registration under the Act, and the dangers involved in non-registration, posed questions about their very survival.

If the problems surrounding non-registration had been the only ones raised by the TUC campaign, then the result would have been to breach, but not destroy, the defences erected against the Act: the majority of TUC unions would still have remained unregistered. But the organisation of the trade-union movement meant that the effects of one union registering could not be insulated from the rest of the movement. The effects of one registration spread throughout the system like ripples from a stone dropped in a pool. A brief glance at two unions, ASTMS and the TGWU, will illuminate the problem.

ASTMS had for some years been successfully converting itself into a general union for non-manual workers. Its ambitions in fields such as insurance meant that it was under heavy pressure to register if – as did indeed happen – the Bank Employees registered.[42] The implications of registration by ASTMS would go far beyond insurance and banking: its aggressive recruiting in the steel industry had resulted in 1969 in a bitter conflict with the Iron and Steel Trades Confederation.[43] The TUC ruling in this affair aroused resentment because of the feeling that the TUC had favoured the established union of manual workers. In engineering also ASTMS had ambitions which were threatened by the United Kingdom Association of Professional Engineers, a non-TUC organisation which would certainly try to register. At the height of the argument about registration the draughtsmen's section of the AUEW, ASTMS and UKAPE were involved in a key dispute over membership in an engineering firm.[44] In short, if ASTMS registered no union organising non-manual workers would be safe from its ambitions.

The case of the TGWU was different, but still immensely delicate. It was not, compared to ASTMS, an especially expansionist body. But apart from being the largest British union, it was also probably the most diverse, having members in most significant occupational groups.[45] As a result, the registration of any of a wide range of TUC affiliates could threaten its interests. Since it organised both among seamen and agricultural workers, the potential registration of the NUS and the NUAW both constituted a danger. These problems were marginal compared to the threat it faced if the GMWU or the EETU/PTU (Chapple's union) registered, since both organisations – but especially the former – were in direct competition for members with the TGWU. The GMWU had been a rather sleepy union for several years,[46] but there were signs that in the wake of the Pilkington revolt it was making a determined effort to recover lost ground. If either the GMWU or the EETU/PTU registered, the fear of poaching could drive the TGWU into registration. Once that occurred, the TUC campaign would have failed.

This, then, was the background to the initial attempt by the General Council to operate a permissive policy on registration. But it quickly became clear that mere advice, however strongly worded, would not be sufficient. Between the March and September Congresses the campaign came very near to collapse, as unions decided either to defy TUC policy, or did their best to delay implementing it. At the end of April the USDAW conference rejected the recommendation of its EC – which was itself openly split – to de-register.[47] Early in May the NUBE Conference took its registration decision and launched its attack on the whole policy of boycotting the Act.[48] At about the same time the NUS conference, as a prelude to registration, rejected an attempt by the left in the union to secure an amalgamation with the TGWU.[49] At the end of May Lord Cooper repeated that he would recommend the GMWU to register,[50] and the following month COHSE, the chief union in the Health Service, announced a similar decision.[51] At the ASTMS Conference in the same month the delegates narrowly supported de-registration, but against the advice of their General Secretary, Clive Jenkins;[52] subsequently, ASTMS was to delay de-registration until the latest possible moment. In June also NALGO's conference declined to commit itself on registration – because of worry over the challenge from professional associations – and voted to leave the matter to its EC to decide. Since Walter Anderson, the Association's General Secretary, strongly favoured registration the decision hardly implied neutrality on the issue, let alone support for TUC policy.[53] Finally, by the end of August the Agricultural Workers' registration seemed imminent.[54]

The TUC did have some successes between March and September. In June the National Union of Railwaymen committed themselves to de-register,[55] and in the same month a conference of the four sections of the AUEW voted to do the same, though in this case a rules revision conference was first necessary.[56] Even the AUEW decision was not simple: in a speech in April to his engineering section Scanlon had criticised the 'vagueness' of TUC policy, and had dwelt on the harsh penalties associated with non-registration,[57] a theme he returned to at the June conference.[58] Whatever the political complexion of the union, it too had institutional interests which could be threatened by the registration of its rivals.

Whatever doubt may have crossed the minds of AUEW leaders, they were nothing to those that afflicted the TGWU. In a speech after the special congress Jack Jones criticised the disarray of the TUC and attacked 'weak' unions – in other words, those which were contemplating registration.[59] It was clear that he felt that, if significant numbers registered, the institutional interests of his own union would compel it to do likewise, for only a few days after the March Congress he told the *Guardian* that he was opposed to registration, but 'clearly if other major unions like NALGO do so then our executive will have to reconsider the position.'[60] In July the union's delegate conference agreed to call a rules revision conference later in the year. This was a necessary prelude to de-registration, but any firm commitment was carefully avoided; Jones told the delegates that the union was willing to make the sacrifices involved in de-registration, but only if others were ready to do the same.[61]

Given the response to the March 'advice' not to register, it was hardly surprising that a renewed attempt should have been made at the September 1971 Congress to have the General Council instruct unions to come off the register. Despite the crumbling away of union resistance to the Act – or perhaps because of it – the supporters of a mandatory policy could not find a majority on the General Council,[62] and the Council faced Congress still committed to the idea of giving strong advice rather than instruction. During the summer, however, a small number of unions with substantial card votes – such as the Mineworkers and the National Union of Public Employees – had become alarmed at the behaviour of some TUC members, and now switched to support of the policy of instructing unions to de-register.[63] This was enough to allow the General Council's position to be rejected, and to allow a small majority for the mandatory line.[64]

This result had all the makings of a Pyrrhic victory. It meant, first, that the bloc votes of a number of large unions had committed the TUC to a policy supported by only a minority of members of the General Council. Second, the debate in September had hardened the lines of division; speakers from smaller unions in particular emphasised that they would decide on registration by reference to their own members, not to the

TUC.[65] Finally, it was unclear how far this new decision represented a significant advance. In moving the motion Scanlon had been very vague as to what sanction might be employed against recalcitrants, stressing that this was a matter for a later Congress,[66] while the attempt to make expulsion automatic on registration gathered only a tiny minority in support. Finally, there was the paradox that two unions which were wavering on the matter of registration – the TGWU and ASTMS – were also among the strongest supporters of a policy of instruction rather than advice.[67] These two facts were, of course, linked: the very pressure which was driving ASTMS to contemplate registration – fear of its competitors – also lay behind its support for a mandatory policy, since if it came off the register it was important that its competitors within the TUC be pressured into doing likewise. Similar considerations affected the TGWU, but with even more force. The TGWU could lose nothing under a mandatory policy: if it were ignored the situation would be no worse than at present, while if the TGWU were forced to defy TUC policy and register it was almost inconceivable that it would be expelled; it was much more likely that the whole campaign of opposition would simply collapse.

Following the Congress decision, the General Council wrote to unions on 24 September 1971 instructing them to come off the provisional register.[68] The results were not encouraging. Three days after despatch of the instruction NUBE reaffirmed its decision to stay on.[69] At the beginning of October a conference of the GMWU decided to remain on the provisional register, and to defer any final decision until June 1972, a delay plainly intended to allow the union to make a final choice in the light of its competitors' behaviour.[70] Three days later the National Graphical Association indicated its intention to defy TUC policy,[71] and was followed shortly after by the Seamen[72] and the Agricultural Workers.[73] The strains within the TUC are illustrated by arguments within the General Council at this time over eighteen unions which had definitely refused to de-register: the majority wanted them merely to explain their behaviour, but a minority led by Scanlon demanded suspension.[74]

During the closing months of 1971 and the early part of the following year a significant group of TUC affiliates continued to disobey the instruction to de-register, either by directly committing themselves to registration or by deferring a decision to de-register. Frank Chapple successfully urged his conference to remain on the provisional register, stressing the institutional interests of the union.[75] The NALGO EC, who had been given the job of deciding on the matter by their conference, were deeply split, and voted to defer any choice until they heard an address from Vic Feather on the matter.[76] A poll of members of the National Union of Journalists led to the reversal of a decision of its EC to de-register,[77] while Equity was moving steadily though acrimoniously towards permanent registration.[78]

The immediate response to the decision taken at the September 1971

Congress was, therefore, discouraging for the TUC. By November of that year, of the four biggest unions only the AUEW had come off the register while two – the GMWU and the EETU/PTU – were inclining towards defiance of the TUC. Yet by the time of the 1972 Congress the campaign against registration had been all but won by the unions: though a number of affiliates did register, and some were eventually expelled, none of the largest did so, while significant waverers such as ASTMS and USDAW fell into line. The explanation for this is twofold: it lies partly in the TUC's ability to exert pressure on its affiliates, and partly in a largely fortuitous combination of events which occurred in the spring and summer of 1972. Both deserve consideration in some detail.

Though the response to the decision of the September Congress to instruct unions to de-register was initially unimpressive, the decision was important in two ways. First, it helped reduce uncertainty a little, and this was beneficial since fear of what rivals would do was one of the main reasons why some unions were unwilling to take the initiative in coming off the register. The most encouraging result came in January 1972 when the TGWU finally held its rules revision conference and at last cleared the way for de-registration.[79] The sanctions implicit in the September decision also began to bite: at the end of January the General Council's General Purposes Committee recommended the suspension of NUBE, which was not only registered but was already using the Act against employers.[80] Since the penalties arising from expulsion were not certain, this represented not so much a new weapon as an intensification of the moral pressure on TUC members to conform with Congress policy.

This sort of sanction was, however, not sufficient by itself. Competition for members between unions organising the same occupations meant that for every union which registered another would contemplate doing so for fear that its ability to recruit would be impaired. The TUC could only be assured of victory if the overwhelming majority came off the provisional register. ASTMS was a key union in this respect, because of the likelihood that it would use the Act to recruit aggressively. The union prevaricated right up to the 1972 Congress, and at the beginning of May 1972 its conference failed to produce the two-thirds majority necessary for de-registration.[81] In the same month Chapple fought a union election in favour of the policy of registration – he even advocated cooperation with the Court[82] – and at the same time the USDAW conference again reaffirmed the registration decision.[83] In June the Iron and Steel Trades Confederation unveiled its plans to register.[84] The pressures of instruction and even expulsion were apparently not enough to hold the line. But at this point the TUC was rescued by three sets of events. None of these was accidental in the sense of being a purely random occurrence. Each arose out of deliberate decisions of policy; but there was a fortuitous element in that they occurred in a particular combination, and at a particular time, when they could give most help to the unions' campaign of resistance.

The first event was the miners' strike of 1972 the outcome of which—embodied in the recommendations of the Wilberforce Tribunal—was a setback for the Government's strategy of fighting inflation by reducing the rate of wage increases in the public sector.[85] This did not bear directly on the Act, but defeat at the hands of the miners was the catalyst which produced a change in Government strategy. During the summer and autumn of 1972 the Government conducted the so-called 'tripartite' talks with the TUC and the CBI.[86] This was indicative of an important shift in thinking: wage inflation was no longer to be fought by introducing greater market discipline into wage negotiations, and by curbing the organisational power of the unions, but by the operation of a compact with the trade union movement involving wage restraint in return for economic expansion, welfare measures and some price control. Since the Act was premissed on essentially liberal policies involving abstention by the Government from attempts at direct wage regulation, this meant the abandonment of the economic—and to some extent political—assumptions on which it had been based. With the benefit of hindsight it is possible to see the opening of the tri-partite talks as the signal that the Act had no long-term future in the regulation of industrial relations. A more mundane consideration was that the unions were now not prepared to arrive at a bargain without the repeal of the legislation.[87]

But if the rationale of the Act had been undermined, its usefulness to the Conservatives had not disappeared. The Tories still tried to use its provisions, receiving, as we shall see in a moment, a bloody nose in the process; and in the summer of 1972 it still looked as if they could win the battle over registration. If they had done so, the Act would at the very least have provided a strong card to be played in any future negotiations. That it became a liability was due to two further sets of events, one concerning the emergency procedures in the legislation, the other involving a complicated set of cases of 'blacking' in the docks.

In the wake of the miners' victory the Government faced the problem of how to treat the negotiations over a pay claim from railwaymen. They decided to use the emergency procedures provided under the Act, and applied to the NIRC for a conciliation pause. When this expired they again applied to the Court, this time for a ballot of all railwaymen on whether or not to accept an offer advised by an outside arbitrator.[88] Since the leadership of the unions involved were against acceptance, the rank and file were being asked not only to accept an offer below what their unions were demanding, but also, in effect, to pass a vote of censure on their leaders. Not surprisingly, they voted by huge majorities to back their unions and to hold out for more.[89] Ask a silly question as one Tory backbencher remarked, and you get a silly answer.[90]

Several features of this episode are worth noting. The Act worked perfectly, viewed from a purely legal point of view: the unions cooperated, albeit reluctantly;[91] the conciliation pause was observed; and the ballot produced a huge poll with a clear decision. But the Government had suffered an important defeat: the final settlement was well above what it had hoped, and its first attempt to use the Act had been a humiliating failure. It established an impression that the Act was accident prone, an impression that was to be strongly reinforced by the episodes involving the dockers.

There is a certain irony in this because the provisions used in the case of the railwaymen were peripheral to the legislation, in the sense that they operated quite independently of the heart of the Act, which concerned registration. Indeed they were measures over which there had been argument and hesitation in the Conservative Party.[92] Conservatives have never been sure about the wisdom of conducting ballots among workers, since they can never quite make up their minds whether industrial militancy is the result of extremist leaders suppressing moderate majority opinion, or whether it is a case of moderate leaders being unable to restrain their own rank and file. The presence in the Act of the ballot provisions was the result of a temporary victory for the first view. Though the outcome of the rail ballot only cast doubt on a marginal part of the legislation, it was an important psychological boost for the unions, and confirmed the warnings about secret ballots which the civil servants had delivered to the politicians. It is not unreasonable to see these events as the beginning of the Government's loss of confidence in the legislation.

The rail ballot produced an important moral victory for the unions, but it was by no means conclusive in the campaign against the Act. The decisive blows came over cases involving dockers which occupied the NIRC during the spring and summer of 1972. The precipitating cause of these cases was technical change in the nature of dock employment.[93] The development of container handling of goods sent by sea meant that the work of loading and unloading containers – 'stuffing and stripping' – was increasingly done by workers in outside depots, who were not dockers. The attempts by dockers to defend their jobs brought them into conflict not only with employers – the container firms – but with the employees of these firms, who in some cases belonged to the same unions as the dockers. The fact that workers were in conflict with each other as well as with employers immensely complicated an already delicate situation. The case which finally brought shop stewards to prison, for instance, was actually initiated by a group of USDAW members.

The docks' cases first appeared before the Court in March 1972. Dockers in Hull began blacking lorries delivering goods from a container firm, and similar unofficial action involving different firms soon spread to Liverpool and London. In the London case blacking was accompanied by picketing of the depots of two container firms.[94] On 23 March 1972 the NIRC granted an order to Heatons, a Lancashire firm, ordering the TGWU to stop its dock members blacking the firm's containers at Liverpool.[95] The union refused to be represented before the Court, arguing that to do so

would breach TUC policy.[96] Six days later, with the TGWU still refusing
to appear, it was fined £5,000 for contempt in refusing to order its members
to stop the blacking, and for aggravating this by declining to appear before
the Court.[97]

Eleven days after this, with the Heatons' case still not settled, a second
firm working out of Liverpool asked the Court for a similar order. Again
the TGWU was unrepresented, and on 14 April the order was granted.[98]
With the blacking still not lifted – indeed extended – the two firms went
back to the Court for a contempt order. On 20 April the NIRC fined the
union a further £50,000, and warned that if its contempt went unpurged
all its assets might be frozen.[99] The immediate effect of this was to break the
boycott of the Court. Three days after the fine was imposed, the Finance
and General Purposes Committee of the General Council decided to allow
unions to defend themselves.[100] At the beginning of May the TGWU
Executive Committee decided by a narrow majority to pay the fine,
though in reality they had little alternative since the Court could have
seized the union's assets. The union also threatened to withhold its
affiliations fees if the TUC did not recompense it.[101] Just over a week later
the union's representative went into court to argue the TGWU case, which
was essentially that it had tried to comply with the Court's instructions but
was unable to secure the cooperation of its members.[102]

The subsequent arguments were to concern the relationship between
the union and the shop stewards who were leading the unofficial action. Sir
John Donaldson, rejecting the union's case, argued that the stewards were
officers of the unions, and indicated that for the TGWU to demonstrate
that it had made a serious effort to implement the Court's orders it must
discipline the stewards by withdrawing their credentials.[103] Whatever the
precise construction which different lawyers could place on the wording of
the Act, there is no doubt that in taking this line Donaldson was reflecting
the intentions of the authors of the legislation. The prospect of another
Betteshanger – when miners had ended up in prison during the Second
World War – had long haunted the Tory policy makers, and they spent the
years of opposition in ingenious attempts to ensure that a direct clash with
workers was avoided. The essence of their solution involved penalties on
corporate bodies, rather than on individuals. The reasoning behind this
was that the former were less inflammatory symbolically than the latter:
fining a union was dangerous, but less so than committing trade unionists
to prison. Thus when Donaldson insisted that the union discipline the
stewards he was undoubtedly acting in accord with the intentions of the
framers of the Act in trying to avoid a direct confrontation with
individuals.

This tactic was destroyed by a most unexpected body: the Court of
Appeal. When the TGWU appealed against the NIRC judgement, Lord
Denning and his two colleagues quashed the fine, on the grounds that since
the union rule book gave no 'implied authority' to its stewards to initiate

industrial action, the TGWU could not be held responsible for the blacking.[104] In short, if the Court wanted to tackle the dockers it must do so directly, and not through the union. This of course destroyed the tactics adopted by both the Act's authors and Donaldson – penalising corporate bodies rather than individuals – and set the scene for the ensuing farce, with the Court desperately trying to avoid jailing anybody, and stewards gleefully inviting incarceration.

An appeal to the Law Lords was set in motion, but in the meantime the NIRC began to act on the basis of the Appeal Court judgement. The day after the decision, Donaldson turned his attention away from the TGWU to the individuals leading the blacking. He ordered the stewards who were leading the blacking of a container firm at Chobham Farm in London to appear before him to explain why an earlier order to lift blacking had not been obeyed. Whatever the 'reasons of state', he remarked, referring to the strikes which would inevitably follow the jailing the the men, 'the Court must uphold the rule of law.' The stewards' response was to refuse even to appear before the Court; in some cases they even expressed delight at the prospect of going to jail.[105] The situation may have been exacerbated because some of the stewards were also active Communists. There is no doubt that Communists – and some groups of Trotskyists – were active in the docks, and were of course anxious to make the legislation look as oppressive as possible. But these are peripheral matters: the underlying problems of economic and social change produced by the container revolution were not manufactured by left-wingers; and there were plenty of non-Communist trade unionists who would have welcomed the well-publicised martyrdom now in prospect.

With the shop stewards now defying the Court it seemed that imprisonment was inevitable. But Lord Denning, having played his part in torpedoing the Court, now helped launch a lifeboat in the form of the Official Solicitor. On 17 June – the day when the dockers were due for imprisonment for contempt – the Official Solicitor, acting at least in part on Denning's instigation,[106] appeared before the Appeal Court on the men's behalf, but without their permission.[107] He secured the quashing of the contempt order on the grounds that the Court had acted on insufficient evidence. Though this saved the day in this particular case it did nothing to alter the basic fact that the Appeal Court had forced the NIRC into a direct conflict with individual stewards. It simply delayed a clash until a new case appeared. This duly happened a fortnight later: in July some of the stewards who had been involved in the Chobham Farm dispute were ordered by the Court to cease blacking and picketing a London depot operated by the Midland Cold Storage Company.[108] Despite strenuous efforts by the unions involved to get a settlement – it was USDAW members who had taken the initial action – no agreement was reached: on 21 July, faced with the refusal to comply with the Court order, Donaldson committed five stewards to Pentonville Prison.[109]

The results were entirely predictable. By the evening of the same day, the docks in London, Liverpool and Hull were at a standstill; lorry drivers who had been counterpicketing the docks withdrew in sympathy; the cold storage workers who had brought the original action expressed their support for the jailed dockers; strikes broke out in other industries, especially engineering; and the publication of newspapers ceased for five days.[110] The General Council of the TUC voted by eighteen votes to eight (with six abstentions) for a one-day national strike though – in line with the constitutionalism which marked their actions throughout – they carefully deferred the date of the strike to allow the possibility of the courts solving the problem without industrial intervention.[111] In the meantime they suspended the tri-partite talks with the Government.[112] This was a serious embarrassment to the Conservatives, since it was very anxious for a settlement with the unions over pay and prices.

The Government and the NIRC were now caught in a trap largely of the Court of Appeal's making. Their chief hope lay in an appeal to the Law Lords against the judgement, which had forced the Industrial Relations Court into a direct clash with the dockers. The Lords, working with unusual speed, did as was hoped. On 26 July they delivered a judgement upholding Donaldson's original decision, and they held the Court of Appeal to be wrong in requiring express delegation of authority in a rule book before a union could be held responsible for the actions of its stewards. The Court's original view that something more was required of the TGWU than advice and requests to its members to cease blacking was also supported. On the same day Sir John Donaldson, recognising that the grounds on which the dockers had been imprisoned had now altered, ordered their release, accompanying it with a by now familiar statement of his views on the importance of the rule of law.[113] The TUC withdrew its call for a national strike, and re-entered the tri-partite talks,[114] though the imprisonment can be held partly responsible for a national dock strike which began almost immediately.

These events finally killed the Industrial Relations Act as a serious measure of industrial relations reform. From the Government's point of view they confirmed the suspicion that the legislation was – to put it mildly – accident-prone. Both of the attempts to use it to solve big problems – the rail ballot and now the blacking in the docks – had been humiliating failures. It was also souring relations with the unions at the point where the negotiations over the economy were at a delicate stage: the suspension by the TUC of the tri-partite talks was probably the single most worrying and annoying outcome of the whole episode from the Government's point of view. Finally, the twists and turns of judicial procedure, and the different decisions over who was responsible for blacking, had led to accusations that the Government was manipulating the law behind the scenes in order to extricate itself from the embarrassing consequences of its own legislation.[115] This does not in fact seem to have been the case: Denning and a Q.C. who frequently appeared for trade unions appear to have stirred the Official Solicitor into action.[116] Nor did the Law Lords need instructing in what judgement to arrive at: the TUC had served notice that they stood between the country and a general strike, and it would have required a quite extraordinary lack of political sensitivity for their Lordships not to see that, whatever the legal niceties, it was necessary that the Court of Appeal judgement must be overthrown. But none of this helped the standing of the courts in the eyes of the unions, or indeed in most other eyes.

The most important contribution made by the jailing of the dockers to the failure of the Act, however, concerned registration. Even at the height of the battle, but before the actual imprisonment, the TUC was having substantial difficulties in securing a united front on de-registration. Early in July the General Council suspended seven unions – including ASTMS and USDAW – for failing to de-register.[117] A number of other unions – including the mighty EETU/PTU – were still not complying with the TUC's requests. The immediate result of the imprisonment was that Chapple's union immediately committed itself to coming off the register, while the Iron and Steel Trades Confederation and ASTMS made moves to obey the General Council's instructions.[118] (ASTMS, however, only produced evidence that it was definitely coming off the register on the morning before it was due to be suspended by Congress.)[119] Less than a month after the release of the dockers USDAW too reversed its decision and voted to de-register.

None of this happened because the union leaders were especially sympathetic to the dockers. On the contrary, both their constitutionalism and their suspicion of grass-roots militancy meant that they were for the most part hostile to such outright defiance of the law. But the imprisonment of trade unionists overrode these reservations. At a more pragmatic level it was also the case that the imprisonment, combined with the Government's strong desire to reach a bargain with the unions, meant that the Act's long-term future was bleak; this in turn lessened the risks of non-registration. When Congress assembled in September, the General Council was forced to recommend the suspension of thirty-four unions. Most were very small, however, only five having memberships in excess of 100,000.[120] All of the big unions had committed themselves to de-registration. Because of the way registration worked, this in itself made the TUC position more secure: one of the main forces working against Congress policy had been the uncertainty felt by the big unions about the intentions of their rivals. Once it became clear that its competitors were going to abide by TUC policy, it became easier for each individual union to take a similar decision.

The TUC's victory in the non-registration campaign can be ascribed to a combination of its own efforts aided by the fortuitous intervention at a key moment of the dockers' case. After August 1972 the Act was dead as a positive force in industrial relations; but it deserves an epilogue for, though dead, it continued to haunt political and industrial life like a malign spirit, until finally exorcised by the new Labour Government in 1974. The Lords' decision which allowed Donaldson to release the dockers did not end the blacking, or the law's involvement in the complexities of the container disputes. The cases before the NIRC became intertwined with the very difficult question of the reform of dock labour, and the disputes continued for some months.

Nor did the unions' victory over non-registration end all the TUC's problems with the Act. There was the difficult question of what to do with those unions which had defied Congress policy by registering. In this respect the TUC behaved with great circumspection: in September 1972 Congress agreed only to a policy of suspension for a year in the hope that the rebels would reconsider; a union could avoid even this if it came off the register by the end of the year.[121] At the 1973 Congress only twenty unions, the majority very small, were expelled. The caution was justified, for not only did some unions de-register when given a stay of execution in 1972 – as did the Power Engineers – but some of those finally expelled had already made moves to de-register even before the Labour Party's victory in the February 1974 general election.[122]

A more serious problem for the TUC concerned the general matter of how it should treat the institutions set up to implement the Act. The most acute problem concerned attitudes to the Court. The General Council had of course at first tried to boycott it completely, but the fines on the TGWU in the early stages of the dockers' dispute forced the Council to allow unions to appear in defensive actions. The AUEW and – to a lesser extent – the TGWU continued to urge a more militant line, while the AUEW engaged in a unilateral boycott of the Court. The Engineers' defiance resulted in a number of conflicts which had the effect of further discrediting the Act – assuming it to have any credit after the dockers' fiasco – in the eyes of almost everyone concerned with industrial relations. At the end of 1972, only a few months after the dockers' imprisonment, Mr James Goad obtained an order from the NIRC instructing the AUEW to admit him as a member, though he already had a rather eccentric record of membership. The union refused either to appear before the Court or to comply with its order, and was fined £5,000 for contempt. As it refused to pay voluntarily, the Court ordered the union's bank to hand over the money from the AUEW account. Since the union still persisted in its refusal to admit Mr Goad, the Court fined it a further £50,000, this time sequestrating its assets.

The Goad affair created problems for almost everybody: for the firm which employed him, since its employees struck in protest at the Court's treatment of the union; for many other employers, since during 1973 the AUEW successfully encouraged part of its membership to engage in a series of one-day strikes in protest at the Court's actions; for the Government, whose attempts to arrive at some sort of wage and price deal with the unions were further threatened by the acrimony surrounding the case; for the TUC whose constitutional strategy involved avoiding disruptive disputes and open conflict with the law; and finally even for Hugh Scanlon, whose irate union withdrew him from the tri-partite talks. Possibly the only participant not embarrassed by the whole affair was the irrepressible Mr Goad who finally added a touch of burlesque to the proceedings by offering to withdraw his action in return for a cash settlement.[123]

Of those who had initially favoured a legislative solution to the problems of industrial relations, none were more disillusioned by the experience of the Act in its twilight days than the large employers who dominate the economy, and their chief spokesman, the CBI. Big business had always had grave reservations about the Tory proposals – particularly their more libertarian aspects – but the actual effects of the Act exceeded their worst fears. After the dockers' episode the Goad case emphasised just how disruptive a combination of union defiance and individual idiosyncrasy could be. The Goad affair was followed by a case involving Joseph Langston, an employee of the Chrysler motor company, the outcome of which indicates just how anxious a large employer could be to avoid disruption. Mr Langston resigned from the AUEW, which had a closed shop in the plant where he worked. He obtained a judgement from a lower division of the NIRC supporting his right not to join a union. Chrsyler had already suspended him, and when he went to collect his pay he was abused and threatened by his workmates. Mr Langston then tried to sue the AUEW but the Court held that this was not provided for in the Act, and while he was appealing against this in a higher court he was dismissed by Chrsyler. He then entered a complaint of unfair dismissal against the firm, which Chrsyler immediately conceded and paid compensation, judging this to be a small price to be paid for industrial peace. Faced with the determination of workers not to tolerate someone who refused to join their union, and the determination of the firm to avoid disruption, even the NIRC judged it impractical to order Mr Langston's reinstatement.[124]

The final, well-publicised fiasco in which the Court was involved concerned Con-Mech, a small engineering firm. For the connoisseur of the tragi-comedy which surrounded the Court this case had every possible ingredient: a colourful and individualistic small employer who disliked unions; allegations that a militant philosophy graduate was stirring up trouble in the firm; the by now customary defiance of the Court by the AUEW; fines and sequestrations on the union; strikes as a result; an attack on Sir John Donaldson by the Labour Government's Secretary of State for Employment; and anonymous benefactors who paid the AUEW's debts to the NIRC in order to prevent a national engineering strike.

In September 1973 there was a strike at the works of Con-Mech because of a dispute about union recognition. The firm applied to the NIRC for an order relieving it from the industrial action, and for an investigation of the case by the CIR. The Court issued the order, the AUEW boycotted the Court as usual, the order was not obeyed, and the NIRC sequestrated £100,000 of the union's assets, eventually confiscating £75,000. It also announced that Con-Mech could apply for compensation for losses arising from the industrial action.[125]

The grievances of the AUEW were now further intensified when the CIR's report on the firm, which recommended recognition of the union, was rejected by the employer. The Court could not give legal force to the ruling of the CIR since the AUEW was unregistered. The union was now suffering with a vengeance those double penalties which the Tories had piled onto unregistered bodies in a bid to win the battle on registration. Not surprisingly, this situation produced a series of one-day strikes which disrupted production in key industries such as motor manufacture and prevented publication of national newspapers. An already delicate situation was exacerbated in April 1974 by the decision of the Court to award £47,000 in damages to Con-Mech. The union as usual refused to pay voluntarily, so its assets were once again seized. The whole affair was made even more complicated by the fact that a Labour Government was now in office, and was committed to repeal of the Act; indeed the repeal Bill had been published the day before the Court awarded damages against the union. The AUEW responded by intensifying its industrial action: on the casting vote of Mr Scanlon the union's engineering Executive Committee called a national strike of indefinite length. Large sections of industry were affected and most newspapers were closed down. At this point the employers stepped in. An anonymous donor – a reliable source has suggested to me that it was the Newspaper Proprietors' Association – paid the money which the AUEW owed the Court, and the strike was called off.[126]

By the time of the Con-Mech episodes, the large employers were thoroughly disillusioned with the Act. In the autumn of 1973 an internal CBI working party on the legislation recommended substantial changes,[127] and in the February 1974 election campaign Campbell Adamson, Director General of the Confederation, remarked that the Act had sullied industrial relations and should be repealed. The publication of this comment – made in what Adamson believed to be a private setting – caused bitterness in the Conservative Party and arguments within the CBI which led Adamson to offer his resignation. His comments were, however, quite consistent with the view the CBI had supported over many years, which took the totally pragmatic line that any reforms could only work with the cooperation of the trade unions. Once it became clear that the TUC was determined to destroy the Act, the Confederation lost interest in it, though some of the smaller firms in its ranks may still have retained some enthusiasm.

Many Conservatives believe that Adamson's remarks contributed to the Tory losses in the February 1974 election. If this was indeed the case Adamson also helped finally destroy the Act, for the Labour Government which came to power as a result of the election quickly repealed the legislation. Its Trade Union and Labour Relations Act, passed in the summer of 1974, had three aims: to abolish most of the institutions and measures connected with the Act; to restore the advantageous legal position enjoyed by the unions before 1971; and to retain and extend those sections of the Industrial Relations Act – chiefly concerning unfair dismissal – which the unions found to their benefit. In connection with the last, Labour's initial Bill made a cursory bow to the liberal tradition by providing some defence against the closed shop in the form of protection against dismissal for those who refused to join a union on religious grounds. During the passage of the Bill a number of opposition amendments in both Houses strengthened the defence against unfair dismissal for refusal to join a union and widened the grounds of objection to compulsory union membership. Labour has, however, used its increased strength in the Commons since October 1974 to reverse these amendments and to widen further the rights of both trade unions and individual workers against employers.[128]

The Act has left an enduring mark on the shape of labour law, in the form of the unfair dismissals provisions and the admittedly now very narrow grounds for objection to compulsory trade union membership. But the greatest influence of the Conservatives' legislation has been in the wider spheres of industrial relations and contact between unions and government. The present administration has frequently maintained – in its refusal to widen the legal grounds of objection to the closed shop, for instance – that all it is doing is returning to the voluntary system which existed before 1971. But in fact voluntary collectivism as traditionally practised has passed away, probably never to return. Labour's legislation has ensured that the law is now very important in the work place, though the law – as in the very extensive legislation affecting dismissals and redundancy – is now shaped to the interests of the trade unions. Industrial relations is also much more collectivist than ever before. The sense of confidence created in the trade union movement by the defeat of the Industrial Relations Act – and by such events as the miners' victories in 1972 and 1974 – means that unions are now more determined than ever to take a central part in the industrial life of the nation. One symptom of this is the rapid extension of trade union membership in general – which the Act facilitated – and of the closed shop in particular.

An even more important change has resulted from the conviction – in both the TUC and the Labour Party – that many of the Conservatives' troubles generally, and over the Act in particular, arose from a failure to consult and bargain seriously with the unions. In this belief lies the origins of the social contract, a development which represents an important shift in the relationship between unions and government as prescribed by the tradition of voluntary collectivism. In the 1950s and early 'sixties government and unions had clearly distinguished spheres of responsibility: unions negotiated over wages, government managed the economy, particularly the level of overall demand, and the two interfered with each other's activities only in times of stress and difficulty. This fairly clear demarcation has now been replaced by a symbiotic relationship in which each has a great deal to say about the other's role: the Government is keenly interested in wage bargaining, the unions in the management of the economy. The Act has thus had an important long-term effect on British politics, though far from the one intended by its authors. Should these developments survive the return of a Conservative Government then the consequences for the political system will be even more profound. It is to this and to other similarly important questions that the final chapter is devoted.

9 Representation and Consent

Laws are for all, and he who seeks to lay them
On others should by rights himself obey them.
Chaucer, *The Canterbury Tales*

A number of separate accounts have been offered of the difficulties faced by the Industrial Relations Act. The purpose of this chapter is to review them and to try to decide if they tell us anything about the problem of enforcing law in our society. Three accounts will be offered in turn, duscussed in order of generality: the first rests on certain views of the way the Act itself was prepared; the second is based on a particular philosophy of industrial relations; the third rests on beliefs about the conditions under which obedience to laws in general can be secured.

EXPERTISE AND CLASS CONFLICT IN INDUSTRIAL RELATIONS

The first explanation – popular with both leaders of the trade unions and the Labour Party – is that the Act's problems arose from the fact that it was manufactured – in Mrs Castle's phrase – by 'legal maniacs'.[1] In other words it was produced by Conservative barristers remote from the realities of industrial life. Supporters of this view tend to see *A Giant's Strength* – the Tory lawyers' 1958 pamphlet – as the Act's ancestor. They also stress the extent to which the legislation departed from the recommendations of authoritative and expert bodies such as the Donovan Commission.

This account is quite unacceptable, both because it is an inaccurate description of the way Tory policy was made and because of its assumption that there is some body of impartial, expert knowledge which could have guided the Conservatives' deliberations. It is true that there is quite a close correspondence between what the final Act contained and what the Tory lawyers proposed, but to assume that the former was a product of the latter is simply to mistake cause and effect. The Conservative lawyers' proposals resemble the Act for exactly the same reason that the views of the Tory trade unionists do: all three are a product of the Conservative mind. The moral and market liberalism which so influenced the proposals may well be congenial to the legal view of life, but it was in the proposals because it was congenial to the Tory view of life.

When we examine the actual mechanisms which were used to arrive at the policy, the notion of legal domination is further undermined. The Party's internal working groups contained members such as Iain Macleod and Joseph Godber, both former Ministers of Labour, and neither with a legal training. Of the four men most closely connected with the proposals – Abbott, Joseph, Carr and Howe – only the last was associated with the Tory lawyers.[2] Joseph, though trained as a barrister, was also at the time front-bench spokesman on industrial relations and vice-chairman of a large building firm; Abbott had long experience in the engineering industry; while Carr not only had a spell as a junior at the Ministry of Labour in the 'fifties but also worked as a foreman and as a senior executive in his family engineering firm.[3]

If it is granted that the Tory proposals were not a product of legalistic ignorance, it may still be objected that the Act's framers ignored the recommendations of bodies such as the Donovan Commission, which had carried out detailed and authoritative investigations of the problems involved. But as soon as we try to treat the Commission's Report as a source of authoritative knowledge it decomposes before our eyes. This is not to imply anything discreditable about the Commission's workings, or to devalue the extremely useful research it produced; but like most royal commissions its final report was the result of political compromise: 'much movement either way', remarked Donovan's research director, 'and there would have been a half dozen minority reports.'[4]

The reception of the various proposals by experts supports the view that there was nothing like an established body of knowledge and recommendations for the Conservatives to ignore. By and large, the view that the law was an inappropriate instrument of reform was accepted by specialists in industrial relations, who tend to stress the value of conciliation, industrial peace and gradual reform;[5] on the other hand economists, more concerned with economic efficiency and wage inflation, tended to favour the use of law to speed up change.[6] The Conservatives did not displace neutral, expert knowledge with amateur prejudice; but they did partly replace one set of values with another. Experts in industrial relations – academics, trade unionists and personnel specialists on the management side – tend to be collectivists: they favour maintaining the stability of the existing institutions of collective bargaining, and the resolution of industrial conflict through these institutions. The Tories tried to inject a large amount of liberalism into the system. A case can be made out for saying that they were wrong to do so, and that the various benefits of the closed shop, for instance, far outweigh anything to be gained by trying to ban it, but such an argument is unlikely to be resolved by recourse to 'the facts'.

The problems of the Act cannot, then, be explained by the real or imaginary shortcomings of its authors. This lets us turn to the second main account offered, which is essentially that the law itself is an inappropriate instrument for reforming industrial relations. What goes on between employer and employee is, so the argument runs, a delicate matter of human relations. The law is too rigid and inflexible to be used in such circumstances. What is important is that human attitudes should change, and laws cannot affect this. The argument was very popular with both Harold Wilson and Vic Feather when they were opposing the legislation,[7] and it also seems to enjoy some support in the Conservative Party today.[8] This is appropriate, since in its implicit acceptance of the importance of piecemeal reform and organic change this view is essentially conservative, an echo of Burke's observation:

> Nations are not primarily ruled by laws. . . . Nations are governed by the same methods, and on the same principles by which an individual without authority is often able to govern those who are his equals or his superiors: by a knowledge of their temper and by a judicious management of it. . . . The laws reach but a very little way.[9]

A moment's contemplation should show this argument to be untenable in our society, for the law demonstrably does reach a very long way. It regulates some of the most delicate areas of the human heart: the conditions under which marriages may be contracted or dissolved; the conditions under which sexual relations may take place; even the conditions under which life may be taken away, as in the laws concerning abortion. There is deep disagreement within the community about what the content of such laws should be, but few would argue that there should be no law on such matters. If it is to be argued that industrial relations are too sensitive for legal regulation, it must be shown that they are uniquely delicate compared with areas where the law does intervene. This has not been done, and it is very doubtful if it is possible to do so. Specifying the conditions under which strikes may occur is surely not a more delicate matter than deciding when an unborn child may have its life ended by an abortion.

There is, however, a variation on this argument which deserves consideration: it can be argued that there was something especially delicate about the Industrial Relations Act both because it was class legislation and because, in attempting to advance the interests of an employing class at the expense of workers, it ventured into a far more explosive area than that covered by a moral issue such as abortion. Supporters of this view might cite Winston Churchill's remark (made in the rather different world of 1911) that 'it is not good for trade unions that they should be brought in contact with the courts . . . where class issues are involved, and where party issues are involved, it is impossible to pretend that the courts command the same degree of confidence.'[10] The trouble with this view is that the Act was not 'class' legislation. Such legislation would surely have had one of two hall-marks: either it would have been the intention of the Act's authors to advance the interests of employers at the expense of workers; or, irrespective of the motives of the framers of the legislation, the measures themselves would have accorded with the wishes of employers and would have advanced their interests. Neither of these is true in the case of the Industrial Relations Act. The Tories sincerely believed that what they were doing was in the interests of the whole community. More important, we have already seen that the Act was not at all what the employers wanted, and mainly as a result of provisions insisted on by the Conservatives against the wishes of business the effect of the legislation was to damage the interests of business by creating industrial disruption. Indeed it was precisely the fact that it was not class legislation that reduced the Act's chances of success, for the fact that it did not accord with the desires of business meant that it received little practical support from employers.

Nor is it possible to sustain the more general case that the law should keep out of industrial relations because of the complexities of class conflict. The law is no stranger to the British scene. The Conservatives did not introduce it into industrial life, though it is true that they replaced a relatively spare framework by a more elaborate design. Nor did the Tories invent the interventionist tradition: policies during the two great wars and under the Labour Government after 1966 were marked by a significant degree of legal regulation of collective bargaining. These interventions, though they had their problems, did not find industrial relations too delicate an area to tackle. The law was kept out of industrial relations in this country for much of the twentieth century not because there is something peculiarly difficult about legal regulation but for a much more simple reason: it suited the interested parties that it should be kept out. Voluntarism had the support of unions because it removed them from the influence of a prejudiced judiciary; it suited the employers' associations because it gave them a key role in collective bargaining; and it suited the Tories because after 1945 it seemed to guarantee peace with the unions. As soon as these interests were threatened then pressures for intervention began to build up. Even the trade unions did not return to abstentionism when they secured the Act's repeal: the package of measures contained in the 'social contract' represent a policy of intervention by the state in favour of union interests.

Just as an examination of the British experience suggests that there is nothing which makes industrial relations immune to extensive legal regulation, so a glance at other countries emphasises the point. If industrial life were especially delicate in the way alleged, then we ought to find that Britain was unusual in attempting to develop a comprehensive legal framework, and we ought also to find that any similar efforts in other countries had ended in disastrous failure. The reverse is true: before 1971

Britain was almost unique among major industrial nations in having a strong tradition of voluntarism. The international norm is indeed one of extensive and relatively successful legal regulation of industrial relations.

The essentially conservative view that there are areas of human activity such as industrial relations which are immune to purposeful regulation by the law will not, therefore, help us to explain the problems encountered by the Act. This leaves us with a third possibility, which rests on the assertion that laws require consent and cooperation if they are to be successfully operated. This was evidently a conclusion arrived at by both major political parties in the light of their experience of legal intervention: Labour's answer was to seek cooperation with the unions through the social contract, while after the summer of 1972 the Conservative Government intensified its efforts to arrive at an agreement through the tripartite talks with the CBI and the TUC.

In a very trite sense this reasoning is obviously correct. Plainly if the employers had been willing to give their support to the Act, the chances of failure would have been diminished; and if the unions had given their support, then success would have been assured. But put in these terms the explanation is not very illuminating. We need to analyse in some detail the nature of both the support and the opposition which the legislation engendered.

Opposition to the Act was most intense among those deeply involved in the conduct of industrial relations. The most visible sign of this was, of course, the resistance of the trade unions, but union opposition was underpinned by a quiet but effective campaign on the part of most employers to emasculate the measures. The CBI, reflecting the views of big business in particular, disliked the liberalism of the Act: instead of the rule of law and open argument in court it wanted the Registrar to operate with a large amount of administrative discretion thus using the power of the state to back up employers and official trade unionism in disciplining workers. It also disliked the attack on the closed shop, perhaps the single measure which also most offended the unions. The advice tendered by the Confederation and other large employers' organisations reflected this extreme coolness: it stressed the importance of great caution before using the new law, and encouraged provisions such as the writing in of clauses specifying that agreements were not to be legally binding.[11] All this was invaluable to the TUC in its campaign to nullify the Act. In addition to advising employers against any speedy use of the new measures, the CBI also began – almost as soon as the Act was on the statute book – to negotiate a conciliation procedure with the TUC which would by-pass its provisions.[12]

The response of individual employers reflected this line. The recent investigation by Brian Weekes and his colleagues illustrates the lengths to which managers were prepared to go to ensure that the legislation did not disturb existing arrangements, especially as they concerned the closed shop.[13] The Court was similarly by-passed: the large industrial undertakings virtually boycotted it, most contentious cases coming from small concerns. During the blacking dispute in the docks, for instance, Ford shifted its business away from a blacked depot and made it very clear that it wanted no involvement in the dispute.[14] Even more important is the fact – pointed to by Thomson and Engleman – that such employers as did use the Court were generally suing workers from companies other than their own.[15] In other words, those who were prepared to use the legislation had a split mind on it: they believed in the use of the law, but only for other firms' workers. Management's implicit attitude was that everyone else's industrial relations needed legal regulation – with the exception of the manager's own firm. The reason is obvious: to sue your own employees would have a disastrous effect on relations; to sue your rivals' employees is much less dangerous. It was the recognition of such problems that had turned groups like the CBI to the idea of using the state as prosecutor. This 'dual' attitude is important in accounting for the reaction of employers; but it is also important in examining the sources of support for the legislation.

In conventional terms, there was widespread support among the population at large for the Act. The Conservatives won the election of 1970 on a platform which included the legislative proposals as a major plank. There is substantial evidence from public opinion polls that for some years there had been widespread disenchantment with voluntary reform; indeed, this was one of the main reasons for Labour's attempts at legislation in 1969.[16] In addition, evidence from polls carried out during the passage of the Bill shows that support for the general idea of legislation was high; during the early stages even a majority of trade unionists seem to have supported the measures. Similarly, almost all the particular proposals commanded widespread assent: over 80 per cent of public and trade unionists supported the ill-fated cooling-off periods, while two-thirds of trade unionists and the public at large agreed with the idea of legally binding agreements.[17] Even given the vagaries of opinion polling, these are impressive figures. Perhaps just as striking is the fact that, even when the legislation was quite discredited among political leaders, trade unionists and employers, the public at large were still unwilling to see it destroyed: in a poll carried out during the February 1974 election campaign only 39 per cent of all electors (55 per cent of Labour, 23 per cent of Conservative) supported abolition.[18] The problems the Act faced were, however, a consequence of the nature and intensity of this public support.

The first of these problems was that, though there existed widespread popular support, the public at large did not have the capacity to make the legislation work. Success depended on the cooperation of union leaders, shop stewards, personnel managers and employers generally. These were precisely the people who were most suspicious of the measures. The problem of intensity complicated this. Within the world of industrial relations opposition was deeply felt and determined. Among the public at large, however, support for the measure was diffuse and lacking in coherence. There is evidence that both knowledge and interest in public policy generally among the electorate at large is low.[19] It is unlikely that many of those who told the opinion polls that they favoured such measures as conciliation pauses and legally binding agreements had very much idea of what the detailed implications of such measures were; rather, such views were an expression of a general feeling that there was something wrong with industrial relations and that something ought to be done about it.

But not only was public support weak in intensity; it was also ambivalent. Just as managers tended to have split minds on the use of the law, so there was a schizophrenic element in the outlook of the electorate. As managers tend to believe that every firm but their own needs regulation by the law, so workers tend to think that all strikes but the ones in which they themselves take part are 'irresponsible' and ought to be curbed by government. The dockers' case provided a classic illustration of this propensity to will a particular end of public policy combined with an unwillingness to will the means necessary for the end: the very cold storage workers who had been responsible for the dockers' embroilment with the Court in the first place expressed their sympathy with the stewards when they were jailed for defiance.[20] This split mind is not a result of some defect of intelligence among the electorate at large. It reflects rather the conflicting pressures which afflict most members of the community: on the one hand, we are citizens with some notion of what is necessary to defend the public interest; on the other, we are workers or employers engaged in a struggle to defend our particular interests, and we find it very difficult to allow the state to restrict our capacity to defend ourselves against enemies or competitors.

TWO SYSTEMS OF REPRESENTATION

The obvious lesson of all this is that if future policies on industrial relations are to be successful they must have the assent of the main parties to the system. But this conclusion does not take us very far, since the obvious problem is: how is consent to be secured? This question is extremely difficult to answer, and one of the main reasons for this is that the problems faced by the Act do not arise from conditions unique to industrial relations; they reflect wider difficulties of the system of government. Historically the development of democracy in Britain has been accompanied by a particular method of popular representation based on competition between political parties for the votes of electors organised in territorial constituencies. This system is in part a means of voicing the interests and views of the community in the political arena, but it is also in the widest sense a method of decision-making and a means of mobilising consent for those decisions. The development of party programmes embodied in such forms as election manifestos allows the electorate a degree of choice between different policy alternatives. Conversely, it is commonly argued that when a decision of government – particularly when it is expressed as a law – arises from an electoral commitment this gives it an added authority and means that it should be complied with.

The system, it is widely recognised, rests on fictions: the electoral system distorts popular choice, while the link between an individual's views and the way he votes is often tenuous. Nevertheless this method of representing views, taking decisions and legitimising those decisions is an important part of our system of government.[21] For the sake of discussion I shall call it the 'parliamentary system of representation'. It was to this that Mr Heath and his Government appealed when they argued that the Industrial Relations Act should be accepted because they had received a mandate to implement it. The Act was indeed the outcome of representation within the parliamentary system. It was drawn up by the Conservatives in comparative isolation from the pressures of interest groups. Individual businessmen of course had a voice in the making of policy, but largely insofar as they were active Conservatives. An employers' spokesman once remarked to me that because the Tories had some businessmen on their backbenches they thought could ignore the employers' organisations, and the way the Act was prepared suggests that there is some truth in the observation. Having drawn up their policies with little reference to interest groups, the Conservatives continued to work within the parliamentary system: they included their proposals in an election manifesto in 1970, and implemented the measures when they won the election.

The parliamentary system of representation is often thought of as the core of the democratic tradition in Britain, but in this century it has been joined by an alternative: a system based on the notion of functional representation, which relies on the representation of corporate interests – workers, employers, farmers and so on – rather than on aggregates of individual voters. In Britain this has taken the form of consultation and negotiation between the Whitehall-based executive and the leaders of functional groups. Whitehall has shown a special predilection for bargaining with peak associations such as the CBI and the TUC, to the point where it has virtually sponsored their entry into the centre of politics. The reasons for the growth of functional representation are complicated, but the most immediate was the feeling on the part of top political decision-makers that the parliamentary system was unable to produce either the necessary level of cooperation or effectiveness needed by a modern state. Thus during the two great wars – but especially between 1939 and 1945 – functional representation expanded rapidly as politicians and civil servants tried to mobilise the whole community for total war.[22]

But functional representation, conceived originally as a supplement to the parliamentary system, now threatens to replace it. In this lies the wider political significance of the Industrial Relations Act. Measures which secure assent according to the parliamentary system are frustrated because of opposition from the functional representatives. Since the two methods of representation are also two means of taking and legitimising decisions, conflicting outcomes occur. This is precisely what happened over the Act. The Government by-passed the functional representatives, believing that to arrive at an agreement with the TUC in particular would involve drastic changes in its proposals. Both the Government and the TUC were thus correct when they accused each other of behaving unconstitutionally, but the Government was referring to the parliamentary part of the constitution, the trade unions to the functional part. The difference was, it should be emphasised, due to nothing as simple as blocks in communication, though these made matters worse: the TUC fully understood the doctrine of the mandate, but since no government for a generation had let it get in the way of functional representation the unions could not see why the Conservatives should start now. The Tories, equally, were fully aware of what functional representation involved – they had practised it before 1964 and were to do so again – but they believed that in this particular case it endangered the essentials of their proposals.

The failure of the Act is often seen as a victory for the unions over government. The situation is actually more serious than this. If it were only a matter of union defiance, then the community might by uniting against the unions have a chance of victory. But the unions' opposition was quietly acquiesced in by the business community, particularly by the large concerns who dominate the economy. The battle between the unions and the Government was only a smaller part of a conflict between parliamentary and functional representation. The existence of such a conflict clearly creates problems of consent and authority; just how serious those problems are depends on whether or not the Industrial Relations Act was a special case of political stress which is unlikely to be repeated, or whether it is an omen for the future. In the past the conflict between the two systems of representation has been successfully managed for a number of separate reasons.

The first of these is that functional representation has tended to dominate where decisions over the details of policy are to be made. This is usually justified on the grounds that argument on such matters cannot be sensibly discussed in public controversy either in Parliament or on the hustings. This mutes any differences, since the functional representatives know that by specifying enough of the 'details' a particular electoral commitment can often be implemented with any offending features removed.

A second reason that a conflict between the two systems has been avoided is that functional representatives are often able to influence at source the proposals produced within the parliamentary system of representation. The political party is a key institution in this respect, since it acts – to adapt Bagehot's phrase – as a buckle joining the parliamentary part of the constitution to the functional part.[23] Functional groups can try to influence particular items in a party manifesto or they can even set up a party as their own creature, as the unions originally did with the Labour Party.

Finally, conflict can be reduced because of the respect which the parliamentary system can still command from functional representatives. This was a very important influence even during the struggle over the Industrial Relations Act. Though the constitutionalism of the General Council was largely of the functional variety, yet there was still evidence of respect for parliamentary representation: after all, repealing the Act after a Labour Party victory at the polls was always a key part of the TUC strategy, while some members of the General Council such as Frank Chapple were prepared to go to extreme lengths in defence of parliamentarianism.

For the reasons mentioned here – division of labour, the fusing role of the political party and the moral authority of parliamentarianism – conflict has in the past been contained. It is clear that the head-on confrontation between parliamentarianism and 'functionalism' – the shorthand by which I shall denote the functional system of representation – only occurred in the case of the Industrial Relations Act because of the combination of a rather special set of conditions: the Tories' long sojourn in opposition; the difficult nature of the problems of industrial relations; the events surrounding the defeat of *In Place of Strife* in 1969; the particular personalities involved in the making of Government policy after 1970 – or, to be more exact, the particular personality of Mr Heath. But such a conflict has arisen since, and will arise again in any part of our society where a well-organised and powerful functional group finds its demands restricted by government. In any area of life where government depends on the cooperation of a functional group it can expect that group to demand a say in decision-making, and can expect defiance if it refuses to share power.

In this respect the failure of the Act was in itself a considerable historical landmark. It dealt a substantial blow to the moral authority of the parliamentary system of representation and its effect in this way has been felt far beyond the narrow confines of industrial relations law. The functional challenge to parliamentarianism spreads by a process of imitation. One of the most striking instances of this has been the increasing tendency of middle-class functional groups to realise and use their bargaining power against the community in general and against the government in particular. Occupations such as doctors, consultants and teachers have generally refrained from threatening collective withdrawal of services for two reasons: the fact that this would offend their middle-class notions of deference to the properly constituted authority of government; and perhaps more important, the fact that it would breach professional ethics which proscribe any action which causes harm to those who consume the services provided by the groups. The success of working-class functional groups in imposing their will on parliamentarianism in recent years has, however, caused their middle-class counterparts to flex their bargaining muscles, as they observe the weakness of parliamentary representation and the necessity of defending themselves in the pressure group jungle. Since the victory of functional representation over the Industrial Relations Act, a number of frightening-looking chickens have come home to roost. Two examples of the increasing challenge of functionalism are particularly instructive, since they go well beyond the particular field of labour law.

The most spectacular – and successful – of these challenges occurred with the miners' strike of 1974. The most important fact about this episode was not merely that a functional group successfully defied the Government, but that the outcome of the subsequent election – the legitimate means of making authoritative decisions under the parliamentary system – made no substantial difference to the miners' position: they would still have been a special case had the Conservatives won, because their power rested on the ability to exercise a stranglehold on the economy.[24] The present Labour Government has also faced the challenge of functionalism. On the question of the abolition of pay beds in the National Health Service, for instance, it has found itself under conflicting pressures from different groups: the unions representing ancillary workers have taken industrial action to try to force the Government's hand on the matter, while sections of the medical profession have threatened counteraction if the Government capitulates. In this case the Government managed to head off the trouble with the aid of the ubiquitous Lord Goodman, who arranged a compromise formula which delayed the phasing out of pay beds. I shall return to the implications of a situation like this – where government is a shuttlecock between conflicting functional groups who can only resolve their disagreements by splitting the difference – at greater length below.

The conflict between the two systems of representation, and the problems this raises for any government seeking consent for its actions, are therefore not confined to the narrow field of industrial relations law. Two separate sets of difficulties for the future demand particular attention. How would a future Conservative Government set about gaining the consent of the functional groups in industrial relations, especially the trade unions? And how can government generally attempt to solve the problem of consent? The two issues are related, but deserve separate discussion.

The future behaviour of a Tory Government is extremely difficult to predict, both because at the moment the Conservatives' public pronouncements are unclear – a reflection of the confusions caused by the general failings of the last Government and the particular failings of the Industrial Relations Act – and because so much will depend on the particular economic situation which the Tories inherit. At the time of writing – June 1976 – a policy pronouncement is promised for the autumn, though whether or not it will significantly clarify matters is far from certain. But even at this stage a number of things appear probable. If there is conflict in the future between the unions and the Tories it is unlikely to concern the narrow field of industrial relations law. The Conservatives are committed – and have been since the October 1974 election – to accepting most of the legislation which Labour has put in place of the Industrial Relations Act.[25] But they have reserved their position on two important matters.

The first concerns the election of union officers. There seems an outside chance that a future Conservative Government might use the law to enforce postal ballots of all members in union elections. A much more likely possibility, however, is permissive legislation – of the sort first promised in the February 1974 election manifesto – allowing unions to obtain financial help from the state towards the costs of running such ballots.[26] Despite the débâcle of the ballot of railwaymen in 1972, and despite the fact that the Government were frightened to use the ballot procedures in the Act in either of the two miners' strikes, the belief apparently persists in the Party that the mass of normally apathetic members is more 'moderate' than the small minority which habitually participates in unions. (The same assumption seemed to underlie the abortive attempt at the beginning of 1976 by the Party's Trade Union Department to raise interest and participation in union elections by publishing lists of approved candidates.) The Conservatives' continued belief in the moderation of rank-and-file union members is a delusion explicable only as a result of the schizophrenic outlook of union members alluded to earlier. Conservatives continually see evidence that workers as citizens are ready to support moderate policies – by, for instance, giving assent to the proposition that there should be a government-regulated incomes policy – and observe at the same time that unions frequently fail to reflect this moderation. They conclude that the views of the rank and file are being perverted by a small, militant minority, whereas it is much more likely that workers are simply failing to carry their opinions as citizens into their trade unionism.

The Conservatives' second reservation about the present state of the law concerns the closed shop. The next Tory Government will not attempt to outlaw it in the fashion of the 1971 Act, but the continued suspicion of it in all sections of the Party is a tribute to the strength of moral liberalism among Conservatives. The most recent publication by the Party on relations with the unions probably sums up the present attitude of most members of the Shadow Cabinet: 'the closed shop is an undoubted encroachment on freedom of choice. Nevertheless . . . there are circumstances in which employers and employees accept [it] as a mutually convenient and orderly way of conducting their relations.'[27] It is, in short, a distasteful but unavoidable fact of life. A future Tory Government will undoubtedly try to regulate it more closely, but in what fashion is at the moment unclear. Three possibilities exist, and it is probable that the present leadership does not know which it would adopt.

The first is to introduce legislation widening the existing narrowly religious objection to compulsory union membership into a wider clause granting exemption on general grounds of conscience. The second possibility – not incompatible with the first – is to set up a public body to oversee closed shops and to guard against their abuse. Finally, there is the option of doing nothing in law but encouraging employers – especially those in the public sector – to either resist closed shops or to concede them only with very generous conscience clauses.[28] The last possibility really amounts to doing nothing of substance. Large employers welcome the closed shop and value peace and discipline far above individual conscience. Nor is the idea of pressuring public-sector employers particularly promising. At the rate closed shops are being gained in public employment, by the time the Tories return to office virtually the whole of the public sector will be covered by compulsory trade unionism, and of a particularly restrictive sort: British Rail's closed shop agreement, for instance, only allows religious objection to union membership where the individual can produce written proof from his denomination that its beliefs are incompatible with joining a union.[29]

The best guess at the moment, therefore, is that the subject on which the Conservatives came into the most bitter conflict with functional groups – the shape and substance of labour law – will not be a major bone of contention in the future. The problem of consent is more likely to arise over general questions of economic policy, and will concern Conservative attitudes to the level of unemployment, to wage determination and to public expenditure. Just how severe these difficulties are depends very much on the economic situation which exists when the Tories come to power. There is a great deal of difference between gaining office in the very near future, with a declining pound, a high inflation rate, a huge public sector deficit and a commitment to cutting public spending sharply, and on the other hand winning an election at the end of the decade when Labour may well have borne the odium of making the most painful reductions in public expenditure and the economy may be poised on the edge of an oil-based recovery.

The uncertain economic future and the Tories' own confusions make prediction difficult, but at least two different responses to the problem of consent are at present being canvassed in the Party. While hardly organised round factions, these views can be associated with particular individuals. They spring from the familiar Conservative dichotomy between liberalism and collectivism. The former, which is linked with members of the present Shadow Cabinet like John Biffen and – more problematically – Sir Keith Joseph, involves the reassertion of market forces in the economy, and one of its most important policy implications arises from the suggestion that control of the money supply is one of the keys to good economic management. The liberals tend to feel that the last great clash with a functional group – the dispute with the miners in 1974 – arose from attempts by government to intervene too deeply and too restrictively in wage determination. The problem of consent is to be solved by letting the functional groups work out their own differences within the overall discipline of a market economy.

A sound political and economic case can be made out for this response, but the suspicion exists that its present appeal to the Conservative Party arises from the belief that it allows government to disengage itself from the acute social conflicts which brought the Tories to grief in 1974: by setting a figure for the expansion of the money supply one can put the economy, so to speak, on automatic pilot. This desire for a painless and impartial resolution to social conflict is also reflected in the support given by *The Times* newspaper – a strong supporter of monetarism – to the idea of a Currency Commission, a group of wise men who would determine the most important matters of monetary policy. But given the existence of strong trade unions and the ever-increasing number of closed shops, combating excessive wage demands through control of the money supply rather than through an incomes policy cannot help but raise the problem of consent. Monetarist solutions involve making workers pay the price of excessive wage settlements in the form of increased unemployment. Even if monetarism works, there is bound to be a transitional period of high unemployment before unions and their members adjust their sights to the new situation. Whether a Tory Government could get through this period without a confrontation with the unions similar to that which took place after 1970 is at least problematical, particularly when one remembers some of the corollaries of monetarism which – according to Peter Walker, admittedly a prejudiced witness, – are being pondered by the Party leadership: abolishing social security payments for strikers' families; changing the law on picketing; and training specialists who can replace strikers in the maintenance of essential services.[30]

It is precisely the recognition of these problems that prompts the collectivist response. Such views are not strongly represented in the present Shadow Cabinet, but they are important because Mr Heath has flirted with them, though he has taken care to keep his options open.[31] They are probably best exemplified at the moment by Peter Walker, his colleague in exile, whom it is not unreasonable to see as an ideological stalking horse for the former Party leader. Walker's views include some proposals which are accepted Tory policy – such as the suggestion for secret ballots in union elections – but they go much further in attempting to incorporate workers. He supports an incomes policy, though how statutory it would be is unclear. (As the present Government has shown, the dividing line between a voluntary and statutory policy is by no means clear.) He also goes far

beyond the present rather vague official Conservative policy on participation in advocating that all firms employing more than 250 people should
be obliged to have a participation scheme. Walker has also advocated state
encouragement of profit-sharing and – the most significant concession to
the functional groups – the creation of an industrial parliament.[32]

Which of these alternatives – or which combination of these – may
finally be adopted is very unclear; party policy is at the moment in such a
state of flux that the skills of the Kremlinologist are required to divine it.
The final factor complicating prediction is that liberal or collectivist
solutions are probably only advocated in an extreme form by a minority.
Most of the Tory leadership is probably agnostic on the matter. Since the
agnostics include Mr Whitelaw, the Party's Shadow Employment
Secretary Mr Prior[33] and – despite her use of liberal rhetoric – Mrs
Thatcher, a great deal is going to depend on how they resolve their
uncertainties under the pressures of office.

The problems the Conservatives face in securing consent from the
functional groups – and from the unions in particular – are clearly affected
by the wider problem of how government generally can solve the problem
of consent. The essential argument of this book has been that the failure of
the Industrial Relations Act did not arise from conditions unique to
industrial relations – such as the alleged inappropriateness of legal
regulation – but sprang from the wider conflict between functional and
parliamentary representation. It follows that some accepted relationship
must be established between the two systems if cooperation and consent is
to be secured. The present Government's reaction has been to turn to one
part of the functional universe – the trade unions – and afford it a large
share in the making of economic policy generally. If this trend continues
the future will lie increasingly with functional groups, and this in turn will
have important consequences for the political system. Government will
become increasingly the art of managing the key organised groups through
consultation and negotiation. This is sometimes called 'corporatism',[34] but
the label, with its overtones of Fascist dictatorship, is probably misleading.
Since the essence of the system is the representation of people in terms of the
functions they perform in the community, 'functionalism' is a more
accurate and less emotionally loaded term. A shift to more functional
representation is quite compatible with some aspects of democracy:
freedom of speech could still exist, and competitive elections still be held.
But elections would not be about the determination of policy in any real
sense; they would be preludes to policy, which would be decided with the
powerful pressure groups through the established procedures of consultation and negotiation.

It does seem that such a shift is inevitable if the country is to have stable
government. This is so for two important reasons. The first relates to the
split-minded attitudes of the citizenry as illustrated by the attitudes of
many managers and workers to the Industrial Relations Act – their

readiness to will the Act through the parliamentary system but their unwillingness to support it as members of functional groups. There are other striking instances of this phenomenon: voluntary incomes policies have, for instance, generally failed though there is widespread popular support for wage restraint. At the beginning of 1975, less than a year after the destruction of the Conservatives' statutory policy and at a time when the Labour Government's attempt at incomes restraint was in tatters, a PEP survey found that a representative sample of the electorate gave overwhelming support (particularly among lower socio-economic groups) to a statutory wages policy.[35] The result of this dual set of attitudes is that the parliamentary system of representation can throw up policies but not the consent necessary for their implementation. One MP has remarked on the fact 'that the power created out of the democratic process is now smaller than it has been for a long time.'[36]

A number of separate accounts have been offered to explain this split state of mind. For Marxists it is the outcome – in Richard Hyman's words – 'of the gap which exists between activity and consciousness':[37] in other words, workers as citizens reflect the interests of a dominant exploiting class in supporting moderation and incomes restraint, but in the workplace the reality of their objective economic position impels them into militancy. Alternatively, Samuel Brittan has argued that it arises from a condition endemic to democracy: citizens are ready to support government action but are unwilling to accept the consequences in terms of restrictions on freedom of action.[38] Whichever account is correct – and Brittan's seems to me the more plausible – the result of this political schizophrenia is to reduce considerably the effectiveness of parliamentarianism as a system of representation.

This discussion leads us to the second reason for the increasing importance of functional groups: the community simply cannot operate at a tolerable level of life without their consent and cooperation. In 1926 the miners were starved and intimidated into submission; now our social and economic institutions are so complicated that even a strike of a few weeks can threaten the whole basis of civilised existence. Since we cannot force the miner – or the surgeon or the power engineer – to do his job, then we must induce him to do it voluntarily. It is plain that the best – but by no means certain – chance of securing voluntary obedience is by securing the assent of the functional groups.

A number of separate schemes have been suggested for coping with the challenge of functional representation. The most straightforward involves trying to disarm the most strategically placed groups by using the law to curb the exercise of their power. John Peyton, a member of the present Shadow Cabinet, suggested in the aftermath of the Tories' February 1974 election defeat that the party should consider outlawing strikes in industries vital for the life of the nation,[39] and the suggestion has recently been revived by Samuel Brittan.[40] The advantage of such a suggestion is that it would require no great institutional reform, and there are precedents for such a measure: there is no right to strike in the armed forces, and before the passage of the Industrial Relations Act it was a crime to strike in a number of industries, including gas, power and sewage disposal. But the problems involved in such a piece of legislation are enormous. It is very difficult to believe that any powerful union would now – after the defeat of the Industrial Relations Act and the miners' victories in 1972 and 1974 – acquiesce in such a measure. An additional problem is that such an Act would – even if it were successful – only strike at a small part of the power of functional groups. Only in a minority of cases such as that of the miners does the power of a group rest on its capacity to put its hand to the community's windpipe and keep it there until government submits to its demands. More usually a group can do as the TUC did in the case of the Industrial Relations Act and frustrate the wishes of government while staying within the law.

A second possible solution to the problem of consent would be to try to strengthen the moral authority of the parliamentary system, especially in the eyes of the functional representatives. This seems to be one of the motives behind some of the current arguments for reform of the electoral system.[41] A government selected as a result of elections on a more proportional system than the present one would probably be composed of a coalition of at least two parties. Whereas at the moment governments never secure the support of over 50 per cent of the electorate – and the present Administration received less than 40 per cent of the votes cast – the parties in a coalition could, on present reckoning, expect to speak for over 60 per cent of voters. Since democracy rests heavily on the notion of the will of the majority, it is conceivable that this would increase the legitimacy of government in any clash with functional groups.

But there are some important difficulties with this argument. It is by no means certain that a coalition would have the necessary decisiveness to impose its will on sectional interests. Coalition governments are not of necessity weak but when they are – as in the French Fourth Republic – the result is to hand over effective power to the civil servants and the most powerful functional groups. An even more important objection, however, is that – as Lord Devlin remarked at the time of the dockers' cases in 1972 – 'there is no magic in a majority'.[42] Functionalism rests on the reality of power in our society: if the miners will not dig coal, then it matters not whether 65 or 45 per cent of electors support the government.

A third possibility in the search for consent is to look for a method of representation – and thus a means of making authoritative decisions – which by-passes both functionalism and parliamentarianism. There exists such a system – perhaps best designated the 'Rousseauist tradition' – which involves the direct assertion of the national will through such a device as a referendum. We have recently experienced an eruption of Rousseauism in the form of the referendum on Common Market entry, and while it was not directly designed to cope with the problem of the power of functional groups it certainly produced an authoritative decision. But the hazards involved in adopting such a system are great. The most obvious danger is that instead of displacing parliamentarianism and functionalism Rousseauism would merely add another system of representation, so that whereas at the moment we have the problem of two modes of representation producing different decisions we could end up with all three systems in conflict. A second difficulty is that referenda cannot resolve the problem of the split-minded attitudes of voters: citizens could still will one set of decisions in a referendum and then refuse to implement them in their capacity as members of functional groups. Finally, it is not clear that the decisiveness of the Common Market result – where turnout was comparatively high and opinion was heavily in favour of EEC membership – could be repeated, especially if referenda became common.

The devices for securing consent discussed so far are all essentially formal and institutional: they involve either changing the law or changing the rules of the constitutional game in some fashion. But the solution which is in practice being adopted is of a more improvised and informal nature. The present Labour Government has sought in a number of important ways to increase the importance of the functional representatives. The most important reflections of this are the emergence of the Labour Party–TUC Liaison Committee as a key institution and the fact that the various versions of the social contract lie at the heart of the Government's policies. Given the ties of history, sentiment and interest between Labour and the trade unions it is not surprising that the unions have been the main beneficiary of Labour's return to power, but the Government is clearly anxious to work with all important functional groups: it has had the closest consultation with the CBI on the new Price Code which appeared in the summer of 1976, while its policy on offshore energy has been worked out in detailed negotiations with the oil companies; indeed, when legislation was recently slipped through which allowed the nationalised energy corporations to apply for unallocated exploration blocks in the Irish Sea the Government apologised to the oil companies for the lack of consultation.[43]

This is not to say that the Government have been colonised by the functional groups: neither the CBI nor the oil companies got everything they wanted, and even the TUC has been denied some things. But it is clear that the criterion of what the relevant functional group finds acceptable is now very important in the mind of government. This ad hoc response to the challenge of functionalism poses a number of important problems, both as regards the taking of authoritative decisions and as regards the proper representation of affected interests. The first of these difficulties concerns what is to be done between groups and the government, or between groups themselves, when there is disagreement as to what a decision should be.

A decision of government can be complied with for one of three possible reasons. First, there are the prudential grounds that if obedience is not forthcoming then the sanctions of the law will be imposed. The lesson of the last few years is that for the most powerful functional groups this is not an effective deterrent where the actions of government seriously threaten the interests of the group. A second ground for obedience is that the group feels that the decision is a correct one; in other words consent can be obtained on the basis of substantive agreement about the content of policy. Finally, consent can be forthcoming because while a particular decision may be disliked it has been arrived at by a method which is considered acceptable, and because the prospect exists of reversing it by the same method; in other words consent can be obtained on procedural grounds.

The great strength of the parliamentary system of representation is that it provides just such a set procedure for making authoritative decisions and for reversing those decisions. Although the system has to rest on some broad notion of what substantive policies are legitimate – a decision to abolish free elections would, for instance, hardly gain acceptance – the essence of parliamentarianism is that if a government wins an electoral majority then it has a right to have its policies accepted and obeyed provided those policies have been cast in appropriate legal form. The essential point is that while the particular rules may not be fair in every detail, and while substantive policies may often be intensely disliked, they do provide a clear means of taking and reversing decisions.

Functional representation at the moment has no such procedural rules. The functional system is a Hobbesian world where decisions arising out of differences between groups come about in two ways: either the very strong impose their will, as the miners did in 1974; or else the contending parties split the difference between them, as occurred in the compromise negotiated by Lord Goodman between the conflicting parties to the argument over pay beds in the National Health Service. The trouble with the latter is that a compromise may not be the most rational solution to a problem, whereas the bias in functionalism as at present practised is towards compromise as a means of producing a substantive decision on which the main parties can agree.[44] But an even greater difficulty is that in a complicated community such as our own it is quite impossible to guarantee that a compromise between conflicting points of view will always be possible; we cannot expect the Lord Goodmans of this world to keep on producing magic formulae. Where conflicting interests are so intense that no substantive compromise emerges then one of two things results: if the dispute is between the government and a powerful group then the challenge from the latter produces the sort of political crisis which the miners precipitated in 1974; or if the dispute is between strategically placed functional groups then the conflict swings from sanction to counter-sanction, with the government left as an ineffective mediator, as very nearly happened over the pay beds dispute.

The response of the present Government to the challenge of functior alism does not, then, solve the problem of consent in the long term though in fairness it must be admitted that Labour has produced a better ad hoc response than anyone had a right to expect when the Party was returned to office in February 1974. Indeed, there are signs that Labour is now the natural party of government as Harold Wilson has claimed. This is not because it is necessarily the party of a majority in the country – it plainly is not – but rather that its instinctive collectivism makes it more suited than the Conservative Party to the workings of functional representation. Labour's essentially ad hoc response to the challenge of functionalism is, however, reflected not only in the reliance on substantive agreement to produce authoritative decisions but also in the range of interests it is willing to consult: it is to the peak associations – especially the TUC – who have already established a customary right of consultation that the present Government turns when it seeks consent for its measures. Because of the structure of the CBI and the TUC this essentially means the representation of big business and big unions, rather than the other interests in the community.

This provides yet again a contrast with the parliamentary system of representation. Functional representation is inegalitarian, giving most weight to those who perform key functions in the community and least to those – such as the old, the sick and the indigent – who have no strategic role to play. The universal franchise, on the other hand, is egalitarian in intent, giving the same weight to all in the community not disqualified from voting by virtue of lunacy or royal blood. In practice the system is admittedly capable of being rigged but there can be little argument that the pensioners' vote, for instance, allows an interest to be represented which would rarely be heard in the functional system. Indeed functionalism is, viewed in this light, an extremely reactionary development. It revives the principle of corporate representation which dominated the pre-democratic constitution and which the liberal-radical supporters of electoral reform in the nineteenth century fought against in their efforts to extend the franchise.[45]

The responses to the challenge of functionalism discussed so far fall into four categories: changing the law so as to restrict the functional groups; strengthening the moral authority of parliamentarianism; replacing existing methods of representation by a Rousseauist reliance on referenda; and finally the Labour Government's response which involves reaching substantive agreements with the most powerful functional representatives. In the light of the difficulties for making authoritative decisions posed by Labour's response a last possibility suggests itself. This would involve giving functionalism an enduring institutional expression in the constitution by, for instance, replacing the present House of Lords by a second chamber selected along functional lines. Such a solution offers substantial advantages. The greatest is that it opens the prospect of a regular procedure by which differences of opinion between the functional and parliamentary systems and between particular functional groups might be resolved. Thus by establishing the second chamber's right to delay or veto certain classes of legislation the conflict between the methods of representation could be institutionalised and a means established of breaking a deadlock between them; a similar possibility exists as far as conflict within the functional universe is concerned.

A second chamber along functional lines would not of itself solve the problem of the narrow range of interests represented by the existing system; indeed if the present Government were to set up such a chamber it would probably be dominated by party placemen and nominees of the TUC and the CBI. But the existence of a second chamber – even one dominated by a narrow range of interests – would open up public discussion about which interests *should* be consulted by government and would force groups such as the TUC to justify their especially privileged position. In addition, with functional representation institutionalised in this fashion there would be a strong incentive for the parliamentary system to concentrate on the representation of those who perform no vital job in the community and who, as a result, are poorly catered for by functionalism.

So much for the advantages. But a second chamber of this sort is one of the oldest chestnuts of constitutional reform. The fact that the idea has been around for a very long time partly reflects the enduring challenge of the functional groups but it reflects even more the extreme difficulties of implementation: who would be represented; in what proportions; how would they be selected; and how – if at all – dismissed? Just to list the questions is to see their enormity. Above all, since the object of the whole exercise is to produce a means by which government can make authoritative decisions there would have to be a consensus about the basis of representation, as otherwise any important group which felt aggrieved at the way the second chamber was ordered would be likely to deny the legitimacy of its decisions.

It is fitting that a book describing events which were a source of widespread pain, difficulty and anxiety should end on a note of puzzlement. It would be pleasant to propose some utopian solution: a Marxist future where greed and sectionalism would vanish along with capitalism and be replaced by the felicities of a workers' state; or a return to an imaginary paradise of sturdy individualism where the restrictions of collectivism would be banished. We are unfortunately faced with difficulties which admit of no utopian solution – indeed of no obvious remedy at all. A solution there must be, however, either in the form of muddling through in the fashion of the present Labour Government or in some more systematic way. If we fail, will we be capable of following the advice of Chaucer's Man of Law – the prescription for any civilised community – which heads this chapter? Or can we preserve what Orwell called our most important trait, 'the respect for constitutionalism and legality'?

Notes

I THE HISTORICAL LEGACY

1. Henry Pelling, *A History of British Trade Unionism*, (Middlesex: Penguin, 1965) p. 50
2. E. H. Phelps-Brown, *The Growth of British Industrial Relations*, (London: Macmillan, 1959) p. 120
3. *Ibid*, p. 124
4. Royden Harrison, *Before the Socialists*, (London: Routledge, 1965)
5. V. L. Allen, *The Sociology of Industrial Relations*, (London: Longman, 1971) pp. 157–184
6. Alan Bullock, *The Life and Times of Ernest Bevin*, (London: Heinemann, 1960) II pp. 156–162; Hugh Clegg, *General Union in a Changing Society*, (Oxford: Blackwell, 1964) p. 108
7. Eric Wigham, *The Right to Manage*, (London: Macmillan, 1973)
8. Hugh Clegg, *The System of Industrial Relations in Great Britain*, (Oxford: Blackwell, 2nd edition, 1972) pp. 200–202
9. Ralph Miliband, *Parliamentary Socialism*, (London: Merlin Press, 2nd edition, 1973) pp. 59–92
10. Michael Stewart, *Keynes and After*, (Middlesex: Penguin, 2nd edition, 1975) p. 62
11. V. L. Allen, *Trade Unions and the Government*, (London: Longman, 1960) pp. 3–33
12. Clegg, *System of Industrial Relations*, pp. 204–206
13. *Royal Commission on Trade Unions and Employers' Associations 1965–1968: Chairman, the Rt. Hon. Lord Donovan, Report*, (London: HMSO, 1968, Command 3623) pp. 14–15 (hereafter referred to as the Donovan Report)
14. J. F. B. Goodman and T. G. Whittingham, *Shop Stewards in British Industry*, (London: McGraw Hill, 1969) pp. 34–38
15. This summary relies heavily on both K. W. Wedderburn, *The Worker and the Law*, (Middlesex: Penguin, 2nd edition, 1971) and Otto Kahn-Freund, *Labour and the Law*, (London: Stevens, 1972). On Wages Councils in particular see Wedderburn p. 217
16. This account has been offered by Kahn-Freund on a number of occasions: see for instance Otto Kahn-Freund, 'Report on the Legal Status of Collective Bargaining and Collective Agreements in Great Britain' in Kahn-Freund, editor, *Labour Relations and the Law: A Comparative Study*, (London: Stevens 1965) pp. 23–24
17. Kahn-Freund, *Labour and the Law*, p. 170
18. Wedderburn, *Worker and the Law*, pp. 309–313; Hugh Clegg, Alan Fox and A. F. Thompson, *A History of British Trade Unions Since 1889*, (London: Oxford University Press, 1964) I p. 434.

19. Wedderburn, *ibid*, p. 24
20. *ibid*, pp. 313ff
21. Dennis Lloyd, 'The Law of Associations', in Morris Ginsberg, editor, *Law and Opinion in England in the Twentieth Century*, (London: Stevens, 1958) pp. 99–115
22. Wedderburn's phrase in *Worker and the Law*, p. 312
23. Kahn-Freund, *Labour and the Law*, p. 229
24. Wedderburn, *Worker and the Law*, pp. 313ff and pp. 326ff
25. Clegg, et al, *British Trade Unions*, pp. 305–312
26. After prevarication the Conservatives set up a Royal Commission which included leading opponents of the unions: *ibid*, pp. 321–324
27. Wedderburn, *Worker and the Law*, p. 320
28. *Ibid*, pp. 395–6
29. Gerald Abrahams, *Trade Unions and the Law*, (London: Cassell, 1968) pp. 114ff
30. Wedderburn, *Worker and the Law*, pp. 309–313
31. *ibid*, p. 313
32. Clegg, et al, *British Trade Unions*, pp. 305–325
33. Wedderburn, *Worker and the Law*, p. 27
34. *ibid*
35. Trades Union Congress, *Annual Reports*, 1962, p. 285; 1964, pp. 352ff; 1965, pp. 376ff
36. K. W. Wedderburn, 'Labour Law and Labour Relations in Great Britain', *British Journal of Industrial Relations*, 1972, pp. 270–290
37. Allen, *Trade Unions and the Government*, pp. 5–7
38. B. C. Roberts, *The Trades Union Congress 1868*–1921, (London: Allen and Unwin, 1958) p. 65
39. *ibid*
40. Henry Pelling, *Origins of the Labour Party*, (Oxford: Clarendon Press, 1965)
41. Allen, *Sociology of Industrial Relations*, pp. 157–184
42. Roberts, *The Trades Union Congress*, p. 341
43. Patrick Renshaw, *The General Strike*, (London: Eyre Methuen, 1975) pp. 215–225
44. Allen, *Unions and the Government*, pp. 3–33
45. *ibid*
46. *ibid*
47. Gerald Dorfman, *Wage Politics in Britain*, (London: Charles Knight, 1974) pp. 35–36
48. *ibid*, pp. 51–72
49. Allen, *Unions and the Government*, p. 34
50. Irving Richter, *Political Purpose in Trade Unions*, (London: Allen and Unwin, 1973)
51. R. D. Coates, *Teachers' Unions and Interest Group Politics*, (Cambridge: Cambridge University Press, 1972) chapter eight
52. For instance: David Maxwell-Fyfe's speech, National Union of Conservative and Unionist Associations 68th Annual Conference *Report* (1947) pp. 57–58; Inns of Court Conservative and Unionist Society, *A Giant's Strength*, (London: Christopher Johnson, 1958) pp. 8–10
53. Paul Smith, *Disraelian Conservatism and Social Reform*, (London: Routledge, 1967) p. 217; Robert Blake, *Disraeli*, (London: Eyre and Spottiswoode, 1966) p. 553

54. Smith, *ibid*, pp. 44–47, 119–125, 213–218; James Cornford, 'The transformation of Conservatism in the late nineteenth century', *Victorian Studies*, 1963, pp. 35–36; Nigel Harris, *Competition and the Corporate Society*, (London: Methuen, 1973) pp. 23–31

55. Keith Middlemass and John Barnes, *Baldwin*, (London: Weidenfeld and Nicolson, 1969) p. 291

56. *ibid*, pp. 48–49

57. Harris, *Competition and the Corporate Society*, p. 57

58. *ibid*, pp. 48–61

59. *quoted, ibid*, p. 116

60. Leon Epstein, 'The Politics of British Conservatism', *American Political Science Review*, 1954, p. 45

61. National Union, 68th Annual Conference *Report* (1947) p. 19

62. Epstein, 'British Conservatism', p. 45

63. *The Industrial Charter*, (London: Conservative and Unionist Central Office, 1947) pp. 21–22

64. National Union, 68th Annual Conference *Report* (1947) pp. 24, 57–58

65. Maxwell-Fyfe in National Union, 71st Annual Conference *Report* (1951) p. 56

66. National Union, 70th Annual Conference *Report* (1950) pp. 44–45

67. Epstein, 'British Conservatism', p. 46

68. Lord Birkenhead, *Walter Monckton*, (London: Weidenfeld and Nicolson, 1969) pp. 274–276

69. National Union, 80th Annual Conference *Report* (1961) p. 115. The speaker was Chairman of the Trade Union Advisory Committee

70. The MP was Tom Iremonger: House of Commons Debates Volume 810, Column 575 (810/575); the original is in HCD 565/1379 and HCD 574/1071

71. Donald Johnson, *A Cassandra at Westminster*, (London: Johnson, 1967)

72. National Union, 71st Annual Conference *Report* (1950) pp. 52–56 and 111–112; 72nd Conference *Report* (1951) pp. 67–68

73. Samuel Brittan, *Steering the Economy*, (Middlesex: Penguin, 1971) pp. 179–226

74. *ibid*, pp. 193–195; Birkenhead, *Monckton*, pp. 285 and 292–294

75. Birkenhead, *Monckton*, p. 280

76. Wigham, *The Right to Manage*, p. 194

77. Jacquez Leruez, *Economic Planning and Politics in Britain*, (London: Martin Robertson, 1975)

78. Brittan, *Steering the Economy*, pp. 227–269

79. According to Harold Watkinson, then a junior at the Ministry of Labour: National Union, 74th Annual Conference *Report* (1954) p. 84

80. National Union, 75th Annual Conference *Report* (1955) p. 77

81. *ibid*

82. Birkenhead, *Monckton*, pp. 298–299

83. For an example see Lord Avon, *Full Circle*, (London: Cassell, 1960) pp. 286–287

84. National Union, 77th Annual Conference *Report* (1957) p. 92

85. National Union, 76th Annual Conference *Report* (1956) pp. 84–85

86. National Union, 79th Annual Conference *Report* (1960) p. 74

87. *ibid*

88. *ibid*

89. TUC *Annual Report* 1964, p. 105

90. National Union, 80th Annual Conference *Report* (1961) p. 118
91. HCD 671/1509
92. The following owes a large debt to Kahn-Freund, 'Labour Law' and to Harris, *Competition and the Corporate Society*
93. Lloyd, 'Law of Associations', pp. 99–115
94. Wedderburn, *Worker and the Law*, pp. 432ff
95. The Resolutions are designed to ensure that public contracts are placed with firms who bargain with unions
96. Allan Flanders, 'The Tradition of Voluntarism', *British Journal of Industrial Relations*, 1974, pp. 352–370
97. Angus Calder, *The People's War*, (London: Panther, 1971) pp. 454ff
98. Harris, *Competition and the Corporate Society*, p. 57
99. Sidney and Beatrice Webb, *Industrial Democracy*, (London: Longmans Green, 1902) pp. 247–276

2 THE CRISIS OF INDUSTRIAL RELATIONS

1. Andrew Shonfield, *Modern Capitalism*, (London: Oxford University Press, 1965) p. 4
2. Angus Maddison, *Economic Growth in the West*, (London: Allen and Unwin, 1964) p. 30
3. The best evidence of this mood of criticism is contained in various documents of committees set up to examine the institutional problems. These include the *Donovan Report* itself; *Report of the Committee on Higher Education*, (London: HMSO 1963, Command 2154); *Report of the Committee on the Civil Service, 1966–1968*, (London: HMSO 1968, Command 3638). For the journalistic literature see Michael Shanks, *The Stagnant Society*, (Middlesex: Penguin, 1961) which went through five printings and two editions in eleven years
4. Clegg, *System of Industrial Relations*, pp. 442ff
5. Brittan, *Steering the Economy*, pp. 292–366; Timothy May, *Trade Unions and Pressure Group Politics*, (Hampshire: Saxon House, 1975) pp. 61–98, for collapses of wage pacts
6. This was essentially the argument of the *Donovan Report*
7. *ibid*, pp. 21–25
8. Andrew Glynn and Bob Sutcliffe, *British Workers, Capitalism and the Profits Squeeze*, (Middlesex: Penguin, 1972)
9. H. A. Turner, 'The Donovan Report', *Economic Journal*, 1969, pp. 1–10
10. *Donovan Report*, pp. 25–26
11. John Goldthorpe, et al, *The Affluent Worker: Industrial Attitudes and Behaviour*, (Cambridge: Cambridge University Press, 1970) pp. 93–115
12. Flanders, 'Tradition of Voluntarism'
13. Figures in the *Donovan Report*, p. 188
14. Goodman and Whittingham, *Shop Stewards*, p. 10
15. William Brown, 'A Consideration of Custom and Practice', *British Journal of Industrial Relations*, 1972, pp. 42–61
16. Clegg, *System of Industrial Relations*, chapter seven
17. *Donovan Report*, p. 25
18. *ibid*, p. 12

19. Clegg, *System of Industrial Relations*, p. 117
20. The figures exclude strikes lasting less than one day or involving less than ten strikers, unless the number of working days lost exceeds one hundred
21. Richard Hyman, *Strikes*, (London: Fontana, 1972) pp. 26–27
22. Michael Silver, 'Recent British Strike Trends: a Factual Analysis', *British Journal of Industrial Relations*, 1973, pp. 71–72
23. Hyman, *Strikes*, p. 31
24. Silver, 'Strike trends', p. 103
25. A. I. Marsh and W. E. J. McCarthy, *Disputes Procedure in British Industry*, (London: HMSO, 1966) p. 25
26. A. I. Marsh, et al, *Workplace Industrial Relations in Engineering*, (London: Engineering Employers' Federation, 1971) pp. 24–25
27. Silver, 'Strike trends', p. 99
28. *ibid*, p. 100
29. *Donovan Report*, p. 19
30. Silver, 'Strike trends', p. 101
31. Hyman, *Strikes*, pp. 39–40
32. Richard Hyman, *Disputes Procedure in Action*, (Heinemann: London, 1972) pp. 64–69
33. H. A. Turner, *Is Britain Really Strike Prone?* (Cambridge: Cambridge University Press, 1969) p. 34
34. *ibid*
35. W. E. J. McCarthy, 'The nature of Britain's strike problem', *British Journal of Industrial Relations*, 1970, p. 230
36. *Donovan Report*, p. 95
37. Silver, 'Strike trends', pp. 66–68
38. Kevin Hawkins, 'The decline of voluntarism', *Industrial Relations Journal*, 1971, pp. 24–41
39. Clive Jenkins and J. E. Mortimer, *The Kind of Laws the Unions Ought to Want*, (Oxford: Pergamon, 1968) p. 2

3 THE COLLECTIVIST HOUR

1. Wedderburn, *Worker and the Law*, pp. 432ff
2. *ibid*
3. TUC, *Annual Report* 1965, p. 376
4. Wedderburn, *Worker and the Law*, pp. 330ff
5. TUC, *Annual Report* 1964, pp. 352ff
6. Wilson to 1966 TUC Congress: *Annual Report* 1966, p. 396. For other instances: *Annual Report* 1964, p. 384; *Sunday Times*, 19 September 1965; Harold Wilson, *The Labour Government 1964–1970*, (London: Weidenfeld and Nicolson, 1971) p. 227
7. Gunter's speech to Congress, *Annual Report* 1965, pp. 400–401; and *Financial Times*, (*FT*)31 January 1965
8. Brittan, *Steering the Economy*, pp. 314–317
9. *ibid*
10. *The Times*, 14 September 1965; *FT*, 4 September 1965
11. *Sunday Times*, 19 September 1965
12. TUC, *Annual Report* 1965, p. 401

13. Allan Fels, *The British Prices and Incomes Board*, (Cambridge: Cambridge University Press, 1972) pp. 26ff

14. *ibid*

15. Hawkins, 'Decline of voluntarism'

16. W. E. J. McCarthy, Donovan's Research Director, quoted in Leo Panitch, 'The Labour Party and the Trade Unions – a study of incomes policy since 1945', (University of London PhD thesis, 1973) p. 279

17. *In Place of Strife*, (London: HMSO, 1969, Command 3888) pp. 20, 28 and 30

18. *ibid*, pp. 14, 19, 23 and 32

19. *FT*, 16 September 1965

20. Peter Jenkins, *The Battle of Downing Street*, (London: Charles Knight, 1970)

21. See chapter six below

22. TUC, *Annual Report* 1960, p. 124

23. *ibid*, pp. 127–129

24. *ibid*

25. *Trade Unionism*, (London: TUC, 1966) pp. 85–95; TUC oral evidence to the Donovan Commission in: Royal Commission on Trade Unions and Employers' Associations, *Minutes of Evidence*, (London: HMSO, 1965–1968) p. 2715. (Hereafter, Donovan, *Evidence*)

26. Trades Union Congress, *Action on Donovan*, (London: TUC, 1968) p. 47

27. So called because they were drawn up at the Bridlington Congress in 1939

28. TUC, *Annual Report* 1962, pp. 294ff

29. TUC, *Annual Report* 1963, pp. 317ff, and *ibid*, 1964, pp. 106ff

30. Donovan, *Evidence*, p. 2706

31. *Trade Unionism*, p. 113

32. The remark is Frank Chapple's

33. Donovan, *Evidence*, pp. 1774 and 1846

34. *ibid*, p. 974

35. *ibid*, p. 976

36. TUC, *Annual Report* 1966, p. 462

37. *ibid*, pp. 312–316

38. *ibid*, 1970, p. 247

39. *ibid*, 1964, p. 357

40. Robert Taylor, 'Jack Jones's T & G', *New Society*, 13 March 1975, pp. 642–644

41. TUC, *Annual Report* 1969, pp. 242–243

42. TUC, *Action on Donovan*, p. 35

43. TUC, *Annual Report* 1970, pp. 180–184

44. For instance see Huw Beynon, *Working for Ford*, (Middlesex: Penguin, 1973) pp. 54ff

45. *Donovan Report*, p. 25

46. *Evidence to the Royal Commission on Trade Unions and Employers' Associations*, (London: CBI, 1965) pp. 16–20

47. Donovan, *Evidence*, pp. 286ff

48. CBI, *Evidence to Donovan*, pp. 23ff; oral evidence in Donovan, *Evidence*, pp. 240–245; CBI *Annual Report*, 1968, p. 34

49. Donovan, *Evidence*, p. 240

50. CBI, *Evidence to Donovan*, pp. 23ff and 32ff

51. Donovan, *Evidence*, pp. 283–286

52. CBI, *Evidence to Donovan*, pp. 29–32

53. *ibid*, pp. 32–34
54. CBI, *Annual Report* 1970, p. 33
55. *ibid*
56. CBI, *Evidence to Donovan*, p. 32
57. CBI, *Annual Report* 1967, p. 34
58. *ibid*, 1970, p. 33
59. The two organisations gave evidence jointly to Donovan: *Evidence*, pp. 269off
60. Royal Commission on Trade Unions and Employers' Associations, *Selected Written Evidence*, (London: HMSO, 1968) pp. 384ff
61. *ibid*, p. 390
62. *ibid*, p. 389
63. *ibid*, p. 391–392
64. Donovan, *Evidence*, pp. 717–719 and 749
65. For an illustration see Donovan, *Evidence*, pp. 710ff. On the Federation's support for national agreements see *Selected Written Evidence*, pp. 431–432
66. CBI, *Evidence to Donovan*, p. 33
67. The CBI first ignored the closed shop, and then responded to the Commission's query by suggesting that any statutory right to join a union be matched by a similar one not to join: *Annual Report* 1967, p. 33
68. Donovan, *Evidence*, p. 836
69. *ibid*, pp. 845–897
70. *ibid*, pp. 575–596 and 2047–2056
71. *ibid*, pp. 2644–2656
72. Society of Independent Manufacturers, in Donovan, *Evidence*, p. 1378
73. For a list of prominent firms who deserted employers' associations to negotiate productivity deals see *Donovan Report*, p. 23
74. Donovan, *Evidence*, p. 715
75. Royal Commission on Trade Unions and Employers' Associations, *Written Evidence of the Ministry of Labour*, (London: HMSO, 1965) p. 43
76. *ibid*, and pp. 8off
77. Donovan, *Evidence*, pp. 655–656
78. Derek Robinson, 'Labour Market Policies', in Wilfred Beckerman, editor, *The Labour Government's Economic Record 1964–1970*, (London: Duckworth, 1972) p. 319
79. Fels, *The Prices and Incomes Board*, p. 69
80. *ibid*, p. 101
81. Donovan, *Evidence*, p. 2190
82. See note 16 above
83. *Donovan Report*, pp. 18–25
84. *ibid*, pp. 12–37
85. *ibid*, pp. 196ff
86. *ibid*, pp. 114–140
87. John Stuart Mill, *On Representative Government*, (London: Everyman edition, 1962) p. 183
88. Flanders' evidence is in Donovan, *Selected Written Evidence*
89. The internal politics of the Commission are described in: Stephen Fay, 'How the doves won', *Sunday Times*, 16 June 1968; and David Howarth, 'How George Woodcock won on points', *The Observer*, 16 June 1968
90. His views are represented in his *Management and Unions: The Theory and Reform of Industrial Relations*, (London: Faber, 1970)

91. *Donovan Report*, pp. 214–215
92. *ibid*, p. 215
93. *ibid*, pp. 288 and 290
94. *ibid*, pp. 291–292 and 297–298
95. Reported in *The Times*, 8 October 1965
96. Iain Macleod, quoted in Eric Heffer, *The Class Struggle in Parliament*, (London: Gollancz, 1973) p. 91; Robert Carr in National Union, 86th Annual Conference *Report* (1968) p. 33
97. Sir Geoffrey Howe in HCD 807/738
98. Heffer, *Class Struggle*, p. 18
99. TUC, *Action on Donovan*, p. 37
100. Donovan, *Evidence*, p. 2190

4 THE PROBLEMS OF LIBERALISM

1. David Butler and Anthony King, *The British General Election* of 1964, (London: Macmillan, 1965) p. 136
2. For instance: National Union *Reports* for 1954 (p. 102); 1956 (p. 80); 1957 (p. 87) and 1960 (p. 69); Harris, *Competition and the Corporate Society*, p. 171
3. National Union, 80th Annual Conference *Report* (1961) pp. 109–118
4. Johnson, *A Cassandra at Westminster*, p. 112; HCD 568/2113–5; 565/1379; 574/1071
5. Charles Fletcher-Cooke, 'Trade Unionism and Liberty', in *Liberty in the Modern State*, (London: Conservative Political Centre, 1957) pp. 69–76
6. HCD 698/4167 and 698/1599
7. Philip Goodhart, *The 1922*, (London: Macmillan, 1973) p. 197
8. *A Giant's Strength*, pp. 7 and 15
9. *ibid*, pp. 21–34
10. *ibid*, pp. 41–42
11. Heffer, *Class Struggle*, pp. 24–29; E. G. A. Armstrong, *Straitjacket or Framework?*, (London: Business Books, 1973) pp. 1–3
12. For early ideas which resemble the proposals see Goodhart, *The 1922*, p. 34; Avon, *Full Circle*, pp. 286–287
13. John Ward, 'The unions have a part', *Crossbow*, 1958, pp. 17–18; *ibid*, pp. 5, 8–9, 10–11; *ibid*, 1959, p. 31
14. *A Giant's Strength*, p. 24
15. *ibid*, pp. 49–50
16. See for instance: *Notes on Current Politics*, 22 January 1962; Conservative Political Centre *Weekly Newsletter* 16 February, 30 March, 25 May, 1 June, 28 September, 7 December 1963; 11 April and 20 June 1964. The attacks increased in frequency and intensity following the 1964 election
17. Leaked in James Margach, 'Tory new deal for workers', *Sunday Times*, 20 April 1962
18. *Industrial Change: the human aspects*, (London: Conservative Political Centre, 1963)
19. *ibid*, pp. 9, 14, 18 and 19
20. HCD 691/1598–1602
21. *ibid*; TUC, *Annual Report* 1964, pp. 355–357
22. For details see: David Butler and Anthony King, *The British General Election of*

178   *The Politics of Industrial Relations*

1966, (London: Macmillan, 1966) pp. 59–64; Alan Watkins, 'The Policy Makers', *Spectator*, 2 April 1965; R. M. Punnett, *Front Bench Opposition*, (London: Heinemann, 1973) pp. 265–266; *The Times*, 1 February 1965

23. *FT*, 31 August 1965

24. List of members in Jenkins and Mortimer, *The Kind of Laws the Unions Ought to Want*, pp. 34–35

25. Andrew Gamble, *The Conservative Nation*, (London: Routledge, 1974) pp. 61–86

26. Watkins, 'The Policy Makers'

27. Heffer, *Class Struggle*, p. 260

28. John Bruce-Gardyne, *Whatever Happened to the Quiet Revolution?*, (London: Charles Knight, 1974) p. 140

29. For instance, see Carr in National Union 88th Annual Conference *Report* (1970) pp. 32–33

30. Gamble, *Conservative Nation*, pp. 94ff

31. Examples of the new mood are: *A Fresh Approach*, (London: CPC, 1965) and the 'new tasks' series, especially: Eldon Griffiths, *The New Competitors*; David Howell, *Efficiency and Beyond*; and Timothy Raison, *Conflict and Conservatism*, all CPC published, and all 1965

32. For a general discussion of the period see Stephen Young and A. V. Lowe, *Intervention in the Mixed Economy*, (London: Croom Helm, 1974)

33. National Union, 83rd Annual Conference *Report* (1965), p. 42

34. *ibid*, pp. 40–43

35. *Putting Britain Right Ahead*. I have been unable to obtain a copy of this pamphlet so am using the version printed in *The Times*, 7 October 1965

36. National Union, 83rd Annual *Report*, p. 40

37. *Putting Britain Right Ahead*

38. National Union, 83rd Annual *Report*, p. 40

39. *ibid*

40. *ibid*, 38–39. For similar criticisms see *Sunday Times*, 10 October 1965

41. Wedderburn, 'Labour law and labour relations', p. 282

42. For Ridley's liberalism see HCD 768/1337–1340

43. *Industrial Advance*, (London: CPC, 1966) pp. 15–20

44. For instance: Armstrong, *Straitjacket or Framework?*, pp. 1–3; Heffer, *Class Struggle*, pp. 24–29; A. W. J. Thomson and S. R. Engleman, *The Industrial Relations Act: A Review and Analysis*, (London: Martin Robertson, 1975) p. 19

45. National Union, 84th Annual Conference *Report*, (1966) pp. 54–55

46. Keith Joseph, in *ibid*, p. 59

47. *Fair Deal At Work*, (London: CPC, 1968)

48. See for instance Fletcher-Cooke, 'Trade Unionism and Liberty'

49. *Fair Deal*, p. 64

50. National Union, 83rd Annual Conference *Report*, (1965), pp. 42–43

51. *ibid*

52. *ibid*; and 84th Annual *Report*, pp. 59–60; and *ibid* for remarks by Heath

53. For examples of this view see *Industrial Change*, p. 7; and National Union, 84th Annual *Report*, (1966), p. 42

54. *Putting Britain Right Ahead*

55. National Union, 84th Annual *Report*, (1966), p. 59

56. *ibid*

57. *ibid*
58. *Fair Deal*, pp. 30–31
59. *ibid*, p. 24
60. *ibid*, p. 51
61. *ibid*, p. 50
62. *ibid*, p. 59
63. *ibid*, p. 58
64. HCD 779/88. The speaker is Enoch Powell
65. *ibid*, 768/1338–9. The speaker is Nicholas Ridley
66. *ibid*, 768/1328–9. The speaker is Ernest Taylor
67. *Fair Deal*, p. 59
68. National Union, 84th Annual Conference *Report*, (1966) p. 59
69. *Fair Deal*, p. 28
70. For Joseph see note 40 above; for Carr see almost any speech on the subject, and for a representative specimen HCD 808/632–651
71. HCD 768/1338
72. *Fair Deal*, p. 56
73. *ibid*, pp. 37–9
74. *ibid*, p. 35
75. *ibid*, p. 34
76. National Union, 87th Annual Conference *Report*, (1969) p. 34
77. The fiasco is described in the *Donovan Report*, Appendix 6
78. For this see Carr in HCD 768/1269 and 1282
79. See Carr's remarks in National Union, 87th Annual Conference *Report*, (1969) p. 34, and HCD 779/66–74; and David Mitchell's speech, *ibid*, 786/740
80. National Union, 83rd Annual Conference *Report*, (1965) p. 41
81. *ibid*
82. *Putting Britain Right Ahead*
83. For instance Heath's speech in National Union, 84th Annual Conference *Report*, (1966) p. 140
84. National Union, 85th Annual Conference *Report*, (1967) p. 96; 88th Annual *Report*, pp. 32–33; HCD 777/61–62; Robert Carr on Granada TVs *State of the Nation*, 20 June 1976
85. National Union, 84th Annual Conference *Report*, (1966) p. 59
86. *Fair Deal*, p. 35
87. *ibid*, p. 23
88. National Union, 87th Annual Conference *Report*, (1969) pp. 34–5
89. J. D. Hoffman, *The Conservative Party in Opposition*, (London: Macgibbon and Kee, 1964) pp. 133–206

5 THE POLITICS OF CONSULTATION

1. *FT*, 30 September 1970
2. For exceptions see David Madel's speech in National Union, 85th Annual Conference *Report*, (1967) pp. 90–91; and Hugh Dykes, 'Trade unions: have we really got the answer?', *Crossbow*, 1968, pp. 32–34. For an early warning by a supporter of economic liberalism see John Biffen, 'School for Tories', *The Guardian*, 27 August 1965

3. See Lord Boyle's letter to the *The Times* supporting Whitelaw in the 1975 leadership contest (11 February 1975): 'no one during the 1966–1970 period was more aware of the danger of introducing an Industrial Relations Bill which tried to do too much.'
4. For a discussion of problems see *The Times*, 12 February and 31 March 1970
5. *Sunday Times*, 12 April 1970
6. *FT*, 7 April 1970
7. *The Times*, 23 February 1970
8. CBI *Annual Report* 1970, p. 33
9. *FT*, 11 April 1970
10. *ibid*, 16 July 1970
11. HCD 803/46
12. On the 'closed' nature of the Document see Arthur Silkin, 'Green Papers and Changing Methods of Consultation in British Government', *Public Administration*, 1973, p. 437
13. *FT*, 16 July 1970
14. *ibid*, 29 July 1970
15. *ibid*, 6 April 1970
16. *ibid*, 20 June 1970; *The Guardian*, 20 June 1970
17. *ibid*, 22 June 1970
18. TUC, *Annual Report* 1970, pp. 503–504
19. Bob Wright to the Confederation of Shipbuilding and Engineering Unions: *The Times*, 25 June 1970
20. TUC, *Annual Report* 1970, pp. 576–588
21. *FT*, 6 August 1970; *The Times*, 6 August 1970
22. *FT*, 17 July 1970
23. See Alan Fisher of NUPE's remarks in *ibid*, 21 September 1970
24. *ibid*, 25 August 1970
25. TUC, *Annual Report* 1971, pp. 247–249
26. *FT*, 9 July 1970; and for Carr's reaction *ibid*, 21 September 1970
27. *ibid*, 25 March 1970 and 21 May 1970
28. *ibid*, 18 August 1970
29. *ibid*, 19 June and 13 August 1970
30. Silver, 'Strike trends', p. 99
31. John Gennard and Roger Lasko, 'Supplementary benefits and strikers', *British Journal of Industrial Relations*, 1974, pp. 1–25
32. Industrial Relations Bill, *Consultative Document*, (London: DEP, 1970) p. 3
33. *ibid*, pp. 3–4
34. *Fair Deal*, p. 31
35. Though for criticism of the CIR as Labour envisaged it see Carr in HCD 779/66
36. *Consultative Document*, p. 5
37. On North American influences generally see R. C. Simpson and John Wood, *Industrial Relations and the 1971 Act*, (London: Pitman, 1973) pp. 64–66
38. *Consultative Document*, p. 7
39. *ibid*, pp. 6ff
40. *ibid*
41. *In Place of Strife*, pp. 19–20. For Carr's criticisms see HCD 779/66
42. *Consultative Document*, p. 5

43. *ibid*, p. 23
44. *ibid*, p. 17
45. On this see *FT*, 16 July 1970; *The Guardian*, 15 July 1970; *The Observer*, 19 July 1970
46. *FT*, 2 November 1970
47. *ibid*, 3 June 1970; *The Times*, 6 April and 3 June 1970
48. *ibid*, 6 October 1970; *FT*, 6 October 1970
49. *ibid*
50. *Industrial Relations Bill: Report of the Special Trades Union Congress 1971*, (London: TUC, 1971) p. 73
51. TUC, *Annual Report* 1970, p. 577
52. *Special Congress Report*, pp. 7−8
53. TUC, *Annual Report* 1971, p. 8
54. *Special Congress Report*, p. 8
55. *ibid*, p. 9
56. *ibid*
57. *ibid*
58. Leruez, *Economic Planning and Politics in Britain*, pp. 242−3
59. A. J. Willcocks, 'Decision making and interest groups in the National Health Service', in Open University, *Health*, (Bletchley: Open University Press, 1972) p. 141
60. House of Lords Debates, Volume 318, Column 22 (HLD, 318/22)
61. *Special Congress Report*, p. 65
62. *FT*, 23 October 1970
63. *ibid*; *The Times*, 23 October 1970
64. CBI, *Annual Report*, 1970, pp. 33−34; *FT*, 12 November 1970
65. Donovan, *Evidence*, p. 1378; *FT*, 9 November 1970
66. *ibid*, 2 November 1970
67. *ibid*, 27 October 1970; *The Guardian*, 27 October 1970
68. *The Times*, 30 October 1970
69. Giles Smith, 'Motor industry puts doubts on labour legislation to Mr Carr', *ibid*, 4 November 1970
70. *FT*, 4 December 1970
71. *ibid*, 2 November 1970
72. See the discussion in chapter four of early−1965−demands for more compulsion; see also HCD 810/1667
73. John Davies, Director General of the CBI, 1964−1969. Of course as a new Minister Davies was too busy mastering his Department to concern himself too much with the details of the Bill.
74. According to Sir Denis Barnes, Permanent Secretary in the Department, speaking on Granada TVs *State of the Nation*, June 20 1976

6 THE PARLIAMENTARY BATTLE

1. HLD 322/936
2. TUC, *Annual Report* 1971, p. 98
3. CBI, *Annual Report* 1971, p. 25
4. HCD 809/532

5. For a general discussion see S. A. Walkland, *The Legislative Process in Great Britain*, (London: Allen and Unwin, 1968)

6. Heffer, *Class Struggle*, p. 201

7. HCD 809/571

8. *ibid*, 810/159

9. Heffer, *Class Struggle*, p. 223

10. HCD 813/1511

11. See the discussion of the Labour Government's policies in chapter three

12. HCD 807/632–651 and 808/961–963

13. *ibid*, 807/637

14. *ibid*, 808/1135

15. *ibid*, 808/1138

16. *ibid*, 808/1178; 808/1192; 810/1309; 810/1274; 810/1405

17. This section of the discussion relates chiefly to the Commons' debates but the points were parallelled in the Lords

18. HCD 810/1374. For similar interpretations by other backbenchers see *ibid*, 810/1472; 810/1908–1909

19. *ibid*, 808/988

20. *ibid*, 808/1221 and 1231

21. For instance: *ibid*, 808/1045, 1157, 1207; 810/1304, 1296, 1367, 1891; and 811/399

22. *ibid*, 807/731

23. *ibid*, 808/1168–1169

24. For a 'legalism' argument see *ibid*, 808/1064

25. For remarks by Mrs Castle approximating a 'class' view see *ibid*, 807/665–666

26. See Mr Wilson's remarks in *ibid*, 808/1233–1234. For other examples of the 'irrelevance' argument see *ibid*, 808/1045, 1057 and 1207; and 810/1734

27. *ibid*, 808/1167; 811/554

28. See the discussion in chapter three

29. HCD 807/667

30. *ibid*; and 807/719

31. *ibid*, 807/686–687 and 709; and 810/116

32. *ibid*, 807/665–666

33. *ibid*, 808/1147

34. *ibid*, 809/909 and 884; for another example see 810/1734

35. *ibid*, 808/1231

36. *ibid*, 808/1234

37. See for instance: *ibid*, 808/1045; 809/946; 810/623, 676 and 963–964; HLD 317/24 and 54–55; *ibid*, 318/207 and 217–218

38. Most notably Norman Atkinson: HCD 808/1167

39. *ibid*, 808/1231

40. *ibid*, 809/936

41. For the former see for instance: *ibid*, 810/631–633, 676, 681, 982; HLD 318/307; *ibid*, 318/213, 217–218 and 266. For the latter see for instance: HCD 808/1057 for Eric Heffer's views

42. *ibid*, 808/1002

43. *ibid*, 808/1001

44. *ibid*, 808/1002

45. *ibid*, 808/1237

46. *ibid*, 810/980
47. Tony Lane and Ken Roberts, *Strike at Pilkingtons*, (London: Fontana, 1971). For Lord Cooper's views see HLD 318/883–886
48. HCD 808/1227
49. For instance: *ibid*, 809/850
50. *ibid*, 808/1052
51. This view emerged especially strongly in debates on the closed shop: *ibid*, 809/676; 810/963–964
52. *ibid*, 808/1047
53. *ibid*; and 809/1054
54. *ibid*, 808/1054
55. For instance Heffer's speech in *ibid* 809/837–842
56. *ibid*, 810/644
57. *ibid*, 808/1167
58. *ibid*, 809/602. Cf 809/589
59. *ibid*, 808/967
60. *ibid*, 808/966
61. *ibid*, 808/1069–1070
62. For related examples see: *ibid*, 810/634–636
63. *ibid*, 810/603
64. *ibid*, 810/57
65. *ibid*, 812/605–606
66. *ibid*, 808/1067
67. See for instance Carr's arguments in *ibid*, 813/296
68. *ibid*, 808/1023–1027
69. *ibid*, 808/1164
70. *ibid*, 808/1024
71. *ibid*, 811/428–443
72. *ibid*, 810/680–686; and various Labour speakers at 810/596–614
73. *ibid*, 810/1667–1668
74. *ibid*, 810/642
75. *ibid*, 810/946 and 813/974
76. *ibid*, 813/942–1003
77. *ibid*, 813/944–945. For further divisions see 813/931, 993–994, 997 and 1003
78. *ibid*, 813/956–960

7 THE CAMPAIGNS AGAINST THE BILL

1. *Special Congress Report*, p. 9
2. TUC, *Annual Report* 1971, pp. 96–98
3. *ibid*, p. 96
4. *Sunday Times*, 20 December 1970
5. *ibid*, 28 February 1971
6. TUC, *Annual Report* 1971, pp. 96–97
7. *Special Congress Report*, p. 73
8. TUC, *Annual Report* 1971, p. 98
9. quoted, *The Times*, 2 December 1970
10. *Special Congress Report*, p. 73

11. *The Observer*, 5 December 1970
12. *ibid*; *Sunday Times*, 29 November 1970
13. *FT*, 16 November 1970
14. *ibid*; and *Sunday Times*, 29 November 1970
15. *FT*, 9 December 1970
16. *ibid*, 16 October 1970
17. *ibid*, 2, 3 and 5 November 1970
18. *ibid*, 8, 13 and 23 November and 8 December 1970
19. *ibid*, 9 December 1970
20. quoted, *ibid*
21. *ibid*, 17 December 1970
22. *ibid*, 16 and 25 February 1970
23. *ibid*, 12 February 1971
24. Widespread stoppages occurred on 1 January 1971, but how much was due to absenteeism is impossible to estimate
25. *FT*, 2 March 1971
26. *Special Congress Report*, p. 98; the voting on the relevant resolution was 5.3 million in favour and 3.9 million against the General Council recommendations
27. *FT*, 19 March 1971
28. *ibid*, 26 and 27 April 1971
29. Walkland, *The Legislative Process*, pp. 21–43
30. *The Times*, 11 January 1971
31. Such as the Writers Guild of Great Britain: HCD 813/982
32. HCD 810/946
33. *ibid*, 810/689–691
34. Feather's speech to the Institute of Directors, reported *FT*, 12 November 1970; also *Sunday Times*, 31 January 1971 and *The Times*, 28 December 1970
35. On the EEF see *The Times*, 11 January 1971; on the nationalised industries *FT*, 27 October 1970; on the motor industry *The Times*, 4 November 1970
36. HLD 317/36ff. Speakers included the chairmen of Tube Investments, Cadbury-Schweppes and Delta Metal, a senior ICI executive and a former chairman of the FBI
37. *ibid*, 318/283
38. *Sunday Times*, 3 January 1971
39. For examples of these fears see HCD 810/965–977
40. *ibid*; and 810/428–443 for attempts by Tory backbenchers to amend the Bill to favour professional associations
41. For the Shipping Federation see *ibid*, 810/946–950; for federations generally see 810/1667–1668
42. *ibid*, 810/993
43. HLD 321/946 and 954
44. HCD 810/642 and 671
45. HLD 321/498
46. HCD 813/933
47. *ibid*, 813/928
48. The NUS wanted explicit exclusion: *ibid*, 813/961; Equity wanted either this or an employment formula which would have amounted to the same thing: *ibid*, 813/974
49. Granada TV, *State of the Nation*, 20 June 1976

50. TUC, *Annual Report* 1971, p. 355
51. HCD 814/335, and *ibid*, 822/1711−1714
52. *ibid*, 814/255ff

8 THE POLITICS OF DEFIANCE

1. For a representative example see J. J. Richardson, *The Policy-Making Process*, (London: Routledge, 1969)
2. Thomson and Engleman, *The Industrial Relations Act*, pp. 44−72
3. TUC, *Annual Report* 1972, p. 91
4. *ibid*, p. 93 and *Annual Report* 1973, pp. 110−111
5. *Special Congress Report*, pp. 59−61 and 81−84
6. 'Croydon' procedures refer to rules governing inter-union disputes adopted as part of the settlement with the Government after the defeat of *In Place of Strife*
7. *ibid*, pp. 40, 42
8. *ibid*
9. TUC, *Annual Report* 1972, p. 428
10. Such as the National Union of Bank Employees: see below
11. *Special Congress Report*, pp. 40−42
12. TUC, *Annual Report* 1972, pp. 440−441
13. *Special Congress Report*, p. 70 for a speech by a qualified constitutionalist supporting a deal with the Labour Party
14. *FT*, 19 March 1971
15. *Special Congress Report*, pp. 55 and 73
16. On registration the voting was 5.0 to 4.2 million, and on strikes 5.3 to 3.9 million
17. TUC, *Annual Report* 1971, p. 435
18. *ibid*, p. 427
19. *Special Congress Report*, pp. 55 and 73
20. *ibid*, pp. 40−42
21. TUC, *Annual Report* 1971, p. 443
22. *Special Congress Report*, pp. 67−68
23. *ibid*, p. 82
24. *ibid*, p. 76
25. *ibid*, p. 74
26. A 'future Congress' would decide the fate of anyone who defied an instruction, Scanlon remarked: TUC, *Annual Report* 1971, p. 428
27. *ibid*, p. 448. The motion received only 234,000 votes
28. *ibid*, p. 433
29. Coates, *Teachers' Unions and Interest Group Politics*, pp. 100−111
30. TUC, *Annual Report* 1973, p. 104
31. *FT*, 11 May 1971
32. For Cooper see HLD 317/278; for Chapple, *FT*, 4 November 1971
33. TUC, *Annual Report* 1972, pp. 327−336
34. *ibid*, p. 97
35. *ibid*, p. 340
36. *FT*, 26 June 1972
37. TUC, *Annual Report* 1971, p. 355

38. *ibid*, pp. 438–439
39. TUC, *Annual Report* 1972, pp. 332–335
40. *ibid*, p. 97; *FT*, 28 April 1971
41. *New Society*, 16 May 1974, p. 367
42. *FT*, 1 March 1972
43. TUC, *Annual Report* 1969, pp. 93–95
44. TUC, *Annual Report* 1972, pp. 93–94
45. Taylor, 'Jack Jones's T & G'
46. Between 1960 and 1969 GMWU membership rose by only 30,000, that of the TGWU by over 200,000
47. *FT*, 28 April 1971
48. *ibid*, 11 May 1971
49. *ibid*, 13 May 1971
50. *ibid*, 24 May 1971
51. *ibid*, 17 June 1971
52. *ibid*, 21 June 1971
53. *ibid*, 25 June 1971
54. *ibid*, 25 August 1971
55. *ibid*, 30 June 1971
56. *ibid*, 15 and 16 June 1971
57. *ibid*, 20 April 1971
58. *ibid*, 16 June 1971
59. *The Guardian*, 27 March 1971
60. *ibid*, 26 March 1971
61. *FT*, 15 July 1971
62. *ibid*, 3 September 1971
63. For NUPE see TUC, *Annual Report* 1971, p. 443
64. The figures were: for instruction, 5.6 million; against 4.5 million
65. See for instance *ibid*, pp. 433–435
66. *ibid*, p. 428
67. *ibid*, pp. 429 and 442
68. *ibid*, p. 336
69. *FT*, 28 September 1971
70. *ibid*, 2 October 1971
71. *ibid*, 5 October 1971
72. *ibid*, 21 October 1971
73. *ibid*, 12 October 1971
74. *ibid*, 26 October 1971 has reports of the General Council meeting
75. *ibid*, 4 November 1971
76. *ibid*, 27 November 1971
77. *ibid*, 18 December 1971
78. *ibid*, 8 March 1972
79. *ibid*, 21 January 1972
80. *ibid*, 25 January 1972
81. *ibid*, 8 May 1972
82. *ibid*, 25 May 1972
83. *ibid*, 1 May 1972
84. *ibid*, 26 June 1972
85. May, *Trade Unions and Pressure Group Politics*, p. 115

86. TUC, *Annual Report* 1972, p. 251
87. *ibid*, p. 252
88. *FT*, 20 April and 20 May 1972
89. *FT*, 1 June 1972
90. Bruce-Gardyne, *Whatever Happened to the Quiet Revolution?*, p. 85
91. *FT*, 21 April 1972
92. For an early disagreement see National Union, 76th Annual Conference *Report* (1957), pp. 84–85
93. David Wilson, *Dockers*, (London: Fontana, 1972)
94. *FT*, 25 May 1972
95. *ibid*, 24 March 1972
96. *ibid*
97. *ibid*, 30 March 1972
98. *ibid*, 15 April 1972
99. *ibid*, 21 April 1972
100. TUC, *Annual Report* 1972, pp. 89–91
101. *FT*, 2 May 1972
102. *ibid*, 10 May 1972
103. *ibid*, 13 May 1972
104. *ibid*, 14 June 1972
105. *ibid*, 15 June 1972
106. Heffer, *Class Struggle*, p. 117
107. *FT*, 17 June 1972
108. *ibid*, 8 July 1972
109. *ibid*, 22 July 1972
110. TUC, *Annual Report* 1972, p. 104
111. Peter Paterson, '1926 and all that', *New Statesman*, 4 August 1972. I have received independent assurances that this is an accurate account
112. TUC, *Annual Report* 1972, p. 104
113. *FT*, 28 July 1972
114. TUC, *Annual Report* 1972, p. 105
115. See for instance John Griffith, 'Reflections on the rule of law', *New Statesman*, 24 November 1972
116. Heffer, *Class Struggle*, p. 317
117. TUC, *Annual Report* 1972, p. 340
118. *FT*, 28 July 1972
119. ASTMS actually appeared on the list of suspended unions: TUC, *Annual Report* 1972, p. 341
120. The list appears in *ibid*
121. *ibid*
122. Brian Weekes, Michael Mellish, Linda Dickens and John Lloyd, *Industrial Relations and the Limits of Law*, (Oxford: Basil Blackwell, 1975) pp. 260–261
123. This account rests on material drawn from various issues of the *FT*, October–December 1972
124. This account is drawn from various issues of the *FT*, December 1972–January 1973
125. This relies on reports in the *FT*, January–March 1974
126. This is drawn from the *FT* for April 1974
127. Thomson and Engleman, *The Industrial Relations Act*, p. 166

128. *ibid*, pp. 157–164

9 REPRESENTATION AND CONSENT

1. HCD 810/1368. For the view that Tory lawyers were the Act's originators see Armstrong, *Straitjacket or Framework?*, pp. 1–3; Heffer, *Class Struggle*, pp. 24–30
2. Howe helped prepare the Tory lawyers' evidence to Donovan
3. *Observer*, 19 September 1970, for a profile of Carr
4. W. E. J. McCarthy in *The Guardian*, 3 September 1970
5. See the symposium on Donovan in the *British Journal of Industrial Relations*, 1968, pp. 275–359
6. Andrew Shonfield, 'A Bill with a clear philosophy', *The Times*, 6 October 1970; Michael Shanks, 'A good Bill but management holds the real key', *ibid*, 15 October 1970. For an important exception to the rule that the Tory proposals were badly received by industrial relations experts see B. C. Roberts, *Trade Unions – The Challenge Before Them*, (Industrial Education and Research Foundation, 1971)
7. For Wilson see HCD 808/1221–1335; for Feather see TUC, *Annual Report* 1971, pp. 421–426
8. Bruce-Gardyne, *Whatever Happened to the Quiet Revolution?*, p. 148
9. Edmund Burke, 'Thoughts on the Causes of the Present Discontent' (1770) in R. J. White, editor, *The Conservative Tradition*, (London: Kaye, 1950) pp. 33–34
10. HCD 26/1022. The remark is quoted on the title page of Heffer, *Class Struggle*
11. *Guidance to Employers on the Industrial Relations Bill* (London: CBI, 1971)
12. TUC, *Annual Report* 1972, pp. 108–110
13. Weekes, et al, *Industrial Relations and the Limits of Law*, pp. 33–63
14. *FT*, 29 June 1972
15. Thomson and Engleman, *The Industrial Relations Act*, p. 149
16. Jenkins, *The Battle of Downing Street*, p. 45; TUC, *Annual Report* 1969, p. 210
17. *Sunday Times*, 20 December 1970
18. David Butler and Dennis Kavanagh, *The British General Election of February 1974*, (London: Macmillan 1974) p. 141
19. David Butler and Donald Stokes, *Political Change in Britain*, (Middlesex: Penguin, 1971) p. 4 and pp. 59–64
20. *FT*, 22 July 1972
21. Peter Pulzer, *Political Representation and Elections in Britain*, (London: Allen and Unwin, 1967) pp. 32–60
22. Samuel Beer, *Modern British Politics*, (London: Faber, 1969)
23. Bagehot's reference – in *The English Constitution* – was of course to the fusing role of the Cabinet
24. May, *Trade Unions and Pressure Group Politics*, p. 115: before the election the miners' case had already been referred to special relativities machinery
25. *The Times*, 16 September for the manifesto
26. This first appeared in the February 1974 manifesto and seems to command wide support in the Party
27. 'A Strategy for Union Members', quoted in the *Daily Telegraph*, 25 June 1976
28. Ronald Butt, 'Tories and the closed shop', *The Times*, 3 June 1976
29. *The Times*, 11 June 1976; cf the *FT* 28 June 1976

30. See the report of Walker's speech to the Tory Reform Group in *The Times*, May 20 1976

31. For a specimen of his rather opaque views see David Wood, 'The Shadow Cabinet also dithers', *The Times*, 26 June 1975

32. Speech to the Tory Reform Group, *The Times*, May 20 1976

33. See his article on pay policies in *The Times*, 15 June 1976

34. Beer, *Modern British Politics*, p. 427

35. W. W. Daniel, *The PEP Survey On Inflation*, (London: PEP, 1975) pp. 14–17

36. Quoted in Anthony King, *British Members of Parliament: A Self Portrait*, (London: Macmillan/Granada, 1975) pp. 117–118

37. Richard Hyman, 'Industrial Conflict And The Political Economy: Trends Of The Sixties And Prospects For The Seventies', *Socialist Register*, (London: Merlin Press, 1973) p. 101

38. Samuel Brittan, 'The Economic Contradictions of Democracy', *British Journal of Political Science*, 1975, pp. 129–159

39. *FT*, 30 March 1974

40. Samuel Brittan, 'An alternative to the Social Contract', *FT*, 24 June 1976

41. In particular the argument of the articles by T. Wilson, 'The Economic Costs Of The Adversary System', and D. K. Stout, 'Incomes Policy And The Costs Of The Adversary System', in S. E. Finer, editor, *Adversary Politics and Electoral Reform*, (London: Wigram, 1975) pp. 99–151

42. Quoted, W. E. J. McCarthy and N. D. Ellis, *Management by Agreement*, (London: Hutchinson, 1973)

43. Ray Dafter, 'British Gas given Irish Sea Area', *FT*, 25 June 1976

44. Brittan has some prescient remarks on the consequences of this in 'The Economic Contradictions of Democracy'

45. A. H. Birch, *Representative and Responsible Government*, (London: Allen and Unwin, 1964) pp. 48–81

Index